Real
Options

Real
Options

A Practitioner's Guide

TOM COPELAND

VLADIMIR ANTIKAROV

TEXERE

New York   London

This book is printed on acid-free paper.

Copyright © 2001 by Thomas E. Copeland.

Published by

TEXERE LLC
55 East 52nd Street
New York, NY 10055

Tel: +1 (212) 317 5106
Fax: +1 (212) 317 5178
www.etexere.com

UK subsidiary office

TEXERE Publishing Limited
71–77 Leadenhall Street
London EC3A 3DE

Tel: +44 (0)20 7204 3644
Fax: +44 (0)20 7208 6701
www.etexere.co.uk

This publication is designed to provide accurate and authoritative information in regard to the subject matter covered. It is sold with the understanding that the publisher is not engaged in rendering professional services. If professional advice or other expert assistance is required, the services of a competent professional person should be sought.

Library of Congress Cataloging-in-Publication Data has been applied for.

ISBN: 1-58799-028-8

Printed in the United States of America

10 9 8 7 6 5 4 3 2 1

PREFACE

There have been many excellent books about the theory of real options, and hundreds of pathbreaking academic articles. Yet there is still the need for a "how to do it" practitioner's guide—the type of reference that you can take off your bookshelf and use to learn how to actually apply the theory to everyday decision-making challenges. We have twelve to thirteen years of experience and dozens of consulting cases that have helped our clients apply real options to major decisions. This book summarizes our experiences with the hope that real options will be used as a primary tool by more decision makers.

WHY READ THIS BOOK?

The central paradigm for making decisions about large investments is net present value. Unfortunately, it is badly flawed and systematically under-values every investment opportunity. Why? Because it is based on expected future cash flows, thereby failing to account for value flexibility. To illustrate a typical net present value (NPV) problem, suppose that we are evaluating an 8-year project that will cost $50 million to design and $300 million to build. The NPV approach says to figure out the expected free cash flows over the 8-year life of the project, to discount them at the weighted average cost of capital, and to subtract out the present value of the required investments. If the resulting NPV investment is negative, *do not* accept the project.

The NPV rule fails to consider flexibility. In the example that we are discussing, management has many options. The project can be abandoned after the design phase, it can be expanded or extended if it does better than expected, and it can be deferred. When optimally exercised, all of these options provide flexibility that adds to the value of the project. Senior managers intuitively know that NPV fails to capture these flexibilities and often disregard (for good reasons) the results of the present value analysis.

In ten years, real options will replace NPV as the central paradigm for investment decisions. This book makes a complex topic simple. We hope that it will speed the day when real options analysis is used every day.

ORGANIZATION OF THE BOOK

Chapter 1 defines real options and gives numerous examples of how real options have made a difference in real world decisions where we have helped clients. Chapter 2, written by John Stonier of Airbus Industrie, is a case example concerning the management challenges involved in implementing a new way of thinking. It describes how Airbus uses real options in its marketing efforts, and the trials and tribulations of changing its management culture. These first two chapters will be useful for top management.

Chapters 3 through 10 are the methodology section of the book. It is written for practitioners and starts with a review of the net present value methodology. Why is NPV unanimously accepted as a wealth-maximizing decision rule by all shareholders? What is the correct definition of free cash flows and the weighted average cost of capital? How does the present value of a project change over time? Chapter 4 then compares NPV, decision trees, and real option analysis (ROA). It also introduces the concept of using a replicating portfolio to value real options.

Chapters 5 and 6 deal with the nitty gritty of valuing various types of simple options (deferral, abandonment, expansion, and contraction of projects) and more advanced types of flexibility (Chapter 6) such as compound and switching options. Chapter 7 shows you how to write your own Excel spreadsheet to value simple options, combinations of them, and compound options. It also shows how to gain greater precision by modeling option lattices with many steps per year rather than just one.

Chapter 8 is the four-step process that we use in most of our client work. We start with the value of the project without flexibility—its net present value. Next, we obtain an estimate of the rate of return volatility for the project by using Monte Carlo analysis to combine the many causal uncertainties (e.g., price and quantity) into one—the present change in the value of the project. The output of this second phase of our solution methodology is an event tree, that is, a binomial lattice that models the stochastic behavior of the underlying risky asset, which is assumed to be the value of the project without flexibility. The third step is to identify the real option decisions available to management and to turn the event tree into a decision tree. The fourth, and final step, is to use the replicating portfolios (or risk-neutral probabilities) to value the project with flexibility. This is its real option value.

Chapters 9 and 10 discuss ways of modeling uncertainties. In Chapter 9, we combine them using Monte Carlo analysis. In Chapter 10, we keep one of them, namely technological uncertainty, separate. The reason is that the exercise price (i.e., the investment dollars) is spent based on the results of activities that one tied to technology, for example in exploration and production decisions of oil companies, the research and development decisions of pharmaceutical companies, and new product development of retailers.

Chapter 11 is case histories and case solutions. It should be of interest to all readers. Finally, Chapter 12 discusses the potpourri of topics ranging from how real option analysis affects the way we think about strategy to the relationship between ROA and game theory.

How to Obtain Supplemental Materials

The end of the chapter questions and problems are not merely the regurgitation of material in the text. They are also new challenges and thoughts that many of our readers will want to have. For this purpose, we have created a downloadable *Solutions Manual to Accompany Real Options: A Practitioner's Guide* that you may purchase by visiting the Monitor Corporate Finance Web site: www.corpfinonline.com or the Texere Web site: www.texere.com. Some, but not all, of our models are also available on our Web site, www.corpfinonline.com.

ACKNOWLEDGMENTS

There are many people to thank. Tom would like to start with loving thanks to Maggie, his beautiful and talented wife, for supporting and encouraging him while he took time and energy away from home life. Also, thanks to Timothy and Michael, his sons. Vladimir thanks his mother Liliana for her unwavering support, his son Teodor for brightening every day of his life, and all his friends for the gift of their friendship.

Our special thanks to John Stonier who authored Chapter 2, providing his insights into the managerial issues involved in implementing real options.

Then there are the many people who commented on this book: Andy Lo (MIT), Eduardo Schwartz (UCLA), Soussain Faiz (Texaco), Steve Ross (MIT), Peter Tufano (HBS), and Peter Carr (Banc of America) were particularly helpful. We would also like to thank Warren Bailey (Cornell), Phil Keenan (General Motors), Chem Inal (McKinsey & Co.), Sam Blyakher (McKinsey & Co.), Max Michaels (McKinsey & Co.), Yiannos Pierides (University of Cypress), Don Rosner (McKinsey & Co.), Rob McLean (McKinsey & Co.), Klaus Droste (Deutsche Bank), Lenora Cannegieter (McKinsey & Co.), Sandeep Vaswani (Monitor), Betsy Bellingrath (Monitor), Albert Wang (MIT), Alan Kantrow (Monitor), Mark Fuller (Monitor), and Myles Thompson (TEXERE).

TOM COPELAND
VLADIMIR ANTIKAROV

December 2000

CONTENTS

Part III

PART I

1 | Getting Started

This is a book about decision making. We take value creation as a company's objective, through its investments in real assets (as opposed to financial securities). The most common applications are the large-scale investments made by firms including green field investments that they build on their own, mergers and acquisitions, and joint ventures. In days gone by, this would have been called a book on capital budgeting—on the make-or-break investments that are strategic in nature.

We call it *A Practitioner's Guide* because it is meant to be a how-to-do-it book. We want it to be a useful tool that shows how to use Real Options Analysis (ROA) in enough detail that today's managers, most of whom are familiar with the use of a personal computer, can work through a problem from start to finish and fully understand the results. This is not easy in a field of knowledge that has been populated with academic papers using Itô calculus to solve abstract problems. We hope that this book becomes worn with use, dog-eared and underlined—a friend to practitioners. For most of the actual work, we will assume nothing more complicated than high-school algebra (although a little higher mathematics does sneak in from time to time). After a few introductory chapters to familiarize the user by providing many examples, however, we get into the methodology of quantifying risk, of designing lattices, and of putting decision nodes into them so that real options analysis can work its magic.

The book is organized roughly into three parts. Part I (Chapters 1–4) is introductory material: examples from fieldwork (Chapter 1); a chapter on the trials and tribulations of Airbus, a company that has come to include real options as part of its everyday thinking, especially in marketing applications (Chapter 2); a review of traditional net present value (NPV) approaches to making investment decisions and a synthesis of the empirical evidence that compares NPV and ROA (Chapter 3); and basic examples of simple options that illustrate the mechanics (Chapter 4). Part II, the middle section (Chapters 5–10) gets down to the use of a four-step process that we recommend for every option problem: (1) estimating the NPV without flexibility, (2) modeling the uncertainties that drive the value of the investment, (3) putting decision nodes into the event tree that is built to reflect the uncertainties, and (4) valuing the real options using a replicating portfolio approach. Part III, consisting of Chapters 11 and 12 of the book shows how to solve two realistic cases (Chapter 11) and discusses some of the more difficult problems such as the relationship between real options and game theory (Chapter 12).

AN ANALOGY—GETTING FROM HERE TO THERE

Suppose you are planning to drive from Boston to Los Angeles. If you are like us, you will get a map (online from the Internet), remember that over long distances the great circle route is actually the shortest distance between two points on the surface of a globe, and you will map out the route along major highways to take advantage of the turnpike theorem, which says that it's preferable to go a little out of your way to take advantage of higher speed paths.

Off you go, following your carefully mapped route—until you encounter a traffic jam, or unplanned detour. This, of course, is unexpected.

Now think about the analogy with capital budgeting decisions. Net present value, or discounted cash flows, deals only with *expected* cash flows, discounted at a constant rate because risk is assumed to be unchanging during the life of the project. Using expected cash flows is like assuming that you can drive across the country using your expected route—no detours, no traffic jams, no bad weather—no ability to respond to uncertainty.

Senior decision makers, most of whom have been knocked around by life's uncertainties, are more than a little cynical about using net present value. The entire concept is based on restrictive assumptions. A typical NPV analysis goes like this. You are going to invest $450 million over the next 2 years ($100 million immediately and $350 million next year) to build a new factory that will last 20 years, generate a new stream of revenues that starts at $80 million at the end of the third year and grows at 8 percent, and incur total costs of $60 million that start in the third year and grow at 6 percent. There is no salvage value, no working capital, no tax, and depreciation is straight line. The weighted average cost of capital is 10 percent. The NPV is –$12.7 million, and its logic suggests that the project should be rejected. But the assumptions are completely unrealistic. The $450 million investment takes place in stages—design, engineering, and construction—and it can be abandoned at each. If the project goes well, it can be expanded (at a cost) or extended (at a different cost). If it goes badly after construction, it can be scaled back, or sold for a floor price. And no one says that the factory has to be built now. It can be deferred until more favorable conditions prevail. There are at least five different types of managerial flexibility to respond to uncertainties.

DEFINITION OF A REAL OPTION

A real option is the right, but not the obligation, to take an action (e.g., deferring, expanding, contracting, or abandoning) at a predetermined cost called the exercise price, for a predetermined period of time—the life of the option. If we had invested in a complete map with all possible alternate routes to Los Angeles, a radio to get weather and traffic updates, and a global positioning indicator to continuously update our location; we would have been investing in flexibility—and the time saved as a result of the additional flexibility would presumably pay for the cost. It is completely unrealistic to expect to travel from Boston to Los Angeles without a detour. And it is equally unrealistic to believe that expected NPV captures the value of flexibility that decision makers have when they undertake projects. We would go so far as to say that NPV systematically undervalues every project.

Like their financial cousins, the value of real options depends on five basic variables (although others may come into the picture), plus an important sixth. The five are:

1. *The value of the underlying risky asset.* In the case of real options, this is a project, investment, or acquisition. If the value of the underlying asset goes up, so too does the value of the option. One of the important differences between financial and real options is that the owner of a financial option cannot affect the value of the underlying (e.g., a share of General Motors stock). But, the management that operates a real asset can raise its value and thereby raise the value of all real options that depend on it.

2. *The exercise price.* This is the amount of money invested to exercise the option if you are "buying" the asset (with a call option), or the amount of money received if you are "selling" it (with a put option). As the exercise price of an option increases, the value of the call option decreases and the value of the put increases.

3. *The time to expiration of the option.* As the time to expiration increases, so does the value of the option.

4. *The standard deviation of the value of the underlying risky asset.* The value of an option increases with the riskiness of the underlying asset because the payoffs of a (call) option depend on the value of the underlying exceeding its exercise price and the probability of this increases with the volatility of the underlying.

5. *The risk-free rate of interest over the life of the option.* As the risk-free rate goes up, the value of the option also increases.

The sixth variable is the dividends that may be paid out by the underlying asset: the cash outflows or inflows over its life. These six variables are illustrated in Exhibit 1.1.

Let's see if we can identify an option and the variables that governed its value at work in the oldest recorded history of a real option. In the writings of Aristotle is the story of Thales, the sophist philosopher who lived on the island of Milos in the Mediterranean. It seems that Thales read the tea leaves and interpreted them as forecasting a bountiful olive harvest that year. In fact, the reading was so favorable that Thales took his life's savings, a modest amount of money, and bargained with the owners of the olive presses to grant him the right to rent their presses for the usual rate during the harvest season in return for his life savings.

Exhibit 1.1   Six variables that drive the real options analysis value.

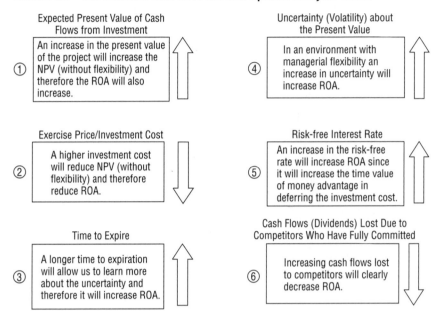

Source: T. Copeland, T. Koller, and J. Murrin, *Valuation: Measuring and Managing the Valuation of Companies,* 3rd edition, New York: John Wiley & Sons, 2000.

Sure enough, the harvest exceeded all expectations, and when the olive growers rushed to the presses to extract the precious oil, Thales was there. He paid the usual rent to the press owners, as required by contract, then turned around and charged the market price—a much higher amount—for use of the presses, which were in high demand. Thales made a fortune, proving for all time, the wisdom of sophists. This is the earliest example, in recorded history, of a real options contract. Can you identify the variables?

The underlying risky asset was the rental value of the olive presses. The driving cause of the uncertainty was the variability of the olive harvest, but the actual variable of interest (the underlying risky asset) was the standard deviation of the value of the rental fee on the olive presses. The exercise price was the normal rental rate, a value that had been written into the contract. The risk-free rate was, presumably, an observable market rate. And the time to maturity was the time until the olive harvest.

The value of the option was the money that Thales paid to the owners of the presses—his life's savings.

If you correctly identified all the variables in the Thales story, you are well on your way. But one or two modern examples might help.

One of my lifelong friends is Professor Steve Ross, now at MIT's Sloan Graduate School of Management. He served on my thesis committee at the University of Pennsylvania. I learned from him then, and continue to learn from him to this day. A few years ago, over lunch in New Haven where he was at that time a professor at Yale, he challenged me with a problem. If I got it wrong, however, I had to buy lunch. Here is the problem. See if you would have to buy lunch—I did that day.

You have the opportunity to buy a toy bank that allows you to put in a dollar today and guarantees you $1.05 with absolute certainty a year later if you do (see Exhibit 1.2). The offer is good for one year. However, interest rates at the real bank are 10 percent right now. How much is the toy bank worth?

Exhibit 1.2 Identifying a simple option.

$1.05 $1.00

Wrong Answer	The toy bank is worthless because you can earn 10% by putting your money in the bank instead of earning 5% with the toy bank (problem: this assumes that the interest rate never changes).
NPV — No Flexibility	

Right Answer	The toy bank is valuable because it is an option (you have the right, but not the obligation, to use it) and because interest rates are uncertain. There is a chance that the rate will fall below 5%. When it does, the option is valuable and will be exercised (the uncertainty in the interest rate is the key to understanding the problem.
Total Value with Flexibility (ROA)	

NPV is misleading because it does not consider the option/flexibility value this toy bank offers.

Source: Steve Ross, Sterling Professor of Economics and Finance at Yale University.

My answer was that the toy bank is worth nothing because I could put my dollar in the real bank and earn 10 percent while earning only 5 percent through the toy bank. I bought lunch because I failed to recognize the toy bank as an option on interest rates. Although currently 10 percent, interest rates are uncertain and there is a finite possibility that rates might fall to less than 5 percent in a year. If they do, the toy bank is worth something. Its value, therefore is the value of a one-year option on interest rates with an exercise price at 5 percent.

A similar and quite serious example, where executives failed to recognize the value of interest rate options, occurred in the life insurance industry. In the late 1960s, interest rates were low and had been low for a long time. As a clause in life insurance policies, life insurance companies granted the policy owners the right to borrow against the cash value of the policy at a fixed rate of interest, say 9 percent, for the life of the policy. Low interest rates, in the 3 to 4 percent range, made it seem that the clause was of little value. But the life of the option was extremely long for some policy holders. I was 22 at the time and my life expectancy exceeded 50 years. How much is a 50-year option on interest rates worth? The question became more than rhetorical when in the early 1980s, rates of interest of U.S. Treasury bills went to 17 or 18 percent. Even I figured out that I had a risk-free profit if I borrowed at 9 percent from the insurance company and invested it at 17 percent in U.S. Treasuries. Millions of other policy holders also exercised their options and as a result, several insurance companies went into default. They failed to realize the option value they were giving up in their rush to sell policies a little over a decade earlier.

THE ASYMMETRIC PAYOFFS OF OPTIONS

Exhibit 1.3 shows a lognormal distribution of values that might be taken by a share of stock. Note that the stock price cannot go negative, but that there is a small probability that it could go to infinity. To value the stock of a large company, it is customary to use discounted cash flow methodology where expected cash flows are forecasted, then discounted back to the present at a risk-adjusted weighted average cost of capital.[1] At expiration,

Exhibit 1.3 Call option payoffs are in the upper tail.

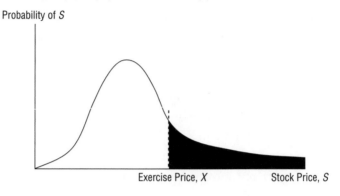

a call option pays off when the stock price, *S*, exceeds the exercise price, *X;* otherwise it is worthless. Mathematically, this is written as

Call option value at expiration: MAX[S − X, 0]

In Exhibit 1.3, this is the area in the upper tail of the distribution (i.e., the region where the exercise price exceeds the stock price). To value the stock, we value the entire distribution, but to value the option, we value the upper tail of the distribution. The option payouts are asymmetric. Exhibit 1.4 shows that the payoffs for a put option are positive when the

Exhibit 1.4 Put option payoffs are in the lower tail.

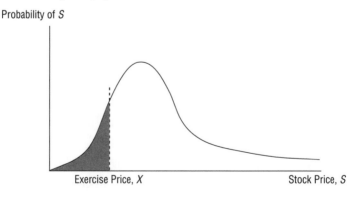

Exhibit 1.5   Options are the "Lego blocks" of finance.

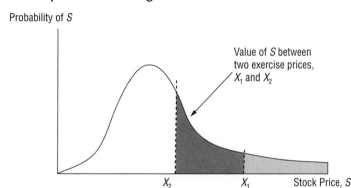

exercise price is higher than the stock price, in the lower tail of the distribution. Mathematically, at expiration

Put option value at expiration: MAX[X – S, 0]

The really interesting implication of these diagrams is that if you can value call and put options, they can be used to slice and dice the payouts of the underlying risky asset into pieces that can be recombined any way you want. Options are the Lego blocks of finance. An illustration is given in Exhibit 1.5. Here we have two call options, one with a high exercise price, X_1, and a second with a lower exercise price, X_2. If we could value both of them, then subtract their values, one from the other, the difference would be the value of the slice of the distribution between X_1 and X_2. Later in the book, we show how to value options using simple algebraic techniques (not Itô calculus); then we can illustrate some of the more interesting Lego block applications.

Real Options Dictionary

Options have a language all their own. You have already been introduced to the basics—the exercise price, the underlying and its volatility, and the maturity date. But there is much more.

A *call option* is the right to buy the underlying asset by paying the exercise price. At the time of exercise, the profit on the option is the difference between the value of the underlying asset and the exercise price. A *put option* is the opposite—the right to sell the underlying asset to receive the exercise price. A call option where the price of the underlying is above the exercise price so that an immediate profit could be made by exercising the option is said to be *in-the-money.* Conversely, if the price of the underlying is below the exercise price the option is *out-of-the-money.*

Options that can be exercised only on their maturity date are called *European options.* Those that can be exercised any time during their life are called *American options.* There are also boundary conditions called *caps* and *floors* that bound the value of the underlying. For example, a mortgage may have a variable interest rate, but with a cap that prohibits the rate from going above a preset level.

TAXONOMY OF REAL OPTIONS

Real options are classified primarily by the type of flexibility that they offer. For example, an option is just what it seems to be—the right, but not the obligation to invest in a project at a later date. A *deferral option* is an American call option found in most projects where one has the right to delay the start of a project. Its exercise price is the money invested in getting the project started. The *option to abandon* a project for a fixed price (even that price decreases through time) is formally an American put. So is the *option to contract (scale back)* a project by selling a fraction of it for a fixed price. The *option to expand* a project by paying more to scale up the operations is an American call. And the *option to extend* the life of a project by paying an exercise price is also an American call.

Switching options are portfolios of American call and put options that allow their owner to switch at a fixed cost (or costs) between two modes of operation. For example, peak load generating equipment, usually gas-fired turbines, is switched on when electricity prices go up and switched off when they come down. The option to exit and then reenter an industry, or to shut down then restart a manufacturing plant are additional examples.

There are also options on options, called *compound options.* Phased investments fit into this category. When you set out to build a factory, you can choose to do so in phases—a design phase, an engineering phase, and construction. You have the option to stop or defer the project at the end of each phase. Thus, each phase is an option that is contingent on the earlier exercise of other options—an option on an option (or options). Finally, options that are driven by multiple sources of uncertainty are called *rainbow options*. Most real options are affected by uncertainty regarding the price of a unit of output, the quantity that might be sold, and by uncertain interest rates that affect the present value of the project. Many real-world applications require modeling as *compound rainbow options*. For example, exploration and production, research and development, and new product development are all compound rainbow options.

REAL OPTIONS ARE EVERYWHERE—WAR STORIES

We have been applying real options in practice for over a decade.[2] These war stories are entertaining and instructive. They show that real options can dramatically change the decisions made by management, that real options fit management's intuition better than NPV, and that the applications are numerous and varied.

We are often asked two questions. First, isn't the option value of managerial flexibility always positive and consequently isn't the use of real options just an attempt to justify projects that should be turned down? Our response comes in two parts. First, the appropriate mind-set is to recognize that the net present value technique systematically undervalues everything because it fails to capture the value of flexibility. And second, while the value of flexibility is always positive, the price that you have to pay for it often exceeds its value. For example, you know that an engine that is capable of switching between two fuels (propane or gasoline) is more flexible and therefore more valuable, but the extra cost of the ability to switch can easily exceed the value of the switching capability, and you would decide to stick with a simpler, less costly engine that uses only gasoline.

The second question is, when is the use of real options likely to change the answer a lot? Exhibit 1.6 is our response. Real options have the greatest value when three factors come together. When there is high

Exhibit 1.6 When managerial flexibility is valuable.

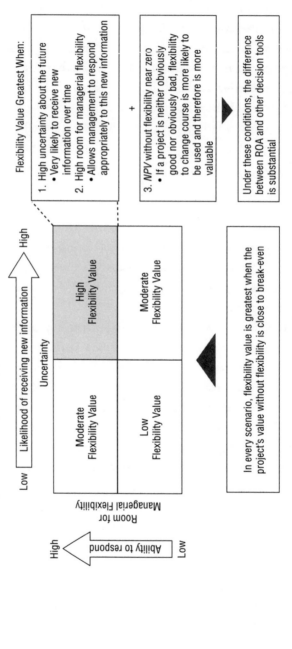

Flexibility Value Greatest When:

1. High uncertainty about the future
   • Very likely to receive new information over time
2. High room for managerial flexibility
   • Allows management to respond appropriately to this new information

+

3. *NPV* without flexibility near zero
   • If a project is neither obviously good nor obviously bad, flexibility to change course is more likely to be used and therefore is more valuable

Under these conditions, the difference between ROA and other decision tools is substantial

In every scenario, flexibility value is greatest when the project's value without flexibility is close to break-even

Uncertainty

Room for Managerial Flexibility	Moderate Flexibility Value	High Flexibility Value
	Low Flexibility Value	Moderate Flexibility Value

Likelihood of receiving new information — Low / High

Ability to respond — High / Low

Source: T. Copeland, T. Koller, and J. Murrin, *Valuation: Measuring and Managing the Value of Companies*, 3rd edition, New York: John Wiley & Sons, 2000.

uncertainty and when managers have flexibility to respond to it, real options are important. But the value of real options relative to NPV is large when the NPV is close to zero, in the gray area. If the NPV is high, then most options that provide additional flexibility will have a very low probability of being exercised, and therefore have low relative value. Conversely, if the NPV is extremely negative, no amount of optionality can rescue the project. It is in making the tough decisions—those where the NPV is close to zero—that the additional value of flexibility makes a big difference. In most of the war stories that follow, the management team was puzzling over an NPV result that did not feel quite right.

Deferral Call Option

Our client was one of several bidders for a lease on government-owned coal lands that gave the right to mine a coal deposit. Management had performed a traditional NPV analysis. The historical growth trend in the price per ton of coal had been estimated and extrapolated, the quantity of coal in the ground was estimated, and so were extraction costs. From these facts, the expected free cash flows were forecast and discounted back to the present at an estimate of the weighted average cost of capital. Then the development costs were subtracted to obtain an estimate of the NPV of the project—$81 million. All of this was standard procedure. Nevertheless, management was concerned because rumor had it that the bids would be somewhat higher. Since the revenue per ton was only one dollar above the current extraction cost per ton, the project was extremely risky—a one-dollar shift could double profits or eliminate them completely. Furthermore, the investment to develop the mineral mine was much larger than the NPV.

When reviewing the NPV results, the management team debated the issue of when to assume the actual development of the mineral lease. They could develop any time up to 5 years after acquiring it. Failure to develop within 5 years would cause the lease rights to revert to the government. Their first thought was to calculate the NPV of five mutually exclusive scenarios: invest now, at the end of the first year, at the end of the second year, and so on. The answer did not change much.

Next, they decided to think of the project as having a deferral option, allowing them to postpone their development decision until the price of coal increased enough to make them relatively certain that they could recover their development costs before the price turned around and fell again. When viewed as a deferral option, the value of the project with flexibility rose to $159.5 million. They actually won the bidding at $99 million and opened the mine a few years later. Since then, good fortune has smiled on them and the property is said to be worth roughly $800 million today.

Note that this example illustrates a fundamental difference between NPV and ROA that will be discussed in detail later on, namely that NPV must consider deferral for one year as a mutually exclusive alternative to deferring for two years, and so on—a total of five mutually exclusive choices. Real Options Analysis combines them into a single present value—a go or no go decision today—with a decision rule about when to develop the lease.

American Put Option: A Cancelable Operating Lease

Conversations with the CFO of a major manufacturer of jet engines revealed that his company was offering customers the right to cancel operating leases of aircraft owned by the jet engine manufacturer. In this situation, competition to put engines on the wings of aircraft was fierce because once on the wings, the engines generated demand for a 30-year stream of spare parts, which had a present value to the manufacturer greater than the engines themselves—so fierce, in fact, that the jet engine manufacturer would buy the plane and lease it to any customer that put the manufacturer's engines onto the wings. He was curious to know how much the right to cancel the leases was worth. The lease could be canceled either predelivery or for a period of time after delivery of the aircraft—a walk-away option. When we valued the options, they turned out to be worth 19 percent of the value of the engines on wide-body aircraft and 83 percent on narrow body aircraft.

Astounded by the value of the options, the CFO asked what to do next, because he feared loss of sales if he stopped offering the cancellation feature. Subsequently, we segmented the market into categories based on the variability of estimated operating income, which in turn depends on the variability of passenger revenue miles (and the cost structure), airline by airline. Those with the greatest variability would value the put option highest and be most likely to exercise it. The jet engine manufacturer decided to stop offering the cancellation feature to these airlines where the value of the cancellation feature was greatest, preferring to lose their business to competitors. A few years later, when the value of planes declined due to a downturn in business, the company suffered fewer cancellations than its competitors, thereby saving millions.

Airbus has stated in public forums that it is using real options to estimate the value of other types of real options to its customers. For example, up to 12 months predelivery, a customer can change the size of the aircraft within a family of aircraft manufactured on the same production line. Having estimated the value of the option, Airbus can be a more effective negotiator. Chapter 2 discusses the trials and tribulations of implementation from a "change management" perspective.

Opening and Closing Mines: Switching Options

Switching options are the right to close an operation that is currently open by paying fixed shutdown costs and the right to open it later for a different fixed cost to a common type of option, actually a portfolio of puts and calls.

There are many examples. Mines can be shut down as the mineral price falls, then reopened later. Factories (e.g., a General Motors assembly plant) can be shut down when demand falls, then reopened when it picks up. Peak load electricity generators (gas-fired turbines) are turned on during days when the spot price of electricity soars, and are turned off again when it falls. Heavy oil is so viscous that live steam must be pumped into the ground to thin it enough to be pumped to the surface. When the well is closed the steam heat in the ground is lost and must be replaced (a fixed cost) when the well is reopened. Trees can be harvested faster (at an extra cost) when prices rise, or slower when prices fall. These are all examples of switching options.

Exhibit 1.7 provides the results of an application of switching options in mining. Not only does the real options approach reveal the added value

Exhibit 1.7   Switching options in mining.

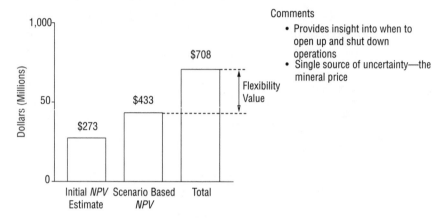

Source: T. Copeland, T. Koller, and J. Murrin, *Valuation: Measuring and Managing the Value of Companies,* 3rd edition, New York: John Wiley & Sons, 2000.

from the ability to close then reopen the mine, but it also provides rules of thumb about when to do so. For example, suppose the price of an ounce of gold is $350 and the extraction cost is $300. If the price falls to $299 per ounce, standard economic theory says the mine should be shut down because marginal revenue is below marginal cost and the company is losing $1 per ounce on every ounce produced. The complications are that fixed costs must be incurred to shut down and to restart, and the price of gold is uncertain. It has a high probability of turning around and rising above $300 the next day. Therefore, the optimal policy is to wait until the price falls enough below the $300 per ounce threshold so that the expected losses from production equal the shutdown costs. Consequently, it is optimal to operate at a loss for a period of time before shutting down. If the mine is already shut down, and the price begins to rise until it finally exceeds the $300 per ounce mark, the mine will not be reopened until the price rises enough so that the expected profit equals the start-up cost. Real options approaches to this problem show that the flexibility to shut down and reopen adds value to the mine, adds more value if the switching costs are low, and tells the mining company exactly what trigger prices to use for optimal operation.

Phased Investment in a Chemical Plant: A Compound Option

A chemical company had estimated the NPV of a new plant to be negative $72 million. The expected investment was planned in three stages, however (see Exhibit 1.8). First was a design phase costing $50 million, followed by an engineering and preconstruction phase that would start in six months and cost $200 million, with construction due to start in a year and cost $400 million. The NPV was only about 10 percent (negative) of the total implementation cost. Furthermore, the operating spread between the cost of the input chemicals and the price of the output chemicals was highly variable, was mean-reverting, and was currently midcycle (see Exhibit 1.9). Net present value scenarios didn't help much because their average was still the original answer of negative $72 million. No one would go out on a limb to guess whether the operating spread would move up or down from its current level, although everyone agreed it was highly variable. A real options approach viewed the project as a series of compound options—each option depending on the exercise of those that preceded it. For example, at the end of the design phase, the viability of the project could be reexamined conditional on the operating spread at that point of time. Either the project would be abandoned or the company

Exhibit 1.8 Compound options in plant construction.

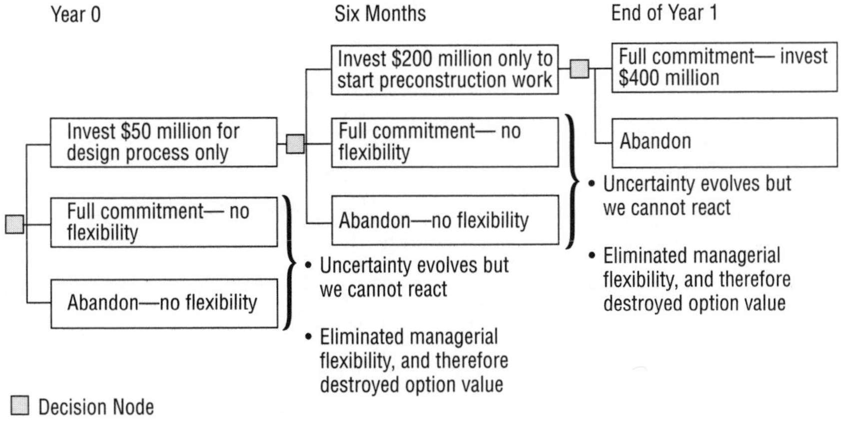

Source: T. Copeland, T. Koller, and J. Murrin, *Valuation: Measuring and Managing the Valuation of Companies,* 3rd edition, New York: John Wiley & Sons, 2000.

Exhibit 1.9   Cyclical and uncertain operating spread.

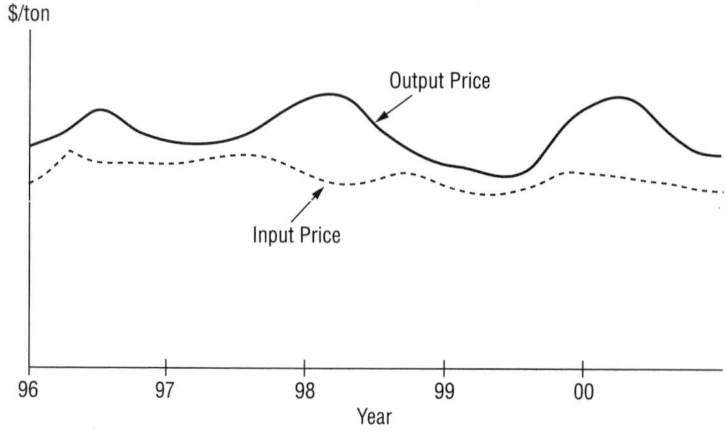

would decide on full commitment to all remaining phases, or the company would commit to Phase II only. Thus Phase II is a call option that is contingent on Phase I. The same is true of a decision one year from now about whether to go ahead with final construction, contingent on the operating spread at that time. The flexibility provided by the phases of the investment added $454 million to the standard NPV, thereby making the value of the project positive $382 million. Consequently, the first phase was started.

Many executive decisions are made in phases without precommitment to undertake all phases regardless of how uncertainties that drive the value of the project might evolve. Examples are new product development and introduction, and expansion into new geographies.

Exploration and Development: A Compound Rainbow Option

This is the most complex and most realistic of the cases reviewed in this chapter. A large integrated oil company was trying to decide whether to go ahead with what would be a $1 billion development of an oil field, with investments in refineries, pipelines, storage, and docking facilities. At present, the field was explored 60 percent by drilling and 40 percent with sonics. A debate was raging among the decision-making team members. Half of them argued in favor of immediate development because it would pull the stream of expected cash flows into the present and create value for shareholders. The other half of the team wanted to continue drilling. They argued that if the field were exploited immediately, the development expense was almost certain to be wrong sized. If there was more oil than expected in the 40 percent that was not drilled, then it would be necessary to construct an additional subscale refinery (an uneconomic result), and if there was less oil than expected, the initial capital investment would be too large, resulting in a wastage. The team was genuinely split. They decided to see if they could learn anything by experimenting with a real options approach. As illustrated in Exhibit 1.10, the decision tree is a compound option with development decisions contingent on the results of further exploration. Furthermore, there were two sources of uncertainty. The price of oil was known at the beginning of the project but would become more uncertain over time. Additionally, there was uncertainty about the quantity of oil in the ground, which is high at the start of the project, but will be reduced over time by drilling.

In this case, the real options analysis indicated that a strategy of drilling over the next 3 years, followed by a much better informed and right-sized field development decision 3 years from now, and a final development decision in 11 years was worth 125 percent more than the base case. The debate was resolved in favor of further exploration, but this need not have been the case. If the resolution of uncertainty that was expected from drilling was low and the cost of drilling high, the answer could easily have been quite the opposite.

Compound rainbow options are perhaps the most realistic and the most complex real options that we will show you how to value. But they cover a wide and important class of decisions: In addition to exploration and development, they are useful for research and development, and new product development decisions.

WHY THE TIME HAS COME FOR PRACTICAL APPLICATIONS OF REAL OPTIONS ANALYSIS (ROA)

The modern breakthrough in valuation of options was made in the early 1970s by Robert Merton, Fischer Black, and Myron Scholes, whose Nobel prize winning work solved a tough problem that had been a challenge

Exhibit 1.10 Compound rainbow option—exploration and development.

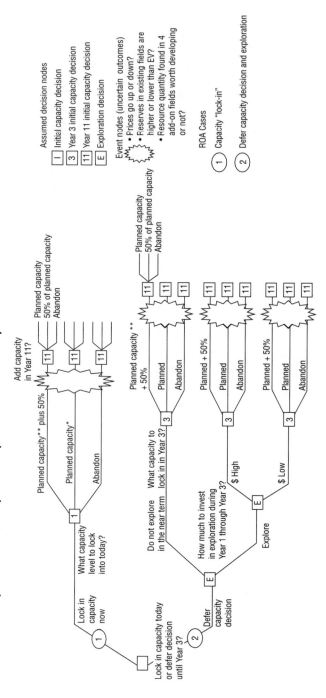

* Simplified for illustrative purposes.
** Capacity planned before ROA analysis.

Source: T. Copeland, T. Koller, and J. Murrin, *Valuation: Measuring and Managing the Value of Companies*, 3rd edition, New York: John Wiley & Sons, 2000.

since the early 1900s. Hundreds of papers, both theoretical and empirical, have followed. The early applications were almost exclusively in the securities pricing arena where data were plentiful and where the market price of the underlying risky security was directly observable. And theoreticians found it convenient to use stochastic differential equations (a graduate level math) as the tool of choice for publishing their advances. This was not a particularly friendly environment for management applications for real options.

Now, at the beginning of the new millennium, the application of real options is just beginning to take off, nearly 30 years after the seminal work of Merton, Black, and Scholes. Why? Some of the reasons are illustrated in Exhibit 1.11. First and foremost, the speed and capacity of personal computers have advanced so rapidly that only recently have managers had at their disposal enough easy-to-access computer power to bring realism and transparency to the table. No longer is Itô calculus a necessary tool. Instead, we can use lattices and algebraic solutions that are

Exhibit 1.11   ROA has many applications.

```
┌─────────────────────────────────────────────────┐
│                Limited Applications…              │
└─────────────────────────────────────────────────┘
┌─────────────────────────────────────────────────┐
│ • Uncertainty driven by world commodity product  │
│ • Higher mathematics necessary for application   │
│ • Limited computer power of PCs                   │
│ • Single source of uncertainty                    │
│ • Simple options                                  │
└─────────────────────────────────────────────────┘

                      ⇩

┌─────────────────────────────────────────────────┐
│               Become Many Applications            │
└─────────────────────────────────────────────────┘
┌─────────────────────────────────────────────────┐
│ • Source of uncertainty not necessarily market priced │
│ • Algebra and Excel spreadsheets                  │
│ • Low cost, fast, powerful PCs                    │
│ • Multiple sources of uncertainty (rainbow options) │
│ • Options on options (compound options, learning options) │
└─────────────────────────────────────────────────┘
```

Source: T. Copeland, T. Koller, and J. Murrin, *Valuation: Measuring and Managing the Value of Companies,* 3rd edition, New York: John Wiley & Sons, 2000.

easy to implement on a PC and easy to understand. Next, early pioneers assumed that real options required that the user identify an underlying asset that was traded in the marketplaces of the world (e.g., commodities markets for oil, coal, or gold). Now we realize that real options can be applied to almost any situation where it is possible to estimate the NPV of the underlying project without flexibility. It is now possible to understand and to value real options for many realistic applications including those that are compound options and that have multiple sources of uncertainty.

CONCLUSION

This book is a practitioner's guide to real options. Why use real options for evaluating major investment decisions? Because Real Options Analysis values the flexibility to respond to uncertain events—net present value techniques do not and consequently undervalue everything. Is real options analysis more difficult to use? Definitely, yes: That is why we are writing this book. Based on over 10 years of experience, we have learned how to apply real options to realistic settings. The next chapter talks about the change process that must accompany implementation.

QUESTIONS

For solutions go to www.corpfinonline.com.

1. What are the six variables that affect the value of a real option?
2. What is the difference between an option and a bet?
3. The value of a call option, C, as a function of the value of an underlying risky asset, S, is graphed below.

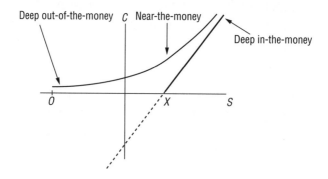

The exercise price is X. Draw another graph with the ratio of the call value to the absolute value of the difference between S and X or the vertical axis and the value of the underlying, S, or the horizontal axis (see below).

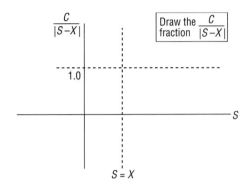

If we interpret the vertical axis as the value of flexibility, C, as a percentage of the (absolute value of) net present value of the project, what do the results say about the relative value of near-the-money options?

4. A runner is on first base, the score is tied in the bottom of the ninth and he has to decide whether to try to steal second. Is his decision an option or a bet? Why?

5. Why does the value of both a call and a put go up when the volatility of the underlying risky asset goes up?

6. Identify the type of option and the five parameters that affect its value in an automobile insurance policy (collision insurance with no deductible).

7. From a real options perspective, what is the difference between a one-off acquisition and an acquisitions program with plans for multiple acquisitions?

8. Graph the payoffs for a call with an exercise price of $50 and a put with an exercise price of $60, both written as a stock whose price is lognormally distributed with a current price of $70 (and pays no dividends).

9. George knew that, at any time during the next five years, he could close down half of his factory and sell the buildings and equipment for $2 million. Of course, the value of the remaining business would

fall by 40 percent. What option is involved and what is the underlying risky asset, the exercise price, the time to maturity, and the volatility?

10. Why do we state that net present value analysis systematically under-values everything?

11. In the middle ages there were laws against usury. They were bypassed in the following way. Suppose you were a baker and needed to finance 100 percent of the construction cost of your bakery with other people's money (a "loan"). Since loans at a positive interest rate are forbidden by usury laws, you enter into the following arrangement with a wealthy merchant. You accept his cash, and give him the deed to your bakery. You promise to buy the bakery from him for $X in five years and he promises to sell the bakery to you for $X on the same date. If you need $100,000 in cash now, and the merchant wants 20 percent interest on his money per year, what should $X be? What options are involved? What risk does the banker accept when he takes the deal?

12. Commercial banks made a large fraction of their fees from committed lines of credit. For a fee (e.g., ⅜ths of a point) on the committed line (e.g., $300 million), they will guarantee your company the right to borrow at a predetermined rate (e.g., LIBOR plus ⅜ths). From the company's point of view, what option are they taking, what is the underlying uncertainty, and what is the exercise price?

13. A Harvard business case called Arundle Partners studies a proposal made by an investment firm (Arundle Partners) to buy the right to sequelize movies produced by motion picture studios during a given year. What option is involved? What is its exercise price? How would you estimate the volatility of the underlying?

14. Your firm is about to build a new operating facility to produce aluminum body race cars. What options might be involved in the decision?

REFERENCES

These are easy-to-read articles on real options that are designed for people who want to get a sound introduction without having to wade through a lot of math.

Chorn, L., and P. Carr. 1997, March 16–18. "The Value of Purchasing Information to Reduce Risk in Capital Investment Projects," SPE paper No. 37948, presented at 1997 SPE Hydrocarbon Economics and Evaluation Symposium, Dallas, TX.

Copeland, T., and P. Keenan. 1998. "How Much Is Flexibility Worth?" *McKinsey Quarterly, 2,* 38–49.

Copeland, T., and P. Keenan. 1998. "Making Real Options Real," *McKinsey Quarterly, 3,* 129–141.

Copeland, T., and J. Weiner. 1990. "Proactive Management of Uncertainty," *McKinsey Quarterly, 4,* 133–148.

Kemna, A. 1993, Autumn. "Case Studies on Real Options," *Financial Management,* 259–270.

Kulatilaka, N., and A. Markus. 1992, Fall. "Project Valuation under Uncertainty: When Does DCF Fail?" *Journal of Applied Corporate Finance,* 92–100.

Ritchkin, P., and G. Rabinowitz. 1998. "Capital Budgeting Using Contingent Claims Analysis: A Tutorial," *Advances in Futures and Options Research, 3,* 119–143.

Trigeorgis, L. 1998. "A Conceptual Options Framework for Capital Budgeting," *Advances in Futures and Options Research, 3,* 145–167.

Trigeorgis, L. 1993, Autumn. "Real Options and Interactions with Flexibility," *Financial Management, 22,* 3, 202–222.

2 | The Change Process

JOHN STONIER*

A FRAMEWORK FOR CHANGE

No change of paradigm comes easily. It took over 20 years before corporate America had widely adopted net present value techniques to replace the payback period as the primary analysis of large budget investments. It always takes a long time to change from one paradigm to another. Inertia is not only a law of physics. It applies to organizational change too. Consequently, pioneers of real options—the new paradigm—are constantly asked the senseless but seemingly necessary question "Why should our company use a new tool that no one else is using?"

This chapter is about how one company is using real options analysis (ROA) to change its thinking about how contingencies should be priced in its sales contracts with buyers. Above all it is about the trials and tribulations of the process of changing the mind-set of a top management team, to use a new more realistic decision-making tool called real options. The successes and failures, the sweat of implementation, and the competitive advantage that was achieved by Airbus Industrie marketing are recorded in this chapter by John Stonier, Marketing Director.

In Diffusion of Innovations, *4th edition,*[1] *Everett Rogers describes five attributes of innovation that determine its rate of adoption. They are illustrated in Exhibit 2.1. First, the new idea has to be better than the old one. It must have a clear relative advantage. It takes a good new theory to kill an*

---

* Marketing Director Airbus Industrie. The opinions expressed in this document are those of the author and do not necessarily reflect those of Airbus Industrie North America or its parent company.

Exhibit 2.1   Attributes of innovation that affect the rate of adoption.

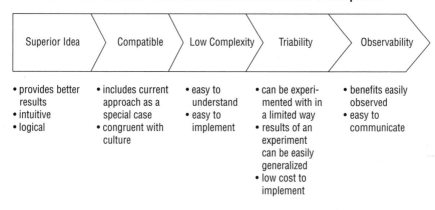

Superior Idea	Compatible	Low Complexity	Triability	Observability
• provides better results • intuitive • logical	• includes current approach as a special case • congruent with culture	• easy to understand • easy to implement	• can be experimented with in a limited way • results of an experiment can be easily generalized • low cost to implement	• benefits easily observed • easy to communicate

Source: Everett Rogers, *Diffusion of Innovations, 4th edition.*

inadequate old one. At Airbus, there was a need to price out the value of flexibility in sales contracts, and to understand its value from the client perspective. Net present value methods failed to do so. Second, the new idea must be compatible with previously introduced ideas. Therefore, it was necessary to be able to show how, when flexibility was removed, the real option analysis reduced to give exactly the same answer as net present value. An analogy in physics is that Einstein's theory of relativity was compatible with Newtonian theory when one assumes a system is at rest. Furthermore, real options are also a net present value concept, therefore, management is not asked to change their basic beliefs. Third, the innovation should have a low level of complexity. This has been a stumbling block for real options, and it shows up as a problem in the case of Airbus. The ROA solution methodology has been simplified by using lattices that employ simple algebra, rather than the alternative—stochastic differential equations. Even so, real options analysis requires executives to estimate and understand uncertainty and the decisions that can be made to respond to it—a new challenge. Next comes triability. Rogers defines it as "the degree to which an innovation may be experimented with on a limited basis." The fact that real options analysis is a model makes it easy to experiment with to see whether it provides intuitive results; this makes it triable. But once an investment is made, it is irreversible. Therefore the cost involved is not recoverable, and triability becomes expensive. The fifth and *final attribute that an innovation should have is observability; its benefits should be easily observed and communicated to others. That is the purpose of this book.*

Keeping these five attributes in mind, let's move on to read the story of Airbus, and reflect on its experience innovating by using real options. What were its successes and failures? [Comments by Tom Copeland are in italics.]

THE AIRBUS INDUSTRIE EXPERIENCE

As a Marketing Director for Airbus Industrie, I am responsible for developing and presenting to airlines the business case for our products—large commercial aircraft—justifying to these airlines why they should purchase our aircraft and not a competitor's. This type of analysis has become increasingly complex and financially oriented as we attempt to explicitly value, to our customers, all elements of a proposed deal extending over many years. I have therefore spent considerable time to understand both the implications and potential limitations of applying conventional financial decision-making tools in the airline industry. This led me to real options.

REALIZING THAT SOMETHING IS WRONG IS THE FIRST STEP TO PUTTING IT RIGHT

In many industries, there seems to be a belief that they are somewhat unique or special and that business processes developed over many years have been created for good reasons—that some Darwinian process at play has shown what will work and what will not. There are usually other justifications of uniqueness like the level of proprietary technology, or the fact that everyone else in the industry is behaving in the same way. Of course, the longer one spends in that industry and the less management cross-fertilization that occurs, the greater that belief. Sometimes it's good to challenge those traditional, deep-seated views.

Working in the North American Marketing arm of Airbus Industrie, my role was to justify to our customers the value of our products, in support of sales campaigns. Over a period of time, I developed a view that we could potentially improve this process. This had implications, not only for the way we were doing business, but also for our competitors and our customers. My basic contention was that the pricing of services that came with the product, a process of bartering between buyers and sellers, was quite inefficient, partially because no one was able to put numbers alongside their intuition.

BACKGROUND ON THE PROBLEM

The economic life of modern commercial aircraft exceeds 25 years, and with a minimum scale to which an airline can economically commit in terms of fleet type, an airline's decision to purchase a new aircraft type is usually a multibillion-dollar decision. This kind of decision comes under considerable financial scrutiny, and airlines use detailed but very conventional capital budgeting techniques in their long-term fleet planning. To quantify the various attributes of an aircraft over its operating life such as fuel burn and maintenance on the costs side, and passenger and cargo loads on the revenue side, airlines use discounted cash flow analysis (DCF) projecting 20 years or more into the future.

To justify the price of our products, in absolute terms, and relative to our competitors, the manufacturers conduct a very similar analysis. Those two perspectives (the buyer's and seller's) of the discounted present value of an aircraft in service with an airline was often the starting point and the basis of a negotiation that led to an eventual sale. Twenty years ago, engineers still dominated airline management. Marketing to this management was traditional product marketing. The vocabulary was range, payload, fuel burn, seating capacity, and so forth. Today, airline management is dominated by financially astute businesspeople. Once it is clear that an aircraft will meet the airline's mission requirements, the discussions turn to life cycle costs, return on investment, and managing risk.

Complicating this analysis was the trend in the industry to include a package of goods (or sweeteners), many of which can be thought of as a form of risk management service beneficial to the airlines (e.g., performance and asset value guarantees, engineering and financing support, and some contractual flexibility). The majority of these services are in fact contingent liabilities for the manufacturer. Historically, we had not explicitly marketed the value of these sweeteners to the customer. In addition, we had not really been able to cost out some of these contingencies. We took provisions, which were essentially accounting charges, a pot of money we could draw against should there be a need some time in the future. The customers would play off the suppliers, one against the other, in a high stakes, winner-takes-all game, demanding various concessions. The pressure to win could be extreme, and sometimes we did things that we later regretted. The trick was to deal with our competitors, meet our profitability requirements, and not get any surprises down the road, which unexpectedly reduced the return of the deal. It seemed that *valuation* of the contingencies was a key aspect of the process.

Not only did we need to better understand the cost to ourselves, but also the value to the airline. By doing this, we could ensure that we were offering the right services and packaging them correctly, giving us the best chance of winning the deal. For example, if a guarantee has an expected cost to the manufacturer of say $3m but the airline values it at $1m, then we would both be better off agreeing on a cash discount on the aircraft price of $2m. This could occur because of asymmetry of information between the two parties or differing perceptions about expected outcomes. Bartering over these various services has always occurred during the marketing and sales process, but not in an efficient manner. This signaling between the buyer and seller has indicated to both parties the respective willingness to bear certain risks in the value chain. However, these soft attributes had been hard to quantify.

The more sophisticated airlines were quite well versed in financial analysis. Despite this fact, we were often both at a loss to realistically model some cost or revenue item. We would scour through the pages of the usual MBA texts. Often the examples seemed self-serving. They appeared to have been reverse-manufactured to demonstrate a point of economic theory that did not fit our real-life problem. A specific example is the valuation of a maintenance cost guarantee. The manufacturer guarantees the level of airframe maintenance costs over the life of the aircraft by placing a ceiling on those costs. While both the manufacturers and the airlines make detailed assessments of the probable life cycle costs, a guarantee caps the downside risk for the airline. It also represents a contingent liability for the manufacturer.

The normal procedure was for the airline to discount all the costs and revenues associated with a project at its weighted average cost of capital (WACC) or a hurdle rate. In this case, thinking that the maintenance cost stream would be less risky if guaranteed, they would discount it at the cost of debt rather than WACC. Of course, when you discount a negative cash flow at a lower rate you get a larger negative cash flow. Could this be right? It was certainly counterintuitive.

THE BEGINNING OF A NEW APPROACH

In desperation, I called Professor Dick Brealey who jointly wrote one of the standard MBA texts on finance used extensively in the industry. From his office at the London Business School, using basic theory on the bond market, he proceeded to convince me that the theory was correct and otherwise would result in a "perpetual subsidy," certainly not something that we would want to suggest could occur in nature. While the airline was quite understanding, our failure to realistically value the guarantee did not help us or the airline understand the trade-offs involved. The negotiations continued. The problem however was filed away in the back of my mind, and one day I would get to the bottom of this disturbing problem.

Another problem was the airline's desire to use a "hurdle rate" rather than WACC in their analysis. This was always a contentious issue for us. When an airline purchases a fleet of new aircraft, it is often trading upfront capital costs against a long stream of cash operating cost savings, the newer aircraft being much more efficient in this respect. The higher the discount rate used, the worse this trade-off looks and the lower the price an airline could justify paying for an aircraft to its shareholders. Could our standard MBA textbook help us this time? Apparently not; while there were several references to the use of a target ROI, and ranking alternatives in the case of limited capital resources, there was no real guidance on what the margin between the hurdle rate and WACC should be. Obviously in the case of limited capital, the project with the highest ROI should be chosen, but what about the case of mutually exclusive projects, where one was the "status quo"? If a firm used a discount rate that was too high, surely it was forgoing an investment that would return value to shareholders (i.e., a return higher than WACC). Strangely, there seemed to be a relationship between an airline's share price and its hurdle rate. When the stock price was high, investing at WACC was fine, but the lower it got, the more unreasonably high the hurdle rate became, in an attempt to turn the airline around.

The use of a relatively high hurdle rate also affected the implicit valuations an airline would put on some of the sweeteners. For example, a cash stream provided by the manufacturer, and costed by discounting at our cost of capital, would have a much lower value to the airline than when discounted at their hurdle rate, thus seeming to destroy value. There were many sleep-disturbed nights thinking about these and other similar problems. Of course, now looking back using a real options lens, the answers are clear.

COULD WE IMPROVE OUR COMPETITIVE POSITION THROUGH BETTER FINANCIAL ANALYSIS?

Specifically, we asked: Would accurate valuation of sweeteners packaged with our aircraft improve our ability to compete? Were we trying to harden up an attribute that our competitors had a cost advantage in? Could we persuade our customers to buy into the valuations? All these questions would have to be addressed before we could commit resources to this project.

As stated, my belief was that the bilateral trading between the airlines and manufacturers was, in a way, unfocused and inefficient. Airlines and manufacturers were making somewhat arbitrary (but heuristic) decisions, about the value of the sweeteners packaged in the overall deal, some of which were significant in the degree of risk taken on. Furthermore, it seemed that the same sweetener was viewed as having different values to different airlines. Could we make the process more efficient through rigorous valuations? Presumably, the benefit of more accurate valuation from both sides of the negotiation was that it would more accurately reflect the ability of both the manufacturers and airlines to bear and manage these risks. There was reason to believe that some of these could be more effectively managed by the manufacturers, and some by the airlines. For example, because the manufacturers are much more concentrated than the airlines, could some or all of the nonsystematic risk be diversified away by holding a portfolio of these liabilities? Another example was that the airlines had traditionally maintained their own aircraft, but were increasingly questioning this practice. Were there synergies for the manufacturers in this area that allowed them to better manage the risks? If we were increasingly required to offer maintenance cost guarantees, would we be better off maintaining the aircraft ourselves?

Changing the Paradigm

I hypothesized that using more realistic valuation techniques could guide us toward exploiting these opportunities and might create a competitive advantage. There was no reason to think that, overall, any of our competitors had a cost advantage in offering these types of services. In some areas, we felt that we had an advantage and in other areas a possible disadvantage. If our competitors adopted the same techniques, or just emulated our strategy toward these various contingencies, I theorized that it could be better for the industry as a whole—a possible win-win scenario. During these high stakes, winner takes all, multibillion-dollar competitions for a major airline's business, the overwhelming desire to clinch the deal can drive the manufacturers to take on what later appear to be inappropriate risks. Would more realistic valuation techniques result in a more considered bargaining process?

Agency and Organizational Issues

The final question was, could we get our own management, including our parent company, to buy into these ideas? There were agency problems within our U.S. sales office and with its relationship with the parent company, located in Toulouse, France. Traditionally, the U.S. office justified its existence on the basis of bringing in offers of potential sales contracts with the all-important North American customers. All analysis of deal economics, and therefore the decision whether to accept the deal, were conducted by the parent. There were also issues concerning the interplay between the various functional groups within the company. Sales directors were implicitly and to a lesser extent explicitly rewarded for bringing potential deals to the table. They often considered any initiative to increase the financial scrutiny of the deal as restricting their ability to be creative and construct offers that would be acceptable to the customer.

The contracts directors were in effect the counterbalance to the sales team. They negotiated the terms of a LOI (Letter of Intent) with a potential customer, and then negotiated the details of the legally binding Purchase Agreement (PA). Inputs to pricing the contract were combined in a single companywide measure of deal profitability, and the directors were given a target to meet in terms of this. Historically, we had found if difficult to account for all contingencies in this measure. Successful directors (and their management) closed deals. There was tremendous pressure to satisfy the airline's demands and also meet the profitability target. This in effect resulted in an incentive to take on unquantified risks. There was a long history of unintentionally including in the contract, concessions that at the time were perceived small, but later turned out to be significant financial liabilities. It seemed management and negotiators were naturally overly optimistic and hopeful about how the future would unfold with regard to these risks. Could better financial analysis provide a counter to this?

THE OPPORTUNITY—A SPONSOR AT THE HIGHEST LEVEL

Around 1998, Airbus Industrie started to plan its transition from a consortium of European aircraft manufacturers intent on achieving market parity with Boeing, to a mature profit maximizing public company. This provided the environment of change required to challenge some of the entrenched processes that had been successfully used in building the company to what it is today. There was a companywide drive to become more financially transparent. It seemed the timing was right.

Early that year, our president raised the question as to why we seemed to be giving away purchase rights to our aircraft. These rights were essentially options on forward sales, and could be considered a contingent liability, as we were legally obliged to provide these aircraft at prenegotiated conditions. If our costs rose unexpectedly due to say exchange rate movements, we could be forced to deliver aircraft at a loss. "Was there an analogy here with stock options, which are quite valuable?" our president asked. This question had occurred to some of us before, however, there is nothing like the words of your president to focus one's energy.

A little more about the industry. Our customers, the airlines, historically have operated in a cyclical environment, not unlike many commodity industries. Demand is driven by GDP growth (consumer discretionary spending) and is subject to shocks such as recession and threat of war. The productive capacity, the aircraft, has high fixed costs and thus supply and demand gets out of balance sometimes. Aggravating this is the historically long lead time on new aircraft. Airlines saw growth opportunities when the economy was good and ordered new aircraft, only to take delivery a considerable time later in less favorable conditions. A type of hysteresis is at play—there was a time lag between airline management making a decision and the effect of that decision on an airline's fleet of aircraft.

From the aircraft manufacturer's perspective, there was also significant leverage involved: The nonrecurring development costs of a new product are enormous, resulting in aggressive market share targets to amortize these costs. The conventional wisdom was that the more purchase rights (or options) we gave away to customers, the more were likely to be exercised. In a finite market, one more aircraft sold is one less order for our competitors. This policy has the added benefit of improving our "bragging rights" to the industry watchers as firm orders and options are being tallied.

So here was our opportunity, a sponsor at the highest level of the company, and an environment of change, but there were still many questions that we had to address regarding how we approached this specific valuation.

COMMENTARY: THE CHANGE PROCESS—A SUPERIOR IDEA

At this point, John has identified a need for change and his CEO is of similar mind and philosophy. Their gut feeling is that NPV is inadequate. It fails to properly value long-term contingencies (e.g., guarantees) and fails to make appropriate trade-offs between capital costs of aircraft today and uncertain cost savings in the future. Real options seem, at least in theory, to be a bet-ter idea. Real options seem, from their perspective, to have a relative advan-tage. Thus, the first necessary condition for rapid adoption of the new idea—real options—was met. It was viewed, at least on an intuitive level, as a potentially superior idea. For example, it explains why contingencies are more valuable to airlines having greater variability in passenger revenue miles. Next, they have to confront the issue of whether it is compatible with Airbus's culture, whether it may be too complex, whether it is triable, and whether its advantages are observable.

CHOOSING OUR WEAPON

One of those questions was the valuation model. Several possible tech-niques were available to model delivery options. Decision Analysis, Real Options Analysis, Monte Carlo analysis, and Inventory Theory. An at-tempt could even be made using traditional DCF techniques. My experi-ence had shown me that the simple mechanics of discounted cash flow were so attractive that anyone could seemingly understand the analysis. Yet in reality, the underlying theory could be very complex. Discounted cash flow was practiced at all levels of the organization, but in reality well understood by few. Time and time again, I had seen detailed cash flows created both internally and by customers that seemed highly plausible but in fact violated some of the underlying assumptions.

In contrast, Real Options Analysis was perceived to be highly com-plex and applicable to only a small number of problems. It is not until one starts to understand the limitations of DCF that you recognize that real options are everywhere. I could in fact see many uses for ROA in our work; the problem was avoiding a "black box" impression of the model from top management, and customers. As will be shown, the mechanics of ROA can often be simplified to a decision tree type analysis, which can be modeled using standard spreadsheet software. This was how we would avoid the black box syndrome. Additionally, the use of ROA to model air-craft delivery options would provide a "skills platform" or option to ex-ploit further valuation opportunities with other contingencies embedded in the sales contracts.

SIMPLE TRIAL SOLUTIONS FOR THE PROBLEM

Our initial cut at trying to value aircraft delivery options was done using the Black-Scholes model developed nearly 30 years ago (published in 1973 to be exact) to value stock options. This "closed form" solution can be solved quite easily. The inputs are readily available, at least as a qualified guess. They are the aircraft price (exercise price), the value of the aircraft to the airline (its PV), the volatility of the PV, the time to exercise, and the risk-free discount rate. When a quick analysis is required, we have found Black-Scholes is often the best approach. Even if the answer was not that accurate, it provided a methodology for framing the problem and determining the variables that affect the valuation.

This simple analysis led us to some interesting observations about what drove the value of the option: The greater the volatility, the greater the value of the option. Our customers, the airlines, had differing volatility of passenger revenue miles and differing financial leverage. Therefore they had differing volatility of earnings. Our aircraft in their hands had a more volatile PV. The options were more valuable to some airlines than others, and we could segment the market in this way.

If there was a value to the customer, was there a cost to our company that we did not currently recognize? If a contingent sale displaced a firm sale, then is an opportunity cost involved? We also realized that the value of the option increases with the time to exercise. The longer the time horizon, the more uncertainty could develop and therefore the greater chance of the value of the aircraft rising above the exercise price. Additionally, the greater the risk of our costs rising above the sales price. Some of the options our customers held had quite long exercise times (several years). Were these options really more valuable than the near term? There were additional thorny details. Was the underlying volatility really a random walk or more like a cyclical or mean reverting process that would limit the growth in value of the option over time? What about the lost revenues? Was there a benefit to the airline taking an aircraft early to block a competitor? Aircraft had a type of "convenience yield"; there was a utility to owning one—its revenue-generating value. Did we need to think about a kind of dividend effect and how that would affect the value of the option?

RECOGNIZING WE DID NOT HAVE THE REQUIRED LEVEL OF FINANCIAL ENGINEERING SKILLS IN-HOUSE

Recognizing that there were more things at play than could be explained using the simple Black-Scholes formulation, we had to go to a greater level of detail. We decided to talk with a local finance professor.* In our initial discussions, we realized that an airline had another option available to it, other than holding a delivery option: a "natural option" to wait and see if any uncertainty would be resolved before signing up for aircraft orders. This is a classical deferral option. The holder of an option was assured a specified price and delivery date, whereas another airline would have to negotiate a price and delivery date dependent on the prevailing conditions at that time. Because the industry is cyclical, the queue length for our products can sometimes get quite long; also, prices firm up as demand rises. Thus the delivery option was valuable because it resolved two sources of uncertainty for the airline, the price and delivery date.

Another complexity was that aircraft options cannot be exercised instantaneously; there is a lead time required to build the aircraft. Once the option is exercised, the airline specifies the level of customization required and the aircraft is built. We were striving to reduce manufacturing lead times significantly, partly by offering a more standardized aircraft: How did this affect the valuation?

The model was now starting to look complex. There were a number of different approaches that we could take to solve the underlying equations. Another consideration was that we wanted not only to value a "generic" aircraft delivery option, but also to have the ability to swap between different aircraft types on the production line—a switching option. This was especially important because we believed we had a competitive advantage in this area. Our product range had been built up over a relatively short period using the same technology platform. This meant that airlines could efficiently operate several aircraft within a family of different sizes and still obtain scale economies. Additionally, these aircraft were produced on the same production line with a very high level of common

---

* Many thanks to Professor Alex Triantis of the University of Maryland for his invaluable help.

parts. This facilitated our ability to allow customers to defer, until as late as possible, the decision as to which size of aircraft within the family they would actually take delivery of. This had a clear benefit to the airlines in managing both market and competitive uncertainty.

CONSTRUCTING THE MODEL

A key element in the modeling was the number of types of uncertainty. We recognized three: the price of the aircraft, the waiting time or queue length, and the aircraft PV (the discounted present value to the customer of the aircraft over its life). Extending the model to value switching options would add an additional degree of uncertainty for every additional aircraft type. As discussed earlier, we wanted to use a "binomial approximation," a large risk-adjusted decision tree, to make the model understandable to both internal management and customers. A two-dimensional tree represented one degree of uncertainty in the vertical axis and time in the horizontal axis. We could extend into one more dimension by using a series of sheets within the spreadsheet program. Expanding further would be problematic without integrating Monte Carlo analysis into our work. We recognized, however, that we could describe both the aircraft price and queue length as deterministic functions of the aircraft PV. Thus the basic delivery option model could be reduced to a two-dimensional tree, and the two aircraft switching option, to a three-dimensional tree.

> ### COMMENTARY: THE CHANGE PROCESS—COMPATIBILITY AND COMPLEXITY
>
> *Airbus was already financially sophisticated. It was comfortable with the language and methodology of net present value, and was experienced with use of Monte Carlo analysis. Since a lattice approach was proposed for option pricing, the fundamental skills that were needed (spreadsheets, algebra, and Monte Carlo analysis) were already being used by management. Therefore, the real options requirements were not fundamentally different from what management was already comfortable with. For example, both NPV and real options discount future cash flows—a familiar overarching framework.*

Management had to become familiar with an entirely new vocabulary (e.g., puts, calls, exercise price), but the solution process was algebraic and therefore within their existing skill set. Therefore, real options was compatible with existing decision-making tools. Complexity is a different attribute of a new idea. Although compatible it may be too complex for rapid adoption. John uses the word "complex" frequently. Here are some examples: "Real Options Analysis was perceived to be highly complex . . . ," "Another complexity was that aircraft options cannot be exercised instantaneously," and "the model was now starting to look quite complex."

Let's not avoid the issue. Real Options Analysis, although intuitive and a better idea than NPV, is more complex. It is best to acknowledge this problem and at every step in the introduction of real options to the organization—seek to simplify. That is a major objective of this book. Next, let's see how they approached the problem of triability.

TESTING THE MODEL

At this point, we were satisfied that we had an accurate model that could hopefully be explained in relatively simple terms to our required audiences. The model quantified the value of holding an option on the future delivery of an aircraft at a predetermined price and delivery date. As the decision tree branched out in time, the nodes represented all the possible values (PV) that the "underlying asset" the aircraft could take in future, between today and when the airline needs to decide whether to actually take delivery.

The value of the option was then just the expected value (the sum of all the outcomes multiplied by their respective probabilities) discounted back to today. A technique called the "no profitable arbitrage" condition was used to determine the appropriate discount rate for each time step and solved in a recursive manner backward to today.

QUANTIFYING RISK

One of the most contentious issues in project evaluation is the choice of the discount rate and therefore the attribution of a level of risk to the project. The most commonly used form of assessing market risk in conventional investment theory is the Capital Asset Pricing Model (CAPM). A market premium is presumed to be paid to shareholders, above the risk-free rate, for bearing the systematic (nondiversifiable) risk associated with an industry or sector. This rate is then used to discount the operating cash flows associated with a project, making adjustments for the relative financial gearing of the company or project. In ROA, in contrast to this, risk is quantified simply in terms of the market volatility of the returns on the underlying asset. Risk-adjusted expected cash flows are discounted at the risk-free rate and the market risk is characterized in the volatility of the modeled cash flows.

With real options, as the underlying asset is often not traded, a proxy for volatility has to be found. This proxy can be a Monte Carlo simulation of the value of the project, another traded asset, or a synthetic portfolio of assets. This proxy may not be easy to find, and represents the greatest theoretical problem associated with real options analysis.

With the measurement of risk being so contentious, it's always a good idea to try to "triangulate" by using different methodologies. In our aircraft delivery option problem, we had a number of possibilities open to us. First, we argued that the market value of an airline was equal to the present value of the sum of all its investments, which were overwhelmingly aircraft. Airlines are nondiversified companies with a single line of business and the aircraft assets dominate their business sheets. It's a mature business with few growth opportunities. Thus the volatility of stock returns was a possible proxy for the volatility of aircraft returns or the PV of an aircraft in service with an airline. We also recognized that part of the volatility was driven by the financial leverage of an airline. In a process similar to unlevering the Beta of a company, we unlevered the measured volatility.

Second, we looked at used aircraft transaction data in the industry. As commercial aircraft are expensive assets and often financed, there are several consulting firms that maintain transactional databases. Historical prices of used aircraft can be used to measure the volatility of price over time, accounting for the fact that aircraft assets have a finite life and depreciate with time. We did not, in the end, use this methodology, but it did help us bracket the volatility.

Third, we created a theoretical model based on the operating cost and passenger revenue stream of an aircraft over its life. We then measured typical passenger demand volatilities on selected routes and applied these to the model to generate aircraft PV volatilities.

Having three different methods to measure volatility of the asset, all of which gave similar answers, significantly helped to address any concerns we had regarding this key input to the model.

COMMENTARY: THE CHANGE PROCESS—TRIABILITY

Although the model was triable in the sense that it provided a reasonable answer for the value of the switching and deferral options, the next section indicates that obtaining buy-in was a real problem because the relevant decision makers were not involved in the development of the real options solution. This made the complexity problem a serious hurdle later on. Another problem was that the model was not only to be judged on its ability to value the aircraft delivery option, but also on its ability to capture that value in the sales process. Buy-in required management familiarity with real option analysis.

ROLLING OUT THE MODEL—INTERNALLY

With hindsight, we realized we had made a mistake by not giving management an ownership role during the model development stage. The reality was our helpful professor and I had "hunkered down" in my office and created a solution to the problem in relative isolation, not wanting to trouble management with modeling intricacies. Additionally due to time constraints, the model had been developed over a period of several months. It was difficult to regain the interest that had originally created the impetus to allocate resources to the problem in the first place. I would face an uphill battle to regain that momentum.

I scheduled a series of management presentations to roll out the model. The presentations included model methodology, inputs, sensitivities, and results. The valuations in general seemed very credible (approximately 10% of the aircraft price); however, the majority of the discussions quickly turned to how we could capture this value in pricing options, and the response of our customers and competitors. While I had been focused for a long time on model methodology and theoretical aspects of option pricing theory, I recognized that I would now have to focus almost entirely on an implementation plan.

INTEGRATING REAL OPTIONS ANALYSIS INTO THE SALES PROCESS AND THE ROLE OF MARKETING

Like most fast-paced corporations, at our company, management time horizons are short. The tactical issues involved in closing a deal always attracted greater management attention than the long-term strategic process of marketing a family of aircraft with all its attributes. Marketing as a function was often seen as sales support. Yet perceptions about products and their value are much more malleable over the medium and long term. In the height of a sales campaign it is almost impossible to get an airline to reverse its position on the value of an attribute or sweetener, as it simply means that the manufacturer can expect to justify a higher price. When airlines get into the negotiating mode, the supply of information and access to working level specialists dry up. We recognized that while our valuation methodology clearly could be used during the negotiation process in helping airline management understand why delivery flexibility is valuable, the transformation of delivery flexibility from a soft to hard attribute (i.e., an explicit recognition of its value in dollar terms) could only come as part of a longer term process outside the constraints of a sales campaign.

COMMENTARY: THE CHANGE PROCESS—OBSERVABILITY

It is hard to say what approach was best to get management buy-in during the heat of battle in the active and competitive sales campaign. But observability requires that the new ideas be clearly communicated to the decision makers who need to know. Due to the constraints of the sales campaign, John decides to try a flanking maneuver via external communications.

EXTERNAL COMMUNICATIONS

To market the valuations to the industry in a much less direct way, I embarked on a process of writing articles in industry publications and talking at conferences. The timing turned out to be very good for a number of reasons. Airlines increasingly recognize their need to manage uncertainty, and along with this are increasingly skeptical of conventional DFC techniques to evaluate the future benefits of a fleet plan. Today, airlines have a significant percentage of their aircraft deliveries as contingent sales.

An unplanned benefit of our analysis had been to solve the "hurdle rate" puzzle described earlier. Airlines recognizing that an investment in aircraft that looks good today may turn sour, say three to five years later, precisely when the majority of aircraft may be going into service, created a buffer between their cost of capital and the investment's implied return. This had been done heuristically; however, it turns out that the spread between a company's cost of capital and hurdle rate is correct when it equals the value of the flexibility given up by making the investment decision today. In the future, we could argue that delivery flexibility should reduce an airline's hurdle rate to invest.

An Unexpected Benefit—Seeing the Bigger Picture around the Problem

Our analysis uncovered many more interesting questions about the way we manage some business risks. With airlines recognizing the value of flexibility, the relatively small number of contingent sales on our order book was growing. In addition, our company was manufacturing an increasing number of aircraft types within a single family on the same production line, and giving airlines conversion rights. There are stiff penalties for failure of a manufacturer to deliver on time, as well as for failure of a customer to take delivery. Due to this, and the fact that production levels had increased significantly over several years, managing our order book was becoming a growing concern. The greater the proportion of contingent sales on our order book, the harder it was to manage the process of ensuring that we met our obligations. A small group of people had managed this process over a long period, starting from when we had much smaller production volumes. To improve our management of the order book, there was a drive to maintain a better flow of information from the customer with regard to its future intentions. Our ROA of the value of delivery options had brought up many questions in this area. For example, we had found that we could double-book some delivery positions, on the basis that not all options were exercised. To what extent could we do this and still meet our obligations? Was there a way that we could diversify some of this risk by double booking options from two airlines that were perceived to be countercyclical? Our worldwide customer base suggested that we could. Was the probability of an airline exercising options related to industry growth, and if so, was there an economic indication that was a good proxy for this? How did competition between airlines affect the value of options and the probability of exercising them? Would competing airlines see the same growth opportunities at the same time and expand by exercising options?

HELPING CONTRACT DIRECTORS IDENTIFY AND MITIGATE RISK IN CONTRACTUAL LANGUAGE

The Black-Scholes formulation was a useful framework to help contract directors recognize possible risk drivers in contract language developed with potential customers during the negotiation process. As mentioned, a common bias affecting negotiators is overconfidence. Companies and individuals tend to have an irrational degree of confidence in their own abilities, and as a result, they tend to overestimate the likelihood of achieving a positive outcome. Negotiators overestimate the upside and underestimate the downside in contingent contracts. A good example was when a company asked for the right of first refusal on every aircraft of a specific type on our production line. The upside appeared to be the opportunity to sell more aircraft to this company at prenegotiated terms and completely shut out a competitor. Luckily we recognized that when the market was tight, prices good, and aircraft scarce, we could be constrained in our ability to direct delivery positions to key strategic campaigns and new customers.

When delivery slots were scarce, we scoured the world in the hope that we could find an airline wishing to defer delivery. The diverse nature of our customer base helped. Usually we could juggle the order book in this way, but not always. Some of this risk could be mitigated in contract design. We could state that a proportion of the delivery slots could be re-purchased at a set cost to the manufacturer.

COUPLING THE MARKETING AND FINANCING ACTIVITY DURING THE SALES PROCESS

In one sense, we were marketing both real and financial assets to our customers, yet the Sales, Finance, and Market departments have historically had quite different "modus operandi." Our marketers want to explicitly quantify, to the airline, the value of all elements of a proposed deal, to justify the highest price possible, either in absolute terms or relative to a competitor's pricing. The finance teams wish to facilitate the sale of our products when financing is necessary, but minimize exposure. This usually resulted in delaying, until as late as possible in the sales process, any commitment. This also meant that, although financing was often a pre-condition to closing the sale, there was little opportunity to explicitly market the value of financing as a driver of the price we could demand. The problem was compounded by the fact that most airlines have a strong delineation between the Fleet Planning and Treasury functions. The Fleet Planning group could make a decision to purchase assets with no regard for the way it would be financed. The working relationships between the manufacturer and airlines were such that the Marketing teams had a close relationship with Fleet Planning and the Finance team with the Treasury, with very little overlap.

BUILDING ON OUR REAL OPTIONS EXPERTISE

Real Option Analysis is not just a methodology but a new way of looking at the dynamics of the investment decision. It also gives insight into which risks are appropriate for a company to bear. With our recently developed expertise, the next problem we attacked was a type of guarantee that is quite common in the industry. We constructed a simple but effective valuation model by making changes to an "off the shelf" closed form solution for an option on a futures contract known as "Black's model." One of the great benefits of this model was the ability of our team to see a guarantee in a different light. Previously, it had been seen as a way to convince an airline to buy into our valuation of a cost driver in their analysis. This was a liability, but sometimes a necessary one, to obtain the desired price for our product. However, the model illustrated how the cost-effectiveness of the guarantee is driven by the asymmetry of expectations about the way the future will unfold between the two parties, the airline and the manufacturer, and their perceived ability to bear that risk. It demonstrated to the team when it was appropriate to use a guarantee as part of the package of sweeteners available, and when it was not. Integral to this was the requirement for the customer to value the guarantee. We now had a better valuation tool we could share with the customers to do this. Our old problem of heuristically risk-adjusting cash flows and the implication of that on cost drivers (negative cash flows), which seemed counterintuitive, could be avoided.

Turning to the big picture, today real options' thinking is still very much in its infancy at Airbus. We have greatly improved our measure of deal profitability by much more comprehensively accounting for cost and risk drivers, yet most of this has been done without an explicit understanding of real options. Contingencies, where necessary, have been quantified stochastically using Monte Carlo analysis or probability theory. This can often be compared to decision tree analysis. As we go forward in time through the tree, the outcome changes at each node. Because of this, however, the discount rate should also change. In real options, the correct discount rate is determined through the "risk neutral" valuation. When I discuss real options internally, often the initial response is that it's nothing new. Explaining why it is—because it gets the discount rate right—is not simple, yet it is clearly very important in determining the correct valuation. This problem is exacerbated because most people are given a discount rate to be used by the Treasury group for all calculations, and in general do not question its appropriateness. In the future, there are many more possible applications for real options at Airbus. The business case for new product development is an obvious choice. However, we will have to be more successful in demonstrating that use of the correct discount rate is not an esoteric and theoretical issue, but critical to correct decision making.

SUMMARY—THE CHANGE PROCESS AND LESSONS LEARNED

The process I went through at Airbus has allowed me to learn a lot about implementing new concepts, and about trying to change mind-sets. With hindsight, there are obviously some things I would have done differently. Here is a list of pointers and lessons learned, for practitioners of real options and companies attempting to implement ROA. It also touches on the implications of using ROA for company structure and management compensation.

Taking Aim

When you first introduce real options to your organization, use an application where you believe you can show clear evidence of the benefits of the analysis. Leave the harder, more contentious problems until later. It may initially seem that those make-or-break decisions are the ones to go for, but most managers will balk at using a new methodology, even if the alternate is mostly intuition. Presumably, that intuition has been observed to work in the past! First generate a consensus base using a simple, clear problem, with observable results requiring only minimal internal company buy-in, and minimal organizational implications. This may be difficult to justify when modeling the problem can take significant resources. Think of it as purchasing an option on the skill set to solve many more (and bigger) problems in the future.

Sponsorship

Change occurs most easily from the top down. It's key to find a sponsor at the highest level, but recognize that top management have short time horizons. They often focus on a problem and then go on to the next, so turnaround time can be important—stay on the radar screen throughout the process. Also seek sponsorship from potential users. During the development stage, keep an open door for anyone who needs to buy into the model. Let them take a stake in the model, by providing input. Avoid the "not invented here" syndrome.

Inertia

Don't underestimate your company's ability to keep going in the same direction. Recognize that people often have a vested interest in maintaining the status quo. They are comfortable with the existing rules, understand them, and have learned how to use them to their advantage in the corporation. Most people are pragmatists and not idealists. They accept the rules and work with them rather than searching for a better way to do things. A recent survey found that only 20 percent of change programs within companies are fully successful. However companies that had internal change centers, and were used to change, did much better. Consider how well your company accepts changes. What do past experiences tell you? Is there an atmosphere of change in the company that you can ride on?

External Help

An external adviser or consultant can be helpful in providing a neutral and nonpolitical expert. In most companies, people find it easier to accept that an existing process can be improved on from an outside source. The cost of a consultant also provides management with an added incentive to make the change process work. In addition, paying for a consultant gives the expectation that the advice is valuable. However, consultants are often criticized for their lack of specific industry knowledge. I have found that the coupling of an internal champion with the theoretical knowledge of an adviser works well. They complement each other's strengths, and it becomes a much more difficult process to ignore their findings.

Intuition versus Analysis

Don't just assume that being right will result in company buy-in. Most top managers are intuitive and heuristic, these are often attributes that we pay managers for having. Some results from option pricing theory are correct, but initially may seem counterintuitive. Often intuition is the easy and expedient way out, it avoids time-consuming analysis especially when timing is critical. It is also harder to prove intuition wrong. Analyzing a previous management decision and what was said is often difficult. Different people within a team always have differing opinions on how the problem was analyzed and the decision was made. Many people find it much more risky to put their faith in a model, which may ultimately make it easier to allocate responsibility for a bad decision. Use the model to confirm and support intuition where possible, rather than pointing out where intuition fails.

Managing the Model

Don't develop a black box that no one understands. A model has to be explainable for the owner, users, and management. Use lots of analogies. It is always good to triangulate and bracket. Use as many different methods as possible to determine key inputs to the model, especially risk. Make sure the new model is consistent with the old one if it exists (i.e., it can collapse into the same solution). Clearly understand the limitations and assumptions behind both the old and new methodologies. Make sure you are significantly more knowledgeable than anyone else in the company about the subject. It's always much easier to shoot down a new idea than to displace an old one. Understand the limitations of using other forms of stochastic modeling, like decision tree analysis.

Rewarding Risk Taking

In conventional investment analysis, managers trade up front relatively certain costs, in return for a stream of distant, more risky (but more valuable) cash flows. With ROA, which also captures uncertainty, this trade can be weighted even further toward taking risks. For example, paying an option premium for the right to exploit a future opportunity should it occur (we know that purchasing a call on a stock is riskier than purchasing the underlying security). Because ROA shows when, based on expected outcomes, it is appropriate to pay this premium, single projects can still fail to meet expectations. This is a predicament for managers, especially if they do not hold a portfolio of such projects. Exercising a put option (an exit strategy) may also be viewed as a failure. Managers need to know that they will be rewarded for taking calculated risks beyond what the company is used to.

Corporate Finance and Company Structure

Many corporations still have a very clear separation of the investment and financing decisions. This usually results in a centralized calculation of the cost of capital by the Treasury group, and the distribution of working rules provided to the operational units for project evaluation and spending limits. It is, however, the operating units that are exposed to and manage the market uncertainty (and private risk), that find ROA of value. Managers responsible for projects are used to trying to model uncertainty through scenario analysis, decision trees, and Monte Carlo analysis, but not used to challenging guidelines for cost of capital, which are often sacrosanct. Yet this may be required to reconcile a risk-neutral valuation of a real option with strict guidelines for the use of a companywide discount rate probably based on the CAPM. Practitioners of real options should search out and develop a real options champion within the Treasury group. Companies that use ROA should be aware of the need for closer coordination between these two activities. There are many more reasons to integrate ROA with Finance and Treasury functions. These are beyond the scope of this chapter but include such issues as diversification and portfolio management, and risk management and hedging strategies.

Competitive Issues

If appropriate to the problem, think hard about the competitive issues associated with implementing an ROA strategy. Are you "hardening up" an attribute you have a comparative advantage in? What are the implications for competitor, customer, and supplier behavior? If negotiations with customers or suppliers are involved, is it beneficial to share the analysis and/or the model? What signals do you wish to send to your competitors?

The Big Picture

The greatest benefit of the process may be the understanding you get of the underlying broader management problem. Don't focus singly on the efficacy of the results of the model. And finally, keep motivated. Remember that it's great to be at the front of the herd, even if no one around you realizes that's where you are! Buy-in is great, but it will probably take some time and effort.

COMMENTARY: THE CHANGE PROCESS—OVERVIEW

Airbus clearly benefited from its explorations into real options analysis. For the purpose of marketing negotiations, it was able to estimate the value of various contract features: the ability given to the airline to change its mind about aircraft seating capacity, guaranteed ceilings on prices, and guaranteed maintenance costs. Airbus was even able to use option pricing to segment its market based on airline-specific parameters, for example, the volatility of airline earnings.

The change process, however, was slow and could have gone smoother in retrospect. What could have been done differently? Real options were a superior idea and compatible with value maximization using lattices. The fact that they used algebra, not calculus, helped but did not entirely cure the problem. A training program, supported by the CEO, and brought to both the contract director group and the sales team, would have helped.

Triability was not an especially difficult issue, except that John and the professor who assisted him worked behind closed doors while they were trying out the new methods. Wider enfranchisement with other managers, and experimentation with some of their more obvious real options problems would have helped.

Finally, even though the benefits have been observable in terms of the Airbus sales and marketing record, the struggle to change was arduous primarily due to the perception of real option analysis being too complex. The separation of the management team responsible for investment decisions from the one responsible for financing decisions did not help either.

QUESTIONS

For solutions go to www.corpfinonline.com.

1. What are the five attributes of an innovation that Rogers suggests have the greatest influence on the rate of adoption of a new idea? Which of them did Airbus have the greatest problem with?

2. What economic issues was Airbus struggling with? Describe how the net present value approach gave counterintuitive answers while real options provided intuitive answers.

3. Why is the value of an option to change the seat configuration on an aircraft a real option? What kind of option is it? How would higher variability in passenger revenue miles affect the value of the option if we used net present value analysis? How would it be affected if we used real option analysis?

4. What might Airbus have done better to improve the earlier acceptance of real options (in terms of superiority, compatibility, complexity, triability, and observability)?

5. What was the effect of organization of investment from financing decisions on the ease of moving from NPV to ROA?

6. How do you think real options analysis might be applied to the Airbus decision to build the 300XX, a 600 passenger aircraft?

7. What differences in Roger's five attributes would shape your approach for convincing top level managers versus analysts to adapt real options analysis?

REFERENCES

Argyris, Chris. 2000. *Flawed Advice and the Management Trap,* New York: Oxford University Press.

Jensen, Michael C. 1998. *Foundations of Organizational Strategy,* Cambridge: Harvard University Press.

Rogers, Everett M. 1995. *Diffusion of Innovations,* 4th edition, New York: Free Press.

3 | Net Present Value

Net present value is the single most widely used tool for large investments made by corporations. Klammer (1972) reported a survey of over 100 large companies indicating that in 1959 only 19 percent used NPV techniques, but by 1970, 57 percent used them. Roughly a decade later, Schall, Sundem, and Geijsbeek (1978) sampled 424 large firms and found that 86 percent of those responding used NPV. It took over two decades for NPV to be widely accepted. Undoubtedly, this rate of adoption was affected by the introduction of pocket calculators and desktop personal computers.

We want to review NPV carefully because it is the foundation for real options analysis. The subjects that we cover in this chapter are many. We start with "the separation principle." It shows that the shareholders of a firm will, regardless of their individual rates of time preference, unanimously agree that the managers of the firm should maximize shareholders' wealth by taking investments that earn at least the market-determined opportunity cost of capital. After that, we move on to the definition of free cash flows of the project, the weighted average cost of capital, and how the present value of a project is expected to change over time. The third section of the chapter explains the equivalence of the risk-adjusted and the certainty-equivalent methods of estimating the NPV of a project. Finally, we summarize the empirical evidence that compares NPV analysis with real options—and conclude that real options is a superior approach.

THE SEPARATION PRINCIPLE

Simply stated, the separation principle is the useful result that shareholders of a firm will agree about the decision rule they want managers to execute on their behalf—namely to undertake investments until the marginal return on the last dollar invested is greater than or equal to the market-determined opportunity cost of capital. Shareholders do not have to take a vote—they will unanimously agree. This is a critical keystone in the theory of decision making because we do not have to construct a complicated rule for the managers that requires that they acquire and use individual owner (shareholder) preferences.

We start our discussion with a single decision maker, call him Robinson Crusoe. His total utility function is shown in Exhibit 3.1. He exhibits positive marginal utility of consumption for consumption today, C_0, and for consumption at the end of the year, C_1. Therefore, he always prefers more to less (sometimes called greed). He also has decreasing marginal utility of consumption at both points of time. As we shall see, this results in risk-adverse behavior. Combining his period zero and his period 1 utility functions, isoutility lines—the dashed lines (labeled TU_1, TU_2, and

Exhibit 3.1   Theory of choice—indifference curves.

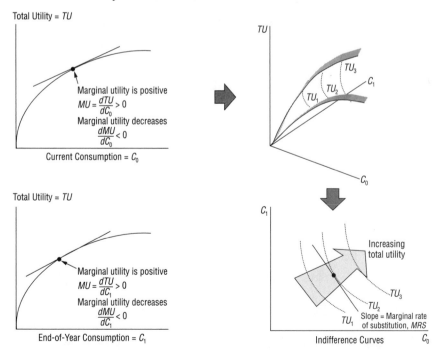

TU_3)—can be projected down onto the floor of the diagram to illustrate lines of equal total utility. Shown in the lower right-hand panel of Exhibit 3.1, these are called indifference curves because they represent, along any one line, the combinations of consumption today and end-of-year consumption that give Robinson Crusoe equal total utility. These indifference curves represent a theory of choice. The slope of a line tangent to an indifference curve, for example at point A in Exhibit 3.2, shows the rate of exchange between consumption today and consumption at the end of the year that will leave Mr. Crusoe with the same total utility. In effect, his marginal rate of substitution is his subjective price of units of consumption tomorrow for units of consumption today. He always requires extra units of consumption tomorrow in return for giving up a unit of consumption today.

Next, we introduce Robinson Crusoe's investment decision by assuming that he lands on a desert island with an endowment of coconuts, $y(C_0, C_1)$, as shown in Exhibit 3.3. The shape of the curve in the right-hand panel comes from the assumption that there are diminishing marginal returns to investment, as illustrated in the left-hand panel. As the amount of investment, I, increases, the rate of return on investment, r, decreases. The right-hand panel is called the production opportunity

Exhibit 3.2   Marginal rate of substitution.

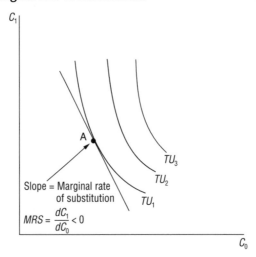

Exhibit 3.3 Production opportunity set—objects of choice.

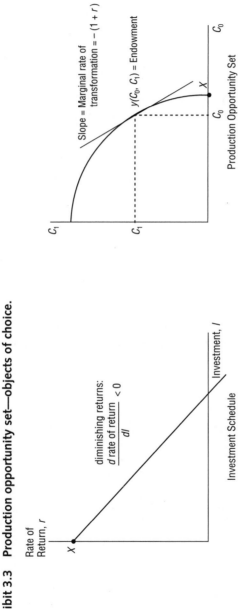

set. The slope of a line drawn tangent to it is called the marginal rate of transformation. It measures the rate of return on the marginal dollar of investment, a rate that is objectively determined by technology. Robinson Crusoe can decide to invest by consuming less than the amount, C_0, of coconuts that are available for consumption today, and investing them (i.e., planting them) for harvest at the end of the year (these are fast-growing trees). Note that point X represents zero investment in both charts. In the right-hand chart, he consumes everything today (and nothing tomorrow) at point X. His marginal rate of return is the slope of a line tangent to his production opportunity set—the marginal rate of transformation.

Having discussed Robinson Crusoe's theory of choice (his indifference curves) and his production opportunity set (his objects of choice), we can combine the two to understand his optimal choice (see Exhibit 3.4). He lands on the island with the endowment of consumption today and consumption tomorrow represented by point A—a combination whose total utility is TU_1. At this point, his marginal rate of substitution, MRS, between consumption tomorrow and consumption today is lower than his marginal rate of transformation MRT, the objective return

Exhibit 3.4   Optimal individual decision assuming no capital market.

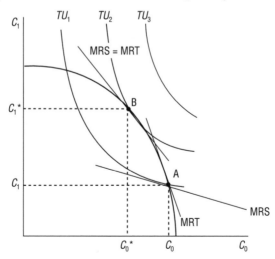

that he can obtain by investing. Therefore, he will choose to invest. He is willing to give up consumption today in return for consumption tomorrow at a rate lower than the rate he can actually get by investing (i.e., by consuming less today). He will continue to invest (consume less) until he moves along the production opportunity set and reaches point B. At this point, he has reached a higher level of total utility, TU_2, and his marginal rate of substitution equals his marginal rate of transformation. He will decide to remain at point B, where he consumes C_0^* today and C_1^* at the end of the period, and invests $(C_0 - C_0^*)$ today.

What happens if we introduce a marketplace with many individuals into the picture? Suppose they individually follow the Robinson Crusoe rule. Won't they all choose different optimal consumption/production points because they all have different preferences for consumption over time, and therefore different indifference curves? The answer is no.

In a frictionless economy with many individuals, there is a market rate, r, that is a borrowing *and* lending rate. If you lend an amount W_0 today at rate r, at the end of the period you receive $W_1 = (1 + r)W_0$. This is graphed in Exhibit 3.5. Robinson Crusoe starts at point A with endowment (C_0, C_1) as before. We can estimate his market-determined wealth by discounting his future consumption at rate r and adding the result to his current consumption as follows:

$$W_0 = \frac{C_1}{1+r} + C_0$$

He knows that his marginal rate of transformation at point A is greater than his marginal rate of substitution, and he begins to move leftward up his production opportunity set. Given the opportunity to borrow or lend at rate r, he moves all the way to point B in Exhibit 3.5. Note that the production output at point B, which is where the market line is just tangent to the production opportunity set, provides him with the greatest feasible wealth, W_0^*. It also provides him with the highest possible total utility, because he will produce the output at point B, then borrow against it at rate r to reach point C, a bundle of consumption with wealth W_0^*. At

Exhibit 3.5 Robinson Crusoe's optimal choice given capital markets.

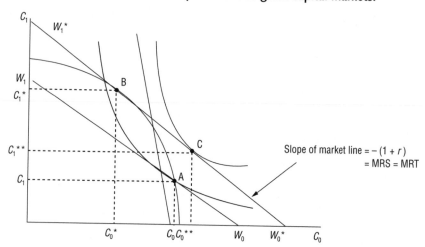

point C, his marginal rate of substitution is the slope of the market line [i.e., $-(1 + r)$]. Also, the same market line is tangent to the production opportunity set at point B. Therefore, if he maximizes his wealth, and his total utility, he will choose to produce the combination at point B, then borrow to move to point C. At point C, his marginal rate of substitution equals the slope of the market line, which in turn equals his marginal rate of transformation.

Exhibit 3.6 concludes this section by illustrating the *separation principle*. Not only will Robinson Crusoe choose point B, but so would every other investor. For example, a second individual might have chosen point C in a world without capital markets, but will choose output combination B given capital markets, then lend at rate r to reach point D on the market line, a consumption combination with higher total utility.

In equilibrium, therefore, all individuals, regardless of their time preferences for consumption today versus consumption tomorrow, will choose to invest until the marginal rate of return on the last unit of investment is just equal to the market rate (at point B). Were the shareholders of a firm, their collective wealth would be maximized if managers follow a simple decision rule—invest until the expected rate of return on the marginal investment equals the cost of capital—the market rate.

Exhibit 3.6   The separation principle.

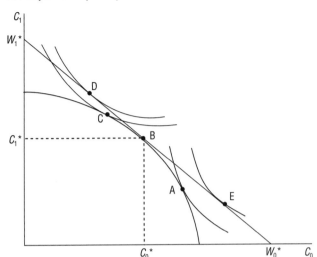

As mentioned, this separation principle means that the wealth-maximizing rule for investment is separate from any information about individual utility functions. And, the separation principle applies equally well for the net present value rule and for real options.

ESTIMATING FREE CASH FLOWS

To operationalize the investment decision rule provided by the separation principle, we need to define the free cash flows from a project, the capital invested in it, and the opportunity cost of capital that is consistent with each of them. Even though we are going to use the real options approach to capture flexibility in decision making, the first step will always be to estimate the present value of the project without flexibility. Therefore, the material that follows is a necessary building block.

To illustrate our approach, which is to estimate the free cash flows that are payable to both sources of capital—debt and equity—we use a simple numerical example and estimate the net present value of the increment in shareholders' wealth in two equivalent ways: discounting the free cash flows to equity at the cost of equity, and discounting the free cash

Exhibit 3.7   Pro forma income statement.

Revenue (Rev)	$1,300
Variable costs (VC)	−600
Fixed cash costs (FCC)	0
Depreciation (dep)	−200
EBIT Earnings before interest and taxes	500
Interest expenses (k_dD)	−50
EBT Earnings before taxes	450
Taxes (T)	−225
NI Net income	225

flows from the project, the entity cash flows, at the weighted average cost of capital. Exhibit 3.7 contains the pro forma income statement for a firm that is going to be created from scratch. Shareholders will contribute $500 of capital and require a 30 percent rate of return, and debt holders will also contribute $500 and expect a 10 percent rate of return. All of this will be invested in equipment costing $1,000, depreciating at the rate of $200 per year, and kept operational by investing $200 per year. To keep the example simple, all cash flows are perpetuities (implying that the change in working capital is zero). Exhibit 3.8 details the exact cash flows assuming that the project is held for 5 years, and that the firm will be sold for its market value at that time. Shareholders will receive the cash, use some of it to pay off the debt ($500), and keep the remainder.

Exhibit 3.8   Equity cash flows for the project.

Year	Inflow	Outflow	Depreciation	Replacement	Interest	Tax	Net Income	Equity CF
0	1,000	−1,000	200	−200	−50	−225	225	225
1	700		200	−200	−50	−225	225	225
2	700		200	−200	−50	−225	225	225
3	700		200	−200	−50	−225	225	225
4	700		200	−200	−50	−225	225	225
5	700	−500	200	−200	−50	−225	225	225 + 1,250

In years 1 through 5, the project returns $700 in cash after the costs of production ($600) are subtracted from revenues ($1,300). Then depreciation ($200), interest expense ($50), and taxes ($225) are subtracted, resulting in net income of $225. Free cash flow to shareholders is calculated by starting with net income of $225, adding back depreciation of $200, which was a noncash charge, then subtracting out annual capital expenditures (i.e., replacement investment) of $200. Thus, annual free cash flows to shareholders is expected to be $225 each year forever. The present value of shareholders' wealth is therefore equal to the expected free cash flows discounted at the cost of equity:

$$S = \frac{\$225}{k_s} = \frac{\$225}{.30} = \$750$$

The present value of bondholders' wealth is the annual interest expense, discounted at the cost of debt:

$$B = \frac{\$50}{.10} = \$500$$

Adding these values together gives the value of the firm, $1,250. Note that the present value of the debt and equity are not affected by the fact that they will be sold at the end of year 5. The new bondholders and equity holders simply take over their streams of cash, paying $500 and $750 respectively. As shown in Exhibit 3.8, the shareholders receive $1,250 in year 5 but must pay $500 to bondholders. Therefore, the increment to shareholders' wealth is $750 after paying bondholders and subtracting out the original amount that equity holders invested, namely $500. Thus the gain in shareholders' wealth is $250.

An alternate and somewhat easier way of computing the gain in shareholders' wealth is to estimate the entity cash flows, also called the free cash from operations, and discounting at the weighted average cost of capital. Operating cash flows are the after-tax cash flows the company (i.e., the entity) would have if it had no debt. These free cash flows are illustrated in Exhibit 3.9. The free cash flows from operations are

Exhibit 3.9   Entity cash flows for capital budgeting.

Year	Operating CF	Depreciation	EBIT	CAPEX	Tax on EBIT	Free Cash Flow
0	−1,000					−1,000
1	700	200	500	200	250	250
2	700	200	500	200	250	250
3	700	200	500	200	250	250
4	700	200	500	200	250	250
5	700	200	500	200	250	250 + 1,250

equal to earnings before interest and taxes (EBIT) minus taxes on EBIT, for example, the taxes the firm would pay if it had no debt (in our case, this is a 50 percent tax rate times EBIT of $500), plus depreciation (a noncash charge of $200), minus capital expenditures each year ($200). Since depreciation and capital expenditures are offsetting, free cash flows from operations equals $250 per year plus $1,250 for selling the firm in year 5.

THE WEIGHTED AVERAGE COST OF CAPITAL (WACC)

The weighted average cost of capital is the weighted average of the after-tax marginal costs of capital. It is appropriate for discounting entity or project cash flows because these cash flows are available for payment to both sources of capital—debt and equity. Note that market value weights are used because the market value of capital committed, not the book value, determines the total cash flow required on investment.

In our simple numerical example, the weighted average cost of capital is estimated to be

$$WACC = k_b(1-T)\frac{B}{B+S} + k_s\frac{S}{B+S}$$

$$= .10(1-.5)\frac{500}{500+1250} + .30\frac{750}{500+750}$$

$$= .02 + .18 = 20\%$$

An interesting question that we discuss later is, Where do we find estimates of the marginal cost of debt and equity? The short answer is that we find comparables. We find other debt with the same risk and assume that its yield to maturity is the same as ours. We use the capital asset pricing model, with all of its flaws, and find other equities that we believe have the same beta as ours and use them to estimate our own cost of equity. Thus, as practitioners we are using priced, comparable securities in the capital markets to estimate the cost of capital for our project. If we discount the entity free cash flows at the weighted average cost of capital, we obtain the same $250 estimate of the increment in shareholders' wealth as we did with the equity approach. Exhibit 3.10 provides the calculations.

It was necessary to know the market value of the debt and equity to estimate the weighted average cost of capital, but it was necessary to know the weighted average cost of capital to know the value of the firm—a case of circular logic. Miller and Modigliani (1966), the authors of this approach, recognized this problem and solved it by recommending that we first determine the firm's target capital structure and use that market value weighting as the capital structure in the estimation of the cost of capital.

Thus, the net present value method is seen to be a direct estimate of the increase in shareholders wealth (assuming no flexibility in decision

Exhibit 3.10   Net present value of entity free cash flows.

Year	Entity FCF	Discount at 20%	Present Value
0	−1,000	1.000	−$1,000.00
1	250	0.833	208.33
2	250	0.694	173.61
3	250	0.579	144.68
4	250	0.482	120.56
5	250	0.401	100.47
5	1,250	0.401	502.35
			$ 250.00

making). If the net present value of a project is zero, it will earn sufficient free cash flows to pay back the providers of debt all of their expected interest payments plus their principle, and to also pay back to equity investors all of the dividends and capital gains that they expect plus their initial capital investment. If the NPV of a project is one dollar, then all of this extra dollar goes to shareholders because they are the residual claimants of the firm.

One of the advantages of discounting the firm's free cash flows at the after-tax weighted average cost of capital is that this technique separates the investment decisions of the firm from its financing decisions. The definition of free cash flows shows what the firm will earn after taxes assuming that it has no debt capital. Thus, changes in the assumed debt-to-equity ratio have no effect on the definition of cash flows for capital budgeting purposes. The effect of financial decisions is reflected in the cost of capital.

Although we have used a simple numerical example, it is sufficient to convey the major issues clearly. For the reader who wants the details of how to start with a realistic set of financial statements, we refer you to *Valuation: Measuring and Managing the Value of Companies,* 3rd edition (New York: John Wiley & Sons, 2000).

THE TIME PATTERN OF NET PRESENT VALUE

Suppose that we take the project free cash flows as given in Exhibit 3.10 and ask how the present value changes over time, first given the assumption that the entity is a perpetuity, then assuming it is a 5-year project. Recall that the NPV of the entity is $250 (i.e., the difference between its present value, $1,250 and the initial investment outlay, $1,000). The instant following the $1,000 cash outflow, it becomes a sunk cost and the value of the entity jumps to $1,250. Assuming a point-input point-output model, the entity throws off $250 in free cash flow on the last day of the first year. On that day, the entity value, which has risen to $1,500, falls to $1,250. Thus, the value of the firm follows the sawtooth pattern illustrated in the left-hand panel of Exhibit 3.11.

Exhibit 3.11 Evolution of expected values through time.

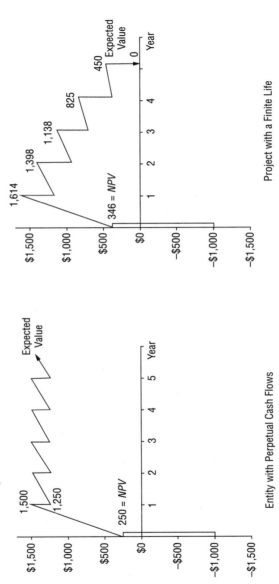

Entity with Perpetual Cash Flows

Project with a Finite Life

Exhibit 3.12   The PV of cash flows from a 5-Year project.

Year	PV Beginning of Year	PV End of Year
0	$ 345.78	$1,614.93
1	1,164.93	1,397.92
2	947.92	1,137.50
3	687.50	825.00
4	375.00	450.00
5	0.00	na

Later on, when we are explicitly modeling uncertainty to value real options, the expected value of the entity will become part of a lattice that emanates from the current value. We have taken this opportunity to describe how the value moves through time, because it isn't usually graphed in exactly this way.

The right-hand side of Exhibit 3.11 assumes that no replacement investments are made and that consequently the free cash flows from the project are $450 per year for five years and the project ends at that time. Exhibit 3.12 provides the calculations for the present value of the project at the beginning and end of each year.

This finite-lived project falls in value over time until its life ends and its value is zero. In either case, with the perpetual entity or with the finite-lived project, the return on capital employed is always equal to the weighted average cost of capital (i.e., 20% in this example).

CERTAINTY-EQUIVALENT APPROACH TO NET PRESENT VALUE

It is possible to estimate the value of a project either by taking its expected future free cash flows and discounting them at a risk-adjusted weighted average cost of capital, or to risk-adjust the cash flows and discount them at the risk-free rate. The answer should be the same either way. As explained later, the certainty-equivalent approach is a common method for valuing options in a lattice.

To illustrate the equivalence of the risk-adjusted and certainty-equivalent approaches, consider a simple one-period example. A project's expected cash flows are $1,000, the risk-free rate is 10 percent, the expected rate of return on the market is 17 percent, and the project's beta is 1.5. If it is an all-equity firm, then its present value is

$$PV = \frac{E\,(FCF)}{1 + R_f + [E(R_m) - R_f]\beta_j}$$
$$= \frac{\$1,000}{1 + .10 + (.17 - .10)1.5} = \frac{\$1,000}{1.205} = \$829.88$$

If the investment outlay is $800, then its net present value is

$$NPV = PV - I = \$829.88 - \$800 = \$29.88$$

And the project would be accepted.

The certainty-equivalent approach reaches the same answer, but by adjusting the cash flows in the numerator. According to the Capital Asset Pricing Model,[1] the beta between a company and the market portfolio is defined as the covariance between the rate of return on the company and the market, divided by the variance of the market return:[2]

$$\beta_j = \frac{COV(R_j, R_m)}{VAR(R_m)}$$

The one-period return on the project is

$$R_j = \frac{FCF - PV}{PV} = \frac{FCF}{PV} - 1$$

Substituting the one-period return into the definition of beta produces a new definition:

$$\beta_j = \frac{COV\left[\dfrac{FCF}{PV} - 1, \; R_m\right]}{VAR(R_m)} = \frac{1}{PV}\left[\frac{COV(FCF, \; R_m)}{VAR(R_m)}\right]$$

By substituting this into the one-period present value equation that uses the risk-adjusted approach, we can derive a certainty-equivalent approach that gives the same answer. The new present value equation becomes

$$PV = \frac{E(FCF)}{1 + R_f + [E(R_m) - R_f]\left(\dfrac{1}{PV}\right)\left[\dfrac{COV(FCF, \; R_m)}{VAR(R_m)}\right]}$$

By recognizing that $[E(R_m) - R_f]/VAR(R_m)$ is the market price of risk in the capital asset pricing model, and using the symbol λ for it, we can rewrite the preceding equation in its certainty equivalent form as follows:

$$PV = \frac{E(FCF) - \lambda\, COV(FCF, \; R_m)}{1 + R_f}$$

This approach adjusts for risk by subtracting a penalty from expected cash flows to first obtain certainty-equivalent cash flows, then it discounts them at the risk-free rate.

In our simple numerical example, the certainty-equivalent risk premium turns out to be $87.13. Therefore, we are indifferent between $1,000 − $87.13 = $912.87 with no risk, and a risky cash flow whose expected value is $1,000 with a beta of 1.5.[3] Either way, the PV is the same:

$$PV = \frac{\$1,000}{1.205} = \frac{E(FCF)}{1 + risk\text{-}adjusted\ rate} = \$829.88$$

$$PV = \frac{\$912.87}{1.10} = \frac{E(FCF) - risk\ premium}{1 + risk\text{-}free\ rate} = \$829.88$$

Later on, when we discuss the methods for valuing real options, we use a similar concept; namely, that we can obtain the same answer using either a risk-adjusted or a risk-neutral approach.

Differences between the Net Present Value and the Real Options Approaches

Both approaches consider all cash flows over the life of a project, both discount cash flows back to the present, and both use market opportunity costs of capital. Therefore, both approaches are discounted cash flow approaches. Yet they are fundamentally different and the NPV approach is a special case of the real options approach. We could say that NPV is a real options approach that assumes no flexibility in decision making.

Sometimes (but not always) the formalism of mathematics helps to clarify the issue. The net present value of a project is often written as

$$NPV = -I + \sum_{t=1}^{N} \frac{E(FCF_t)}{(1 + WACC)^t}$$

Note that the uncertainty of cash flows is not explicitly modeled in the NPV approach. One merely discounts expected cash flows. In reality, there are many paths of possible free cash flows that might be realized between the start of the project and its finish. None of them are mapped out when we use NPV. That is because the NPV approach is constrained to precommitting today to a go or no go decision. It uses only information that is available today. Mathematically, this is equivalent to taking the maximum of a set of possible mutually exclusive alternatives:

NPV rule: MAX(at $t = 0$) $[0, E_0 V_T - X]$

The analogy used in Chapter 1—the decision to drive across the country—applies here. The problem solution is to compare all possible mutually exclusive routes to determine their value, $E_0(V_T - X)$, then to choose the best among them. Real options takes a different perspective. Mathematically, a call option is an expectation of maximums (not a maximum of expectations):

ROA rule: E_0 MAX(at $t = T$) $[0, V_T - X]$

From an options perspective, a project is undertaken, at a future time, if and only if $V_T > X$. If we use the NPV rule, the project is accepted at

$t = 0$ if and only if the expectation at time zero is that $E_0 V_T > X$. The two approaches will be the same if there is no uncertainty, because then the actual future value, V_T, will equal the current expectation of the future value, $E_0 V_T$. Returning to the analogy of a trip from Boston to Los Angeles, the real options paradigm assumes that we will be making decisions down the road, based on the future scenarios that we might encounter. Decisions are made when information about the state of nature is revealed (MAX at $t = T$). For example, we will deviate from our planned route if construction forces a detour, but we will make the optimal decision given information available at the future date, $t = T$.

EMPIRICAL EVIDENCE

There is plenty of evidence that NPV techniques are the primary quantitative criterion being used for evaluating major investment decisions. As mentioned earlier, surveys indicated that by 1970 more than half of the large corporations were using NPV and that by 1978 usage had risen to 86 percent.

One of the few pieces of empirical evidence where the market reacts favorably to the acceptance of positive NPV projects was published by McConnell and Muscarella (1985). They studied the effect of the announcement of capital expenditure plans for a sample of 658 companies over the 1975–1981 time interval. As shown in Exhibit 3.13, the market reacts favorably to the announcement of unexpected increases in capital spending. It is interesting to note that the market reaction to announcements by industrial firms was 1.3 percent in a two-day period and was statistically significant. To see why it was significant, remember that there are roughly 125 two-day periods per year for trading. If we could earn 1.3 percent each two-day period, our total annual return would be roughly 403 percent.

The announcement period returns of regulated public utility firms were not statistically significant—probably because rate of return regulation limits returns to merely equal the cost of capital—thereby neither creating nor destroying shareholder value. Because we do not actually

Exhibit 3.13 Common stock returns on capital expenditure announcements.

	Sample Size	Announcement Period Return	Comparison Period Return	t-Statistic
Industrial firms				
All budget increases	273	1.30%	.18%	5.60
All budget decreases	76	−1.75%	.18%	−5.78
Public utility firms				
All budget increases	39	.14	.11	.07
All budget decreases	17	−.84	.22	−1.79

Adapted from J. McConnell and C. Muscarella, "Corporate Capital Expenditure Decisions and the Market Value of the Firm," *Journal of Financial Economics,* September 1985, 399–422.

know whether the company was using NPV or any other capital budgeting technique, we cannot say for sure that the McConnell-Muscarella evidence supports the NPV method.

There have been only a few empirical studies that compare NPV with real options methodology. Exhibit 3.14 provides a list of companies that claim to be using real options. We were able to find four empirical studies that compare NPV with real options, Paddock, Siegel, and Smith (1988), Bailey (1991), Quigg (1993), and Moel and Tufano (2000). Perhaps an experimental economics paper will fill the void.

Paddock, Siegel, and Smith (1988) collected data on company bids for the bids for the right to develop offshore oil leases in 21 tracts. They calculated the values of the leases using a government-discounted cash flow model and using a deferral option. They found that the two modeling approaches give highly correlated values but that, on average, they are only half of the actual winning bids. The slightly higher value produced by the deferral option approach was inadequate to explain the high prices that were paid. The authors speculate that the high bids may be the result of a "winner's curse" problem. Therefore, the article provides only limited support for the real options approach.

Exhibit 3.14   Companies that have used Real Options (through 2000).

Company	When	Use
Enron	1994	New product development, switching options for gas fired turbines
Hewlett-Packard	Early 1990s	Production and distribution
Anadarko Petroleum	1990s	Bidding for oil reserves
Apple	1995–1996	Exit decision for their PC business
Cadence Design Systems	1990s	Options-based method for valuing licenses
Tennessee Valley Authority	1994	Power purchase options
Mobil	1996	Development of a natural gas field
Exxon	1990s	Oil exploration and production
Airbus Industrie	1996	Valuing delivery options
ICI	1997	New plant construction
Texaco	1990s	Exploration and production
Pratt & Whitney	1989	Cancelable operating leases

Bailey (1991) uses the stock prices of seven palm oil and rubber plantations between January 1983 and December 1985 to compare real option with discounted cash flow valuation. He argues that the option to open and close operations is not captured by the discounted cash flow approach. For six out of seven companies, the real options model fits the actual stock prices better than the DCF model, and in 2 out of 7 cases the difference is statistically significant.

Quigg (1993) studies 2,700 land transactions in Seattle and finds empirical support for a model that incorporates the option to wait to develop land. The owner of the undeveloped property has a perpetual option to construct an optimal size building at an optimal time. Quigg builds an option model with two sources of uncertainty—the development cost (exercise price) and the price of the building (the underlying asset). Her test procedure was to first collect 2,700 land transactions in Seattle between 1976 and 1979 and to break the sample into five categories (commercial, business, industrial, low-density residential, and high-density residential). Next, regressions were used to estimate property prices as a function of building and lot sizes, building height and age, and dummy variables for location and season. Third, the standard errors of the regressions were used to estimate the variances needed for the option model, namely the variance developed property values and of development costs. The final step was to calculate option-based prices, assuming that the building would be built (i.e., that the option would be exercised) when the ratio of its price to the development cost was greater than (one plus) the market rate of the interest.

Quigg's results support the option-pricing approach. The option model prices were, on average, 6 percent above the intrinsic value suggested by the regressions. In a "horse race" where actual transaction prices are regressed against either the option value or the regression value, the option model r-squared was higher in 9 of 15 cases, and the slope coefficients in the option regressions were closer to one in seven out of 15 cases. Furthermore, when the option premium was added to the multiple regression, it was a significant variable in 14 out of 15 cases.

Moel and Tufano (2000) studied the annual opening and closing decisions of 285 developed North American gold mines during the period 1988–1997. They find strong evidence to support the hypothesis that the real options model (specifically a switching model) is useful for explaining opening and closing decisions. As predicted by a real options model, mine closings are influenced by the price of gold, its volatility, the firm's operating costs, proxies for closing costs, and the size of reserves.

CONCLUSION

This chapter has covered some of the fundamental concepts of investment decision making. First, we saw that the separation of the optimal rule from individual time preferences of owners of the firm is possible. Therefore, there is a single rule that maximizes wealth of all shareholders: Undertake all investments that are expected to earn rates of return higher than the opportunity cost of capital. So doing will maximize the wealth of all shareholders, and they will support the rule unanimously.

Our second task was to learn how to estimate cash flows and the weighted average cost of capital, requiring that their definitions be mutually consistent. With the entity approach, the operating free cash flows are discounted at the weighted average cost of capital, and the market value of debt outstanding should be subtracted from the value of the firm to arrive at an estimate of the market value of equity. The alternative equity approach causes the free cash flows to equity to be discounted at the cost of equity. Either way, the results are the same. Also, the expected cash flows discounted at the risk-adjusted rate result in the same answer as the certainty-equivalent cash flows discounted at the risk-free rate.

We also graphed the expected changes in the present value of a project over time, a somewhat novel way of thinking about projects that will be extended later on in a lattice framework that shows the possible paths that value may take when we model uncertainty explicitly. And finally, we visited the issue of the fundamental differences between the NPV and the real options approaches to decision making. In Chapter 4, we go into the mechanics of pricing simple real options such as the right to defer the start of a project, the right to expand or contract its scale, the right to abandon it, and the right to extend its life.

Questions and Problems

For solutions go to www.corpfinonline.com.

1. The separation principle is illustrated in Exhibit P3.1.
   Suppose that the market (borrowing/lending) rate increases. What happens to (1) the current amount of investment, and (2) shareholders' wealth? Explain your results.
2. An investment schedule is shown in Exhibit P3.2.
   Suppose that it shifts to the right (e.g., the dotted line). How does the production opportunity set change?
3. The internal rate of return on a project, IRR, is defined as the return that equates the present value of the cash inflows, with the present value of the cash outflows:

$$NPV = 0 = -I + \sum_{t=1}^{N} \frac{E(FCF_t)}{(1+IRR)^t}$$

Exhibit P3.1

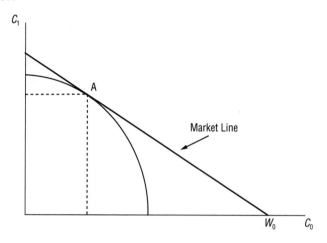

Exhibit P3.2

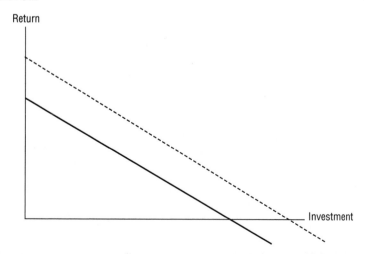

The project should be accepted when $IRR > WACC$. What is the IRR for the following project cash flows? Should the project be accepted?

Year	E(FCF)
0	$ 400
1	400
2	−1,000

4. Compute the NPV and the IRR for projects A and B. Assuming that they are mutually exclusive, which project should be accepted? How does your answer tie into the separation principle?

Expected FCF

Year	Project A	Project B
0	−$1,000	−$1,000
1	0	100
2	0	200
3	300	300
4	700	400
5	1,390	1,250

5. Based on the income statements and balance sheets for the following project, calculate the expected cash flows. If the company's WACC is 10 percent, what is the NPV of the project if the original investment was $1,400?

Forecasted Income Statement

	Year 1	Year 2	Year 3	Year 4	Year 5
Revenue	$1,000	$1,000	$1,000	$1,000	$1,000
Variable costs	−200	−200	−200	−200	−200
Fixed cash costs	−100	−100	−100	−100	−100
Depreciation	−200	−200	−200	−200	−200
EBIT	500	500	500	500	500
Interest income	15	20	25	30	35
Interest expense	−90	−80	−70	−60	−50
EBT	425	440	455	470	485
Taxes at 50%	−212	−220	−227	−235	−242
Net income	213	220	228	235	243

Forecasted Balance Sheet

Assets:					
Cash	$ 50	$ 50	$ 50	$ 50	$ 50
Marketable securities	100	150	200	250	300
Accounts receivable	100	100	100	100	100
Inventories	200	200	200	200	200
Gross property, plant, equipment	1,000	1,000	1,000	1,000	1,000
Accumulated depreciation	200	400	600	800	1,000
Net PPE	800	600	400	200	0
Total	1,250	1,100	950	800	650
Liabilities:					
Accounts payable	$ 100	$ 100	$ 100	$ 100	$ 100
Accruals	0	0	0	0	0
Short-term debt	200	150	100	50	0
Long-term debt	700	650	600	550	500
Retained earnings	50	0	0	0	0
Common	200	200	150	100	50
Total	1,250	1,100	950	800	650

6. Plot the NPV of the project in question 5 as it changes over time. Next, suppose that the project becomes a perpetuity because capital expenditures to replace worn-out facilities are equal to annual depreciation. What is the new NPV? Plot the NPV of the project, given the replacement investment, over time.

7. Suppose that the WACC on a project is 10 percent and that the risk-free rate is 5 percent. The expected cash flow on this one-year project is $5,000 (at the end of the year). What is the present value of the project? What are the certainty equivalent cash flows?

8. Extend the single-period certainty equivalent model to multiple time periods.

9. The big difference between the NPV and the ROA approaches to decision making is that the former is the maximum of a set of mutually exclusive alternatives, evaluated at the present time.

$$MAX(at \ t = 0) \ [0, E_0 V_t - X]$$

While the latter is an expectation of maximums, evaluated in the future contingent on the state of nature, for example:

$$E_0 \, MAX \, (at \, t = T) \, [0, \, V_T - X]$$

To illustrate the difference, consider the following simple problem.

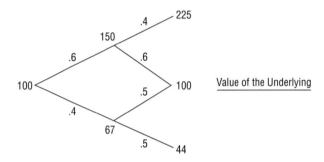

The value of the underlying is illustrated above along with its objective probabilities.

(a) Suppose we must invest $110 today to proceed with the project and that there are no further investments. What is the NPV of the project?

(b) Suppose, instead, that we have to invest $20 today but have the choice of investing $80 at the end of the first year. How does the NPV solution change?

(c) Can we use the same risk-adjusted discount rate to solve both (a) and (b) above?

10. What explanation would you give to rationalize why discounted cash flows work well when valuing companies, but real options work better when valuing projects?

References

Bailey, W. 1991. "Valuing Agricultural Firms: An Examination of the Contingent Claims Approach to Pricing Real Assets," *Journal of Economic Dynamics and Control, 15,* 771–791.

Copeland, T., T. Koller, and J. Murrin. (2000). *Valuation: Measuring and Managing the Value of Companies,* 3rd edition. New York: John Wiley & Sons.

Davis, G. 1996, May. "Option Premiums in Mineral Asset Pricing: Are They Important?" *Land Economics.*

Klammer, T. 1972, July. "Empirical Evidence on the Adoption of Sophisticated Capital Budgeting Techniques," *Journal of Business,* 387–397.

McConnell, J., and C. Muscarella. 1985, September. "Corporate Capital Expenditure Decisions and the Market Value of the Firm," *Journal of Financial Economics,* 399–422.

Miller, M., and F. Modigliani. 1966, June. "Some Estimates of the Cost of Capital to the Electric Utility Industry, 1954–1957," *American Economic Review,* 333–348.

Moel, A., and P. Tufano. 2000. "When are Real Options Exercised? An Empirical Study of Mine Closings," forthcoming in *Review of Financial Studies.*

Paddock, J., D. Siegel, and J. Smith. 1988, August. "Option Valuation of Claims on Physical Assets: The Case of Offshore Petroleum Leases," *Quarterly Journal of Economics, 103,* 3, 479–508.

Quigg. L. 1993. "Empirical Testing of Real Option Pricing Models," *Journal of Finance, 48,* 2, 621–640.

Schall, L., G. Sunden, and W. Geijsbeek. 1978, March. "Survey and Analysis of Capital Budgeting References," *Journal of Finance,* 281–297.

Titman, S. 1985, June. "Urban Land Prices under Uncertainty," *American Economic Review, 75,* 505–514.

4 | Comparing Net Present Value, Decision Trees, and Real Options

In Chapter 3, we reviewed the finer points of net present value methodology. It will always be the starting point for real options analysis (ROA) because we need the present value of a project without flexibility as a base case. We begin this chapter by focusing on the basic differences between the three most popular decision-making techniques—net present value, decision trees, and real options. We then discuss the key assumption that drives ROA—the Marketed Asset Disclaimer (MAD). Toward the end of the chapter, we describe the differences between financial and real options, introduce the Black-Scholes model, and explain why it usually does not make sense to use the Black-Scholes formula in a real options setting (although it may be useful as a rough approximation).

This chapter is your first exposure to the basic algebra of real options, and in an oversimplified setting, to the basic idea of the no-arbitrage condition that we employ to value these options. Later on, we gradually complicate the types of problems that we tackle as well as the solution methodology. For now, we keep the examples as simple as possible.

A SIMPLE DEFERRAL OPTION

In their book, *Investment under Uncertainty*, Dixit and Pindyck (1994) provide a simple example of a deferral call option. (It is always best to start simply.) Consider a decision that you must make today either to invest in a $1,400 project right now, or to defer until the end of a year. Once made, the investment is irreversible (in other words, its salvage value is zero). To have perpetual level cash flows, the depreciation of the project each year is compensated by replacement investment of equal magnitude. The price level of output is $200 now, and there is a 50-50 chance that it will go up to $300 at the end of a year or down to $100. In either case, the price change is assumed to be permanent. Therefore the long-term expected price level is also $200. The first unit is sold at the beginning of the first year of operation. The cost of capital is 10 percent.

If we apply standard NPV analysis to this project, we need to forecast the expected cash flows, discount them at the cost of capital, and subtract the amount of the investment. The algebra looks like this:

$$NPV = -1,600 + \sum_{t=0}^{\infty} \frac{200}{(1.1)^t} = -1,600 + 2,200 = 600$$

Note that the expected cash flows that went into the numerator are based on a 50-50 chance of the price going permanently to either $300 or $100.

Although the NPV is positive $600 and we are tempted to take the project, there is a mutually exclusive alternative, a deferral option that allows us to invest at the end of the year. Let's calculate the value of this alternative, assuming for the moment that it has the same risk and that we can still discount the cash flows at 10 percent:

$$NPV = .5MAX\left[\frac{-1,600}{1.1} + \sum_{t=1}^{\infty} \frac{300}{(1.1)^t}, 0\right] + .5MAX\left[\frac{-1,600}{1.1} + \sum_{t=1}^{\infty} \frac{100}{(1.1)^t}, 0\right]$$

$$= .5MAX\left[\frac{-1,600+3,300}{1.1}, 0\right] + .5MAX\left[\frac{-1,600+1,100}{1.1}, 0\right]$$

$$= .5\left[\frac{1,700}{1.1}\right] + .5[0] = \frac{850}{1.1} = 733$$

The key concept is that if the price falls to $100, the present value of the cash flows is only $1,100, less than the required investment of $1,600, and we can decide not to invest. On the other hand, if the price increases to $300, the present value of the cash flows is $3,300, which exceeds the cost of the $1,600 investment, and therefore we exercise our deferral option by actually investing $1,600. Weighted by its probability of 50 percent and discounted at 10 percent, this decision is worth $733 today.

Thus, we are better off by deciding today to defer, rather than to invest. The value of the deferral option is the difference between the two alternatives, namely $733 − $600 = $133.

Next, suppose that the volatility of the price increases but its expected value stays the same. For example, there may be a 50-50 chance that it goes either to $400 or $0. How does the answer change? First of all, the NPV remains unchanged because the expected price is still $200.[1] The value of the deferral option will increase, however. The intuition is that there is more to be gained by waiting to see how the price uncertainty resolves itself. The calculations are as follows:

$$NPV = .5MAX\left[\frac{-1,600}{1.1} + \sum_{t=1}^{\infty}\frac{400}{(1.1)^t}, 0\right] + .5MAX\left[\frac{-1,600}{1.1} + \sum_{t=1}^{\infty}\frac{0}{(1.1)^t}, 0\right]$$

$$= .5MAX\left[\frac{-1,600+4,400}{1.1}, 0\right] + .5MAX\left[\frac{-1,600+0}{1.1}, 0\right]$$

$$= .5MAX[2,545.45, 0] + .5MAX[-1,454.55, 0] = .5[2,545.45] = 1,272.73$$

The value of the deferral option has increased from $133 to $673. In this example, the value of waiting to decide has increased with the volatility of

Exhibit 4.1   High volatility of the underlying risky asset increases the value of an option.

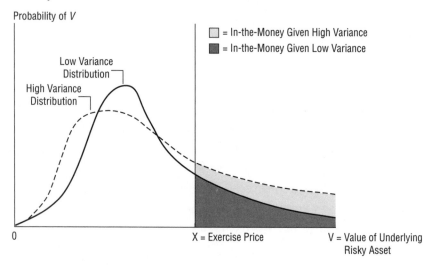

the outcome. This is a general result for options. An interesting macro-economic implication is that when uncertainty increases in the economy, due perhaps to political unrest, then one would predict that investment would decline in response because it becomes worth more to "wait to see what happens."

In Chapter 1, we also talked about the fact that uncertainty increases the value of options. Take a look at Exhibit 1.3 again. It is replicated in Exhibit 4.1 and has been overlaid with a distribution that has higher volatility—the dotted line. The probability of exceeding the exercise price, X, increases as a result of the higher volatility. This is why volatility increases the value of options.

A SIMPLIFIED COMPARISON OF NET PRESENT VALUE, DECISION TREE ANALYSIS, AND REAL OPTIONS ANALYSIS

Consider another simple deferral option. You have to decide right now whether to precommit to a project that will cost $115 million next year with absolute certainty, but will produce uncertain cash flows—a 50-50 probability of either $170 million or $65 million. The alternative to pre-commitment is to wait to the end of the year to decide, and this right costs $$C_0$. We discuss how much it really is later on. For the time being, we think of it as the cost we have to pay for flexibility. The risk-free rate is 10 percent.

Estimating the Net Present Value

How should we go about estimating the net present value of the project? We know the capital outlay and can calculate the expected cash flows, but we still need a risk-adjusted discount rate. Usually practitioners use the Capital Asset Pricing Model, and search for company-level betas that are presumed to have the same risk as the project that is being valued. Suppose that we conduct an extensive search and find a "twin security" that has cash flows that are perfectly correlated with those of our project (and therefore have the same beta) and that has a market price of $20 per share. Exhibit 4.2 shows the payoffs of our project and of the twin security. Note that the twin security has cash payoffs that are exactly one fifth of the

Exhibit 4.2   Cash flows of a project and a twin security.

	Project to Be Valued	Twin Security
Cash in up state	$170	$34
Cash in down state	65	13

payoffs of our project, therefore they are perfectly correlated. To obtain the risk-adjusted discount rate, k, we can use our knowledge of the expected cash flows and the current price as follows:

$$V_0 = \frac{q(V_u) + (1-q)(V_d)}{1+k}$$

$$20 = \frac{.5(\$34) + .5(13)}{1+k}$$

$$k = 17.5\%$$

where q and $(1-q)$ are the *objective* probabilities of obtaining the up state and down state volatilities respectively.

Since our project and the twin security have the same risk, we can now value the project by discounting at 17.5 percent:

$$PV = \frac{.5(\$170) + .5(\$65)}{1.175} = \$100$$

This is the *risk-adjusted discounted cash flow method* for estimating the present value of a project. The net present value subtracts the present value of the end-of-year outlay to which we precommit. Since the outlay is required to be $115 for sure, we can discount it at the risk-free rate. Its present value is $115/1.08 = $106.48. Thus, the net present value (NPV) of the project is $100 − $106.48 = −$6.48. Therefore, we would reject the project.

A more elegant approach for solving the problem is to create a portfolio composed of securities whose values we know have exactly the same payouts as our project. We can then use *the law of one price*. It says simply that to prevent arbitrage profits, two assets that have exactly the same payouts in every state of nature are perfect substitutes and must, therefore, have exactly the same price (or value). Let's use a portfolio of m shares of the twin security and B bonds to replicate the payouts of our project. In the up state, this portfolio must pay off as follows:

Replicating portfolio payoff in the up state: $m(\$34) + B(1 + r_f) = \$170$

And in the down state it pays off:

Replicating portfolio payoff in the down state: $m(\$13) + B(1 + r_f) = \$34$

We now have two equations and two unknowns, m is the number of shares of the twin security and B is the number of risk-free bonds. The solution is $m = 5$ and $B = 0$. Therefore the present value of the replicating portfolio is

Present value of the replicating portfolio: $m(\$20) + B = 5(\$20) + 0 = \$100$

The results are straightforward (although trivial). Since the twin security is perfectly correlated with the project, with payouts exactly one-fifth of those of our project, the value of the project must be exactly 5 times the value of the twin security, that is, it must be 5($20) = $100. This is called the *replicating portfolio approach*. We shall use it frequently for valuing real options. There is an alternative approach that is frequently used, called the *risk-neutral probability approach*, that is mathematically equivalent. We shall present and explain both approaches in greater detail later on. For now, a good way to think about them is that the replicating portfolio approach discounts expected cash flows at a risk-adjusted rate, while the risk-neutral probability approach discounts certainty-equivalent cash flows at the risk-free rate.

Decision Tree Analysis

This is a long-standing method for attempting to capture the value of flexibility. Let's use it as our first attempt at valuing the alternative to pre-committing to take the investment. Instead, a mutually exclusive alternative is to wait until the end of the period before committing. Exhibit 4.3 shows the cash payouts for the various alternatives.

Exhibit 4.3   Cash payoffs for precommitment and for deferral.

	Precommit	Investment	Net precommit	Defer
Up state	$170	$115	$55	MAX[$55, 0]
Down state	65	115	−50	MAX[−50, 0]

The decision tree analysis (DTA) allows the decision maker to defer until the end of the period and choose whether to spend $115 million based on knowledge of the state of nature. The net present value of the decisions is estimated by discounting the expected cash flows, given the right to defer, at the weighted average cost of capital, as follows:

$$NPV = \frac{.5(\$55) + .5(\$0)}{1 + .175} = \frac{\$27.5}{1.175} = \$23.40$$

The NPV of the project has increased from −$6.48 million given the inflexible precommitment alternative to $23.40 million with the ability to defer. Consequently, the value of the deferral option, using the DTA approach is $23.4 − (−$6.48) = $29.88 million.

At first glance, this seems to be a good approach, but on close reflection the DTA method is wrong. Why? Because *the DTA approach violates the law of one price.* The risk-adjusted discount rate of 17.5 percent is appropriate for a 50-50 chance of either $170 or $65, and for any pattern of cash flows that are perfectly correlated (i.e., that are a constant multiple) with it. But the cash flows of the deferral option are very different. Look at Exhibit 4.3 again. The cash flows in the fifth column (55 or 0) are not perfectly correlated with the net cash flows of the project (55, −50). To value the cash flows provided by the deferral option, we need to use the replicating portfolio approach.

Real Options Analysis

To conform with the law of one price when we evaluate the deferral option, we can form a replicating portfolio that is composed of *m* shares of the twin security, with a price of $20 per share, and B dollars of the risk-free bond whose present value is $1 dollar per bond. The payouts of the replicating portfolio must be the same as the payouts of the deferral option (column 5 in Exhibit 4.3). At the end of the period, the replicating portfolio has the following payouts:

Replicating portfolio in the up state: $m(\$34) + B(1 + r_f) = \$55$

Replicating portfolio in the down state: $m(\$13) + B(1 + r_f) = \$0$

In the up state of nature, each of the m units of the underlying risky asset (the twin security) pays $34 and our holdings of B units of default-free bonds pay 8 percent interest. In the down state, the m units of the twin security each pay $13 and B units of the default-free bond still pay 8 percent.

Solving these two equations for the two unknowns, we find that $m = 2.62$ shares of the twin security and $B = -\$31.53$, which implies that we borrow $31.53 (recall that the risk-free rate is 8%). To double-check, put these values into the preceding equations. Except for a small rounding error, the results check.

Replicating portfolio in the up state: $2.62(\$34) - \$31.53(1.08)$
$$= \$89.08 - \$34.05 = \$55.00$$

Replicating portfolio in the down state: $2.62(\$13) - \$31.53(1.08)$
$$= \$34.06 - \$34.05 = \$0$$

Because the replicating portfolio has the same payouts as the project with the deferral option, by the law of one price, it should have the same present value. The present value of the replicating portfolio is:

Present value of the replicating portfolio: $m(\$20/\text{share}) - B(\$1.00)$
$$= 2.62(\$20) - \$31.53 = \$20.87$$

The value of the flexibility to defer is equal to the difference between the value of the project given precommitment, −$6.48 million, and the value with the flexibility to defer, $20.87 million. The value of deferral is therefore $27.35 million.

If we had used the correct risk-adjusted discount rate applied to the expected cash flows from the project given deferral, the DTA approach would have provided the same answer. That risk-adjusted discount rate is calculated as follows:

$$PV = \$20.87 = \frac{.5(\$55) + .5(\$0)}{1+k}$$

$$k = 31.9\%$$

This confirms that when the DTA approach used the appropriate discount rate for the project assuming inflexible precommitment (i.e., 17.5%), it was using the wrong rate for the cash flows of the project with flexibility as provided by the deferral option. In general, the DTA approach will give the wrong answer because it assumes a constant discount rate throughout a decision tree, when the riskiness of the cash flow outcomes changes based on where we actually are located in the tree.

Valuing the deferral flexibility is straightforward if we use a replicating portfolio approach. First of all, what are the payouts for the option, as opposed to the project with flexibility? They are shown in Exhibit 4.4. The deferral option allows the decision maker to avoid negative outcomes in the down state of nature. Replicating portfolios for the option are as follows:

Replicating portfolio in the up state: $m(\$34) + (1 + r_f)B = \$0$

Replicating portfolio in the down state: $m(\$13) + (1 + r_f)B = \$50$

Exhibit 4.4 Payouts of project compared with option.

State of Nature	Payouts for Project with Flexibility	Payouts for Project without Flexibility	Option Payouts
Up state	MAX[$170 − $115,0] = $55	$170 − $115 = $55	$ 0
Down state	MAX[$65 − $115,0] = $0	$65 − $115 = −$50	$50

Solving these two equations for the two unknowns, we find that $m = -2.38$, and $B = \$74.93$, therefore the value of the replicating portfolio and the value of the option is:

Present value of the option: $m(\$20) - B = -2.38(\$20) + \$74.93 = \$27.34$

This demonstrates that we can obtain the market value of flexibility either by taking the difference between the value of the project with flexibility and its value without flexibility, or by valuing the flexibility option directly from the differential cash flows that it generates.

INTUITION OF THE REPLICATING PORTFOLIO APPROACH

The replicating portfolio consists of m units of the twin security and B units of the risk-free bond. Let C_u be the option payoff in the up state and C_d be its down state payoff. Also, let V_u be the value of the underlying

$$m\,V_u + B(1 + r_f) = C_u$$
$$-[m\,V_d + B(1 + r_f) = C_d]$$

$$m = \frac{C_u - C_d}{V_u - V_d} = \frac{\textit{Incremental option payoff}}{\textit{Change in the value of the twin security}}$$

twin security in the up state and V_d its value in the down state. When we solve for the number of units, m, of the twin security in the replicating portfolio, it turns out to be the ratio of the incremental option payoff to the change in the value of the twin security—a hedge ratio. Thus the hedge ratio, m, multiplied by the value of the underlying risky asset (the twin security), V_0, minus the

$$m\,V_0 - B_0 = C_0$$
$$m\,V_0 - C_0 = B_0$$

value of the call option, C_0, gives a risk-free payout, B_0, as shown in the above equation. If one holds m units of the twin security and its value goes up, the capital gain will be exactly offset by a capital loss in the short position created by writing one call.

THE MARKETED ASSET DISCLAIMER

The frustrating part of the twin security approach is that it is practically impossible to find a priced security whose cash payouts in every state of nature over the life of the project are perfectly correlated with those of the project. Therefore, it is nearly impossible to find market-priced underlying risky assets. Early applications of real options analysis used the prices of world commodities as the underlying risky asset, but made the somewhat arbitrary assumption that the volatility of the underlying project without flexibility was the same as the observed volatility of the world commodity. For example, the volatility of the price of gold was assumed to be the same as the volatility of the value of a gold mine that had the right to defer opening. Unfortunately, the volatility of gold is not the same as the volatility of a gold mine.

If you are trying to value real options on a research and development program, or the right to shut down and then reopen a General Motors automobile assembly plant, where do you find a twin security? Instead of searching in financial markets, we recommend that you use the present value of the project itself, without flexibility, as the underlying risky asset—the twin security. What is better correlated with the project than the project itself? We are willing to make the assumption that the present value of the cash flows of the project without flexibility (i.e., the traditional NPV) is the best unbiased estimate of the market value of the project were it a traded asset. We call this assumption the *Marketed Asset Disclaimer (MAD)*. To see how it might be applied to the problem at hand, assume that we abandon our futile search for a twin security, and use the present value of the project without flexibility, as well as the cash flows that it is expected to generate in each state of nature.

If we use the MAD assumption, the payouts of the twin security are the same as those of the project itself, $170 in the up state and $65 in the down state, and the present value of the project is $100. The replicating portfolio now becomes:

Replicating portfolio in the up state: $m(\$170) + B(1 + r_f) = \$55$

Replicating portfolio in the down state: $m(\$65) + B(1 + r_f) = \$0$

Solving the two equations for the two unknowns, we have $m = 0.524$ and $B = -\$31.54$. Therefore, the present value of the replicating portfolio is the same as the present value of the project with flexibility:

$$\textit{Present value of the project with flexibility: } m(\$100) - B = .524(\$100) - \$31.54$$
$$= \$52.40 - \$31.54 = \$20.86$$

This is exactly the same answer that we obtained earlier using the twin security approach, but it is much more practical because we can use the MAD assumption as the basis for valuing real options on any real asset where we are able to estimate the traditional net present value without flexibility.

Note that the MAD makes assumptions no stronger than those used to estimate the project NPV in the first place. Therefore, if a decision maker is currently using NPV to value a project without flexibility, there is no reason to use a different set of assumptions for real options analysis. And what are the assumptions? Most important among them is the assumption that the comparables are really comparable—that the distribution of rates of return of the priced securities is correlated with the project sufficiently well to be usable. We all know how imprecise the use of comparables is, but it's the best we can do. And if it's okay for NPV analysis, then we can reasonably assume that the PV of a project without flexibility is the value it would fetch were it a marketed asset (estimation of project volatility is discussed in detail in Chapters 9 and 10).

THE RISK-NEUTRAL PROBABILITY APPROACH

There is a second, intuitive, and easy-to-use approach to valuing real options called the risk-neutral probability approach. It starts out with a hedge portfolio that is composed of one share of the underlying risky asset and a short position in "m" shares of the option that is being priced; in our example this is a call option, the right to defer. The hedge ratio, m, is chosen so that the portfolio is risk free over the next short interval of time. The hedge portfolio is riskless because if the value of the underlying risky asset goes down, so too does the value of the call option written on it, but since we are short the call option, our wealth goes up. If the hedge ratio is exactly right, the loss on the underlying asset is exactly offset by the gain on the short position in the call option and the result is risk free.

Continuing with the same example, and making the MAD assumption, the end-of-period payouts on a riskless hedge are shown in Exhibit 4.5. We proceed by equating the end-of-period payoffs on the hedge portfolio, because if we can find a value of the hedge ratio m that equates the two, the portfolio will return exactly the same cash flows in either state of nature and will, in fact, be riskless:

$$uV_0 - mC_0 = dV_0 - mC_d$$
$$170 - m(55) = 65 - m_0$$
$$m = \frac{(u-d)V_0}{C_u - C_d} = \frac{(1.7 - .65)100}{55 - 0} = 1.909091 \qquad [4.1]$$

where: u = Up movement = 1.7
$\quad\quad d$ = Down movement = .65
$\quad\quad V_0$ = Starting value = 100
$\quad\quad C_u$ = Call value in up state = 55
$\quad\quad C_d$ = Call value in down state = 0

To check our result, let's see what the payouts of the hedge portfolio are, given that we are long one unit of the underlying and short 1.909091 units of the call option:

Hedge portfolio payoff in the up state: $170 - 1.909091(55) = 65.00$

Hedge portfolio payoff in the down state: $65 - 1.91(0) = 65.00$

Exhibit 4.5 Payouts on a riskless hedge.

End-of-Period States	Hedge Portfolio Payouts	Payoff of Underlying
Up state	170 – mMAX[170 – 115, 0]	170
Down state	65 – mMAX[65 – 115, 0]	65

Knowing that our hedge portfolio is riskless allows us to substitute the algebraic value of the hedge ratio, m, into the present value of the hedge portfolio and to solve the resulting equation for the present value of the call option. First, the present value of the hedge portfolio is

$$V_0 - mC_0 = 100 - 1.909091\, C_0$$

Next, the hedge portfolio will earn the risk-free rate and the resulting payoff will be identical in either the up or the down state. In the following equation, we took the present value of the hedge portfolio, multiplied the result by one plus the risk-free rate, and set the result equal to the payout in the up state:

$$(V_0 - mC_0)(1 + r_f) = uV_0 - mC_u$$

$$(100 - 1.909091C_0)(1.08) = 1.7(100) - 1.909091(55)$$

$$C_0 = \frac{\left[\dfrac{(170-100)}{1.08-100}\right]}{(-1.909091)} = 20.86$$

Not only is the numerical result the same as that obtained using the replicating portfolio approach, but also, by substituting the equation for the hedge ratio, m, into equation 4.1 and solving for the call value, C_0, we obtain

$$C_0 = \left[C_u\left(\frac{(1+r_f)-d}{u-d}\right) + C_d\left(\frac{u-(1+r_f)}{u-d}\right) \right] \div (1+r_f) \qquad [4.2]$$

We define the expressions in parentheses as "risk-neutral" probabilities, p and $(1-p)$, so that the equation becomes

$$C_0 = \frac{[pC_u + (1-p)C_d]}{(1+r_f)} \qquad [4.3]$$

In other words, the present value of the call is equal to the expected payouts multiplied by probabilities that adjust them for their risk. In this way, the numerator becomes a certainty-equivalent cash flow that can be discounted at the risk-free rate. Note that the risk-neutral probabilities sum to one.

$$\left[\frac{(1+r_f)-d}{u-d}\right]+\left[\frac{u-(1+r_f)}{u-d}\right]=\left(\frac{u-d}{u-d}\right)=1 \qquad [4.4]$$

The risk-neutral probabilities are not the same as the objective probabilities that we usually think of when estimating the probability that an event will occur. They are simply a mathematical convenience to adjust the cash flows so that they may be discounted at the risk-free rate. At various times, the risk-neutral probabilities have also been called risk-adjusted probabilities and hedging probabilities.

As this book progresses, we use the replicating portfolio approach on some occasions and the risk-neutral probability approach on other occasions.

MORE ON THE RISK-ADJUSTED AND RISK-NEUTRAL APPROACHES

Exhibit 4.6 shows a two-period example of a project that has a current value of $100 with objective probabilities, $q = .6$, and $(1 - q) = .4$, of moving up by 20 percent or down by 16.67 percent each time period. Given a weighted average cost of capital of 5.33 percent, we have a mutually consistent set of assumptions. The present value, the objective probabilities multiplied by the payoffs, and the risk-adjusted discount rate are a triad of assumptions that must be mutually consistent with each other. Given any two, we can solve for the third. Note that the *expected* present value follows the dashed line in Exhibit 4.6, that is, $V_0 = \$100$, $V_1 = .6\,(120) + .4(83.33) = \$105.33$, and $V_2 = .36\,(144) + 2(.6)(.4)(100) + .16(69.44) = \$110.95$. Thus the expected present value grows at a rate equal to the cost of capital (i.e., 5.33% per year).

Normally, a capital budgeting NPV calculation estimates the expected free cash flows, uses comparables to estimate risk-adjusted discount rate, then deduces the third part of the PV triad—the PV itself. An

Exhibit 4.6 Present value event tree for an underlying risky asset: Risk-adjusted discount rate approach.

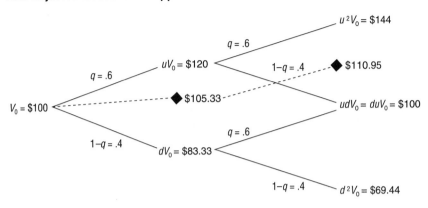

$$PV = \frac{.6^2(144) + 2(.6)(.4)100 + (.4)^2 69.44}{1.0533^2} = \frac{51.84 + 48 + 11.11}{1.1095}$$

$$PV = \frac{\$110.95}{1.1095} = \$100$$

equivalent alternative would be to obtain the market price (i.e., the PV) of a marketed twin security, one that has perfectly correlated expected cash flows in every state of nature, then use these two pieces of the triad to estimate the third, the risk-adjusted discount rate.

Next, suppose that the risk-free rate is 3.00 percent. We could use a certainty-equivalent approach, as discussed in a capital asset pricing model context in Chapter 3. To accomplish this, we discount the project's certainty-equivalent cash flows at the risk-free rate to obtain the same PV (i.e., $100). The risk-neutral probabilities were derived in equations 4.2 and 4.3 and are

$$p = \frac{(1+r_f) - d}{u - d} = \frac{(1.03) - .833}{1.2 - .833} = .53722$$
$$1 - p = (1 - .53722) = .46278$$

Exhibit 4.7 shows the restatement of the present value calculations in a world where all investors are risk neutral. Note that the risk-neutral

Exhibit 4.7 Present value event tree for an underlying risky asset: Risk-neutral approach.

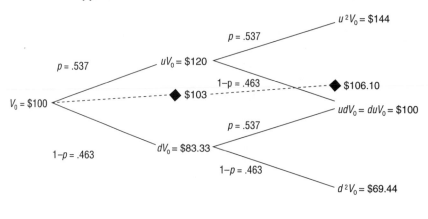

$$PV = \frac{(.537)^2 \,(144) + 2(.537) \,(.463) \,(100) + (.463)^2 \,69.44}{1.03^2} = \frac{41.56 + 49.73 + 14.87}{1.0609}$$

$$PV = \frac{\$106.16}{1.0609} = \$100$$

probabilities of favorable payoffs are lower than the objective probabilities, and the risk-neutral probabilities of unfavorable payoffs are higher. Thus, the expected certainty-equivalent payoffs are lower than the objective payoffs. However, they are discounted at a lower rate, the risk-free rate. Consequently, the present value of the project is the same using either approach.

Next we turn to options that are written on the underlying risky asset. Suppose we have a two-period American call with an exercise price of $95.00. Let's value it using both approaches. Exhibit 4.8 shows the objective probabilities and payoffs. We use the replicating portfolio method to value the call at node D. If the value of the live call, C_u, is greater than the value of the call if exercised, we will decide to hold the call. The replicating portfolio end-of-period payoffs in the up and down states are

$$m \, u^2 V_0 + (1 + r_f)B = 49$$
$$m \, ud \, V_0 + (1 + r_f)B = 5$$

Exhibit 4.8   Option valuation: Objective probabilities.

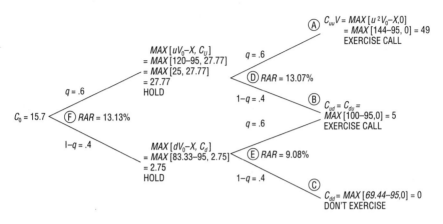

Solving the two equations for the two unknowns yields

$$m = 1 \text{ and } B = -92.23$$

Therefore, the present value of the replicating portfolio at node D will be

$$C_u = mu\,V_0 + B = 120 - 92.23 = 27.77$$

This is greater than the $25 payoff if we exercise the option at node D. Therefore, we hold (i.e., we keep our option alive to exercise later). Similar calculations for nodes E and F produce the following results:

$$\text{At node E: } m = .1636, B = -10.88, C_d = 2.75$$
$$\text{At node F: } m = .6823, B = -52.53, C_0 = 15.70$$

We have also calculated the risk-adjusted rate of return at each node by finding the rate that equates the present value of the option with its expected cash flows, discounted at the risk-adjusted rate (RAR). For example, at node D

$$C_u = \frac{qC_{uu} + (1+q)C_{ud}}{1+RAR}$$

$$27.77 = \frac{.6(49) + .4(5)}{1+RAR}$$

$$RAR = 13.07\%$$

The risk-adjusted return changes from node to node reflecting the changing risk of the payoffs.

Exhibit 4.9 shows the same valuation, but uses the risk-neutral probability approach. For example, the calculation at node D is

$$C_u = \frac{pC_{uu} + (1-p)C_{ud}}{1+r_f}, \quad p = \frac{1+r_f-d}{u-d} = \frac{1.03-.833}{1.2-.833} = .53722$$

$$C_u = \frac{.53722(49) + (.46278)5}{1.03} = 27.80$$

The answer, except for a small rounding difference, is the same as that obtained using the replicating portfolio approach. The advantage of the risk-neutral probability approach is that the risk-neutral probabilities remain constant from node to node. Consequently, the risk-neutral approach is computationally easier to implement than the replicating portfolio approach.

Exhibit 4.9 Option valuation: Risk-neutral probabilities.

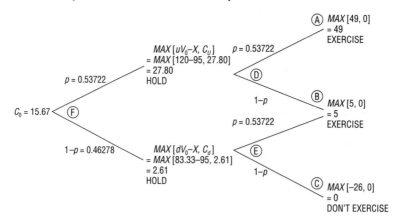

But why do the risk-neutral probabilities remain constant from node to node while the risk-adjusted rates and hedge portfolios change? To answer this question let's revisit the valuation of an underlying risky asset and a call option with exercise price X written on it, as illustrated in Exhibit 4.10.

Other parameters such as the exercise price, X, the up and down movements, u and d, the risk-free rate, r_f, and the weighted average cost of capital (WACC). The objective probabilities of up and down movements are .6 and .4, respectively. The present value (at node F) can be derived by discounting the expected cash flows at the weighted average cost of capital, as follows:

$$V_0 = \frac{.6(\$150) + .4(\$67)}{1.168} = \$100$$

Risk neutral probabilities, p and $(1 - p)$, are derived by equating the present value with certainty equivalent payoffs which we discounted at the risk-free rate, as follows:

$$V_0 = \frac{puV_0 + (1-p)dV_0}{(1+r_f)}$$

$$V_0(1 + r_f) = puV_0 + dV_0 - pdV_0$$

$$p = \frac{(1+r_f) - d}{u - d}$$

Note that the risk-neutral probability does not depend on the state of nature (node). It is a function of only the risk-free rate, and the up and down movements, u and d.

Another way of showing the same result is valid when we are pricing options is to pick a node, say node D, to solve for the replicating portfolio parameters, m (the hedge ratio), and B (the number of default free bonds), and the value of the call at node D, C_D. Having done so, we will prove that the result using replicating portfolios is equal to the risk-neutral value.

Exhibit 4.10 Underlying risky asset and a call.

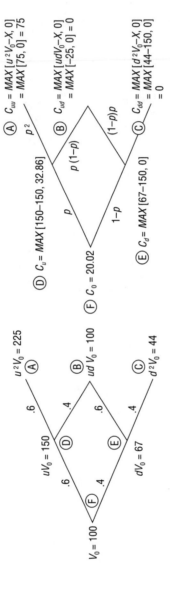

Parameters

$u = 1.50 \qquad r_f = 5\% \qquad X = 150$
$d = .67 \qquad WACC = 16.8\%$

First, solve for m at node D using the replicating portfolio approach

$$mu^2V_0 + B(1+r_f) = 75 = C_{uu} \text{ at node } A$$
$$-[mud\,V_0 + B(1+r_f) = 0 = C_{ud}] \text{ at node } B$$
$$\overline{\qquad\qquad\qquad\qquad\qquad\qquad}$$
$$mu\,V_0\,(u-d) = C_{uu} - C_{ud}$$

$$m = \frac{C_{uu} - C_{ud}}{u\,V_0(u-d)}$$

Next, use the node B equation to solve for the number of risk-free bonds, B

$$mud\,V_0 + B(1+r_f) = C_{ud}$$

$$B = \frac{C_{ud} - mud\,V_0}{(1+r_f)}$$

Finally, the value of the replicating portfolio at node D is

$$C_D = mu\,V_0 - B$$

To prove that this value gives the same result as the risk-neutral approach, substitute the values of m and B into the above equation for the value of the replicating portfolio, as follows:

$$C_D = mu\,V_0 + B = \frac{C_{uu} - C_{ud}}{u\,V_0(u-d)}\,u\,V_0 + \frac{C_{ud} - mud\,V_0}{1+r_f}$$

$$= \frac{C_{uu} - C_{ud}}{u\,V_0(u-d)}\,u\,V_0 + \frac{C_{ud}}{1+r_f} - \frac{C_{uu} - C_{ud}}{u\,V_0(u-d)}\,\frac{ud\,V_0}{1+r_f}$$

$$= \frac{C_{uu} - C_{ud}}{u-d}\left[1 - \frac{d}{1+r_f}\right] + \frac{C_{ud}}{1+r_f}$$

$$= \frac{C_{uu} - C_{ud}}{u-d}\left[\frac{1+r_f-d}{1+r_f}\right] + \frac{C_{ud}}{1+r_f}$$

$$= \left(\frac{1+r_f-d}{u-d}\right)\frac{C_{uu}}{1+r_f} - \frac{C_{ud}}{u-d}\left(\frac{1+r_f-d}{1+r_f}\right) + \frac{C_{ud}}{1+r_f}$$

$$= \left[\left(\frac{1+r_f-d}{u-d}\right)C_{uu} + \left(\frac{u-1-r_f}{u-d}\right)C_{ud}\right] \div (1+r_f)$$

$$= \frac{[pC_{uu} + (1-p)C_{ud}]}{(1+r_f)}$$

This proves that we obtain the same value for the call option using either the risk-neutral approach or the replicating portfolio approach.

COMPARING REAL OPTIONS TO THE BLACK-SCHOLES APPROACH

The famous paper by Fischer Black and Myron Scholes (1973) for the first time, provided a closed-form solution for the equilibrium price of a call option. Although Black prematurely died of cancer, Scholes later won the Nobel prize in economics, along with Robert Merton, for their work.

The Black-Scholes model was the beginning of hundreds of papers that priced various types of options and empirically tested their predictions. It is important to remember the seven assumptions embedded in the Black-Scholes model to understand its limitations for use in real options analysis. The Black-Scholes model assumes:

1. The option may be exercised only at maturity—it is a European option.
2. There is only one source of uncertainty—rainbow options are ruled out (e.g., the interest rate is assumed to be constant).
3. The option is contingent on a single underlying risky asset; therefore, compound options are ruled out.
4. The underlying asset pays no dividends.
5. The current market price and the stochastic process followed by the underlying are known (observable).
6. The variance of return on the underlying is constant through time.
7. The exercise price is known and constant.

To be realistic, most real options problems require analysis that is capable of relaxing one or more of the standard Black-Scholes assumptions. For example, most investment decisions are compound options because they progress in phases, and there are usually several correlated sources of uncertainty. The need to be realistic will cause us to venture far from the Black-Scholes equation, which follows:

$$C_0 = S_0 N(d_1) - X e^{-r_f T} N(d_2)$$

where: S_0 = The price of the underlying (e.g., a share of common stock)

$N(d_1)$ = The cumulative normal probability of unit normal variable d_1

$N(d_2)$ = The cumulative normal probability of unit normal variable d_2

X = The exercise price

T = The time to maturity

r_f = The risk-free rate

e = The base of natural logarithms, constant = 2.1728 . . .

$$d_1 = \frac{\ln (S/X) + r_f T}{\sigma \sqrt{T}} + \frac{1}{2\sigma \sqrt{T}}$$

$$d_2 = d_1 - \sigma \sqrt{T}$$

Today, many pocket calculators have Black-Scholes routines built in, and there are numerous personal computer applications. In Chapter 7, we show how a binomial model, which is based on discrete mathematics and simple algebra, approaches the Black-Scholes model as a limit. For now, however, let's work through a simple numerical example that shows exactly how to use the Black-Scholes model. After that, we will discuss the intuition behind the model.

Exhibit 4.11 provides data for Digital Equipment Co. that was taken out of the *Wall Street Journal* on October 4, during the late 1970s when it had not yet paid a dividend. For close-to-the-money calls on Digital Equipment, the assumptions of the Black-Scholes model are closely approximated. Therefore, we should be able to use it to give reasonable estimates of the price of the calls. Most of the necessary information to value the call is in Exhibit 4.11. The stock price, the exercise price, and the number of days to maturity are given for each option. The risk-free rate is estimated by using the average of the bid and ask quotes on U.S. Treasury bills of approximately the same maturity as the option. The only missing piece of information is the instantaneous variance of the stock (underlying security) rate of return. We shall use the implicit variance estimated from one call price in valuing the others. The implicit variance is calculated by simply using the actual call price and the four known exogenous

Exhibit 4.11 Data needed to price Digital Equipment calls.

Exercise Price	Call Prices Oct. 4			Closing Stock Price
	October	January	April	
$35	$11⅞	$12⅞	n.a.	$46¾
40	6⅞	8	n.a.	46¾
45	2¹⁵⁄₁₆	4¼	6	46¾
50	¼	1¾	3	46¾
Maturity date	Oct. 21	Jan. 20	Apr. 21	
Days to maturity	17	108	199	

Maturity Date	Treasury Bill Rates on Oct. 4			
	Bid	Ask	Average	Risk-Free Rate
Oct. 20	$6.04	$5.70	$5.87	5.9%
Jan. 19	6.15	6.07	6.11	6.1
Apr. 4	6.29	6.21	6.25	6.2
May 2	6.20	6.12	6.16	6.2

parameters in the Black-Scholes formula to solve for the instantaneous variance. We did this using the January 45s on Digital Equipment, which were priced at $4¼ on October 4. The estimate of the instantaneous variance was approximately 7.84 percent (this is a standard deviation of 28%).

Substituting our estimates of the five parameters into the Black-Scholes valuation equation, we estimate the value of the April 45s as follows:

$$C_0 = S_0 N(d_1) - Xe^{-r_f T} N(d_2)$$

where: $r_f = .062$, $T = 199/365$, $S_0 = \$46.75$, $X = \$45.00$, $\sigma = .28$

$$d_1 = \frac{\ln\left(\dfrac{S}{X}\right) + r_f T}{\sigma\sqrt{T}} + \frac{1}{2\sigma\sqrt{T}}$$

$$d_2 = d_1 - \sigma\sqrt{T}$$

If we plug the parameter values into d_1, it equals .4514. Since this is a unit normal variable with mean zero and variance one, it implies that we are .4514 standard deviations above the mean. The cumulative normal probability, $N(d_1)$, is the probability from minus infinity to a point .4514 standard deviations above the mean, as illustrated in Exhibit 4.12. Using probability tables for normal distributions (see Appendix A), the cumulative normal probability is $N(d_1) = .5 + .1741 = .6741$. A similar calculation results in $d_2 = .2446$, and $N(d_2) = .5 + .0969 = .5969$.

The estimated call price turns out to be $5.58, whereas the actual call price was $5.00. If we repeat the procedure for the October 45s (now $r_f = 0.59$, and $T = 17/365$), the estimated call price is $2.28, whereas the actual price is $2.94. Since both of the estimated prices are lower than the actual prices, our estimate of the instantaneous variance is probably too low.

Exhibit 4.12 Estimating the cumulative normal probability.

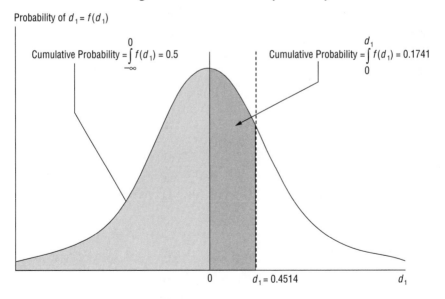

$$N(d_1) = \int_{-\infty}^{d_1} f(d_1) = \int_{-\infty}^{0} f(d_1) + \int_{0}^{d_1} f(d_1) = 0.5 + 0.1741 = 0.6741$$

It is interesting to compare the intuition behind the Black-Scholes model with that of the replicating portfolio method that was explained earlier. First, let's write the replicating portfolio approach:

$$m V_0 - B_0 = C_0$$

The basic idea is to find the right number of units of the underlying risky assets, V_0 plus some bonds, B_0, so that the portfolio has exactly the same payout in each state of nature as the call. Because the market prices of the individual components, V and B, are known, the value of the call option is exactly the same as the value of the replicating portfolio. Next, look at the Black-Scholes formula:

$$S_0 N(d_1) - Xe^{-rT} N(d_2) = C_0$$

It turns out that $N(d_1)$ is the number of units of the underlying necessary to form a mimicking portfolio, and that the second term is the number of "bonds" each paying \$1 at expiration. To explain the second term in greater detail, $N(d_2)$ is the probability that the option will finish "in-the-money" (i.e., with the stock price greater than the exercise price), and Xe^{-rT} is the exercise price at maturity discounted back to the present at the risk-free rate for T units of time.

Thus, the idea behind the Black-Scholes formula and the replicating portfolio is the same. The main difference is that Black-Scholes starts from Itô calculus (the calculus of stochastic differential equations), while the replicating portfolio concept is an algebraic approximation over the next short interval of time that approaches the Black-Scholes equation in the limit as the number of discrete subintervals per unit of time becomes large.

COMPARISON OF FINANCIAL AND REAL OPTIONS

The underlying for a financial option is a security such as a share of common stock or a bond (or interest rates), while the underlying for a real option is a tangible asset, for example, a business unit or a project. Both types of option are the right, but not the obligation, to take an action.

The fact that financial options are written on traded securities makes it much easier to estimate their parameters. The security price is usually observable, and we can estimate the variance of its rate of return either from historical data or by calculating the forward-looking implied variance from other options on the same security (as we did for Digital Equipment). With real options, the underlying risky asset is usually not a traded asset; therefore, we make the Marketed Asset Disclaimer assumption that we can estimate the present value of the underlying without flexibility by using traditional net present value techniques. Although we have not yet discussed exactly how to estimate the volatility of the underlying (see Chapters 9 and 10), we shall use simulation techniques as our primary tool.

Another important difference between financial and real options is that most financial options are side bets. They are not issued by the company on whose shares they are contingent, but rather by independent agents who write them and buy those that are written. Consequently, the agent that issues a call option (by writing it) has no influence over the actions of the company and no control over the company's share price. Real options are different because management controls the underlying real assets on which they are written. For example, a company may have the right to defer a project and may choose to do so if its present value is low. However, if the company comes up with a new idea that raises the present value of the underlying project (without flexibility), the value of the right to defer may fall, and the company may decide not to defer. Usually, the act of enhancing the value of the underlying real asset also enhances the value of the option.

Finally, with both financial and real options, risk—the uncertainty of the underlying—is assumed to be exogenous. This is a reasonable assumption for financial options. The uncertainty about the rate of return on a share of stock is, in fact, beyond the control or influence of individuals who trade options on the stock. However, as discussed in greater detail later on, the actions of a company that owns a real option (e.g., to expand production) may affect the actions of competitors, and consequently the nature of uncertainty that the company faces.

CONCLUSION

In this chapter we have started describing the methodology of real options, albeit at a rudimentary level. We compared net present value methodology with decision trees, and with real options analysis and learned that NPV implicitly assumes no flexibility in decision making, that DTA does but that it is inadequate because it assumes a constant discount rate even when uncertainty is clearly changing based on the changing payouts at various parts of the decision tree. ROA corrects both deficiencies. It models the flexibility of decision making, and because it forms replicating portfolios based on the law of one price, it eliminates arbitrage opportunities and correctly prices the project with flexibility. In Chapter 5, we describe how to value most simple options: options to expand or contract a project, options to abandon, and compound options. Later on, we extend our understanding to include options to switch from one mode of operation to another (e.g., to switch off and on, or to exit and reenter an industry). And we discuss phased investments with multiple sources of uncertainty.

This chapter also discussed two equivalent but seemingly different approaches to valuing simple options: the replicating portfolio approach, which may be thought of as discounting expected cash flows at a risk-adjusted rate, and a risk-neutral probability approach, which is equivalent to discounting certainty-equivalent cash flows at a risk-free rate.

Mainly for the purpose of review, the Black-Scholes call pricing formula was discussed. Its assumptions are much too restrictive for use in most real options applications, but it is useful at this stage to understand how it compares with the lattice methodology that we are going to use.

And finally, we discussed the main differences between financial options and real options, a topic that is useful for those of us who cut our teeth on financial options and frankly wonder what the big deal is about real options.

QUESTIONS AND PROBLEMS

For solutions go to www.corpfinonline.com.

1. A project runs for two periods and then is sold at fair price. Its present value without flexibility is $30 million and the initial investment is $20 million. The annual volatility of the project's present value is expected to be 15 percent and its WACC is 12 percent. At the end of the second period there is an option to expand, increasing the value of the project by 20 percent by investing an additional $5 million. The risk-free rate is 5 percent.

   (a) What is the project's NPV without the option to expand?
   (b) What is its ROA with the option to expand?
   (c) Is the project's ROA value different from its NPV without the option to expand? (Prove your answer).
   (d) What is the project's ROA value with the option to expand? When and under what conditions should the option to expand be exercised?

2. A project runs for two years and then is sold at fair price. The project requires an initial investment of $155 million. Its present value without flexibility is $150 million, with annual volatility of 20 percent and a WACC of 12 percent. At any time during the next two years the remaining assets of the project can be sold for $140 million. The risk-free rate is 5 percent.

   (a) Should this project be undertaken?
   (b) How valuable is the option to abandon?
   (c) When and under what conditions should the option to abandon be exercised?
   (d) Should the project be undertaken without the option to abandon?

3. A project runs for two years and then is sold at fair price. Its present value without flexibility is $15 million with annual volatility of 15 percent and a WACC of 12 percent. The risk-free rate is 5 percent. The project requires $16 million of initial investment. At any time 35 percent of the operations can be contracted with expected scrap value of $5 million.

    (a) Should we undertake the project?

    (b) When and under what conditions should the option to contract be exercised?

    (c) What is the value of the option?

4. A company operates under a hard budget constraint and has a WACC of 12 percent. In the current year it can spend a maximum of $80 million on a new investment. The management is considering two alternative projects: project 1 and project 2. Each of the two projects would run for two years and be sold at a fair price. Both of the projects require $80 million initial investment and have present values without flexibility equal to $100 million. However, project 1 has an annual volatility of 40 percent and project 2 has an annual volatility of 20 percent. Both projects allow the management to contract operations by 40 percent at any time during the next two years. With project 1 the cash received from contracting would be $33 million and with project 2 it would be $42 million. The risk-free rate is 5 percent.

    (a) Using a Decision Tree Analysis (DTA), answer the following questions: Which project should the company select? When and under what conditions would the options to contract be executed with each project? What is the value of the option to contract with project 1? What is the value of the option to contract with project 2?

    (b) Using a Real Options Analysis (ROA) answer the following questions: Which project should the company select? When and under what conditions would the options to contract be executed with each project? What is the value of the option to contract with project 1? What is the value of the option to contract with project 2?

    (c) Do the DTA and ROA valuation results suggest the same optimal execution for the options? Do the DTA and ROA valuations show the same value for each of the two projects? Do the DTA and ROA valuation select the same project as a winner?

5. Using the description of the project in Problem 1, calculate its ROA value using both replicating portfolio and risk-neutral valuation techniques.

   (a) Do the two approaches provide the same value?

   (b) Do the two techniques use the WACC of the project without flexibility?

6. Two companies are developing a 50-50 joint venture with an NPV of $25 million. The annual volatility of the venture is 20 percent and its WACC is 12 percent. The risk-free rate is 5 percent. One of the companies wants to buy the right from the other to acquire its 50 percent share in a year for $15 million.

   (a) Using a two-period model (six months per period), what is the maximum price the company should be ready to pay for the option?

   (b) Using a three-period model (four months per period), how does the option price change?

   (c) How can we use the Black-Scholes formula to solve this problem? What is the option price if we use the Black-Scholes formula?

   (d) Which of the three prices would you use to make a decision and why?

   (e) What price would you use if the buyer wants the right to buy the share at any time during the year?

7. A company is contemplating acquiring a patent on a new drug which expires in three years. The market analysis suggests that the present value of introducing the drug to the market is $120 million with an estimated annual volatility of 15 percent. The required investment to start operations is $140 million with a WACC of 12 percent. The risk-free rate is 5 percent. The company feels that it can successfully introduce the drug within the next two years if the NPV turns positive.

   (a) If the company buys the patent, when (what year) would it introduce the drug to the market if at all?

   (b) Using a two-period model estimate, what is the maximum price the company should consider for the patent?

   (c) How would that price change if any of the following estimates are changed:

     —The present value is $130 million.

     —The risk-free rate is expected to be 7 percent.

—The required investment is $125 million.

—The expected volatility is 20 percent.

8. An equipment manufacturing company provides its clients with an uncancelable capital lease. The present value of operations for a client is $15. The annual volatility for the first five years is 20 percent. The lease is for 12 years and by that time the equipment is exhausted and the present value of operation zero. The clients' operations do not generate a positive cash flow for three years. The annual lease payments are $2 million and they start at the end of year three until year 12. A client has approached the company with a request for a cancellation option at the end of the second year of the lease. The WACC for the client is 12 percent and the risk-free rate is 5 percent. How valuable is this option to the client?

9. A company is considering alternatives to enter a foreign country market. It can either take a green field approach and build its own facility or acquire a local producer within the next two years. The present value of a green field project is $45 million with annual volatility of 17 percent. The required investment is 43 million. The company believes that within the next two years it can sell its new facility for $20 million. The present value of the local factory is $35 million with annual volatility of 15 percent. The asking price for the next two years is expected to be $40 million. What should the company do? Would its choice change if the option to sell the new project is not available? What would be the optimal choice for the company if the market stabilizes and the volatility of both alternatives drop by 5 percent?

10. A company is negotiating a lease for a new manufacturing facility. The estimated present value of the operation is $20 million. Due to market uncertainty it has an annual volatility of 25 percent. The annual lease payments of $2.5 million start in year 3 and last for 10 years. The present value of the lease payments for the first two years are. . . . The company is offered two cancellation options. The first option allows the company to cancel the lease at the end of year two with a payment of $1 million. The second option allows it to cancel the lease at any time until the end of year three with a payment of $2 million. Which option should the select?

REFERENCES

Black, F., and M. Scholes. 1973, May–June. "The Pricing of Options and Corporate Liabilities," *Journal of Political Economy,* 637–659.

Brennan, M., and L. Trigeorgis, eds. 1999. *Product Flexibility, Agency and Product Market Competition: New Development in the Theory and Application of Real Options Analysis.*

Dixit, A., and R. Pindyck. 1994. *Investment under Uncertainty,* Princeton, NJ: Princeton University Press.

Dixit, A., and R. Pindyck. 1995, May–June. "The Options Approach to Capital Investment," *Harvard Business Review,* 105–115.

Hurn, A.S., and R.E. Wright. 1994, March. "Geology or Economics? Testing Models of Irreversible Investment Using North Sea Oil Data," *The Economic Journal.*

Ingersoll Jr., J., and S. Ross. 1992. "Waiting to Invest: Investment and Uncertainty," *Journal of Business, 65,* 1, 1–29.

McDonald, R., and D. Siegel. 1986, November. "The Value of Waiting to Invest," *Quarterly Journal of Economics,* 707–727.

Merton, R. 1973, Spring. "The Theory of Rational Option Pricing," *Bell Journal of Economics and Management Science,* 141–183.

Pindyck, R. 1998, December. "Irreversible Investment, Capacity Choice, and the Value of the Firm," *Journal of American Economic Review, 78,* 5, 969–985.

Pindyck, R. 1991. "Irreversibility, Uncertainty and Investment," *Journal of Economic Literature, 28,* 1110–1148.

PART II

5 | Numerical Methods for Simple Options

This chapter walks through numerical methods for solving simple options such as a simple call (deferral option), a simple put (abandonment option), and options to scale up (expand) or scale down (contract). We also explore combinations of these simple options, because most projects allow all of them to be considered simultaneously. We then show an important difference between NPV and ROA, that in many situations where NPV is forced to treat future courses of action as mutually exclusive, ROA can combine them into a single value with a decision rule for choosing among them. We explore the effect of dividend payments by the underlying risky asset on American call options such as a deferral or an expansion option. They would never be exercised early unless the underlying risky asset dropped in value, for example, when it pays a dividend.

METHODOLOGY FOR MODELING THE STOCHASTIC PROCESS OF THE UNDERLYING ASSET

The methodology that is used depends on characteristics of the underlying asset that needs to be modeled and on the features of the option that is contingent on it. For example, does the value of the underlying asset follow a multiplicative series through time or an arithmetic series? And does the underlying asset pay out cash flows (dividends) or not?

A *multiplicative or geometric process* starts with a value, V_0, at the beginning of a lattice, then moves up or down by multiplying V_0 by an up-movement factor, $u > 1$, or a down-movement factor, $d < 1$. Although it is not strictly necessary, we usually assume that $u = 1/d$. Later on, we show

how these up and down movements are related to the volatility of the underlying asset. Exhibit 5.1 shows the up and down movements in a lattice (in this case, a binomial tree) and the associated probabilities. To illustrate the example numerically, we have chosen to divide the time to maturity into four steps with $V_0 = \$100$ and $u = 1.1$ and $d = 1/1.1 = .90909$. Note that the tree is *recombining*. In other words, the branches come back to the same points. In every even-numbered time period (e.g., 0, 2, 4, etc.), the middle point is exactly $100. In odd-numbered time periods, the geometric average payoff is also $100.[1] In the limit, as the number of time intervals becomes very large, the distribution of outcomes at the end branches approaches a lognormal distribution, as illustrated in Exhibit 5.2. In the uppermost branch of Exhibit 5.1, the value approaches positive infinity (although with zero probability), and the lowest branch value approaches zero because d^T approaches zero in the limit as T, the number of time intervals, approaches infinity. If the underlying risky asset is a common stock, the lognormal distribution is a reasonable approximation of its probability distribution, because we know that stock prices cannot go negative (due to the limited liability provision of share ownership). Multiplicative stochastic processes are chosen by practitioners most of the time.

Exhibit 5.1   Multiplicative stochastic process.

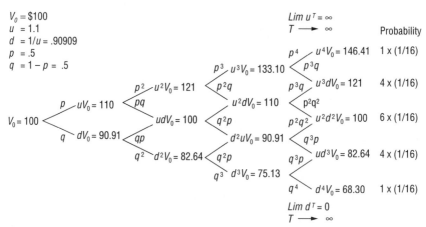

Exhibit 5.2   Lognormal distribution.

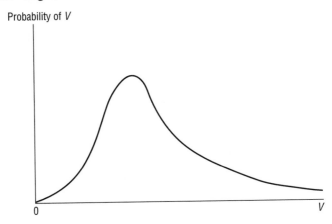

If there is a reason to believe that the value of a project might go negative, it may be better to model the value of the underlying as an *arithmetic* or *additive process*. The up and down movements in the lattice are assumed to be additive, rather than multiplicative. An example is shown in Exhibit 5.3. Now the value changes by adding the up movement to the value in the previous period, or by subtracting the down movement.

Exhibit 5.3   Additive stochastic process.

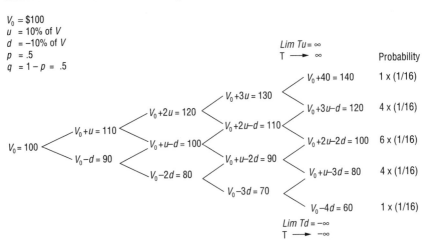

Consequently, the changes in value at each node are no longer proportional to the value in the previous node as they were with the multiplicative process. For example, adding $10 to the starting value of $100 raises the value 10 percent, but adding $10 to $130 in the fourth time period adds only 7.69 percent. Thus, the rate of increase in values in the arithmetic (additive) process is slower and the rate of decrease faster than the multiplicative process. If the-up-and-down movements are equally likely ($p = q = .5$), and they often are, then in the limit, the additive process approaches a normal distribution as shown in Exhibit 5.4.[2] A normal distribution is symmetric and has values in the left tail that go to minus infinity. Like the multiplicative process, the additive process is also recombining.

There are many problems where the underlying asset is *dividend paying* (or cash flows from the project to its owners). To preserve the recombining property of the event trees that describe the evolution of the price of the underlying through time, we usually assume that dividends paid are proportional to value in a multiplicative tree, and are constant and additive in an additive tree. Exhibit 5.5 illustrates both cases. We have assumed that a dividend equal to 5 percent of the value is paid in the multiplicative process, and that in the additive process the dividend is a constant $5.00 each period. Note that the trees are still recombining—a

Exhibit 5.4 Normal distribution.

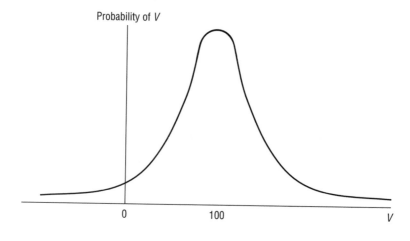

Exhibit 5.5   Value trees with dividends.

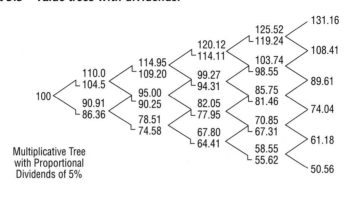

Multiplicative Tree
with Proportional
Dividends of 5%

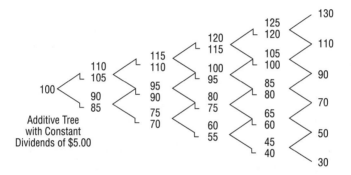

Additive Tree
with Constant
Dividends of $5.00

convenient result that follows from the dividend assumptions—proportional for the multiplicative process and constant for the additive process. Also, the limiting distributions (for the predividend values) are still lognormal for the multiplicative process and normal for the additive process. Finally, the obvious result of paying dividends is that the values at the end branches are lower than they were in the no-dividend case. As the project generates free cash flows that can be dividended out, the remaining value is reduced by the amount of the free cash flow (dividend).

For the time being, we are sticking to examples where we are modeling the stochastic process of the value of the underlying. It is also possible to start by modeling the cash flows of the underlying risky asset and then to construct the resulting value-based event tree. We cover this alternative in a later chapter.

MODELING SIMPLE OPTIONS

The remainder of the chapter shows how to value simple options on the value of the underlying risky asset. The taxonomy of simple options was given earlier in the book. We shall give examples of abandonment put options; the option to contract—also an American put; the option to expand—an American call; and the option to extend the life of the project—an American call. We shall see that American call options will always be exercised on their maturity date and are equivalent to European calls, unless the underlying pays a significant dividend. Since the exercise price of the option is not adjusted for the decline in the value of the underlying on the dividend date, early exercise can be forced by the dividend. For example, if the expected free cash flow from a project is positive and significant, the value of the project declines over time and this may force the early exercise of an American call option. After exploring these simple options one at a time, we will take a look at them in combination.

ABANDONMENT OPTIONS VALUED INDIRECTLY

If one has the right, but not the obligation, to rid oneself of a risky asset at a fixed (predetermined) price, it is called an *abandonment option.* Abandonment options are important in research and development, in exploration and development of natural resources, in new product development, and in merger and acquisition programs. For the first three applications, abandonment amounts to "trimming" an event tree if the outcome from an experiment is unsatisfactory. In many of our client settings, there is a strong and wasteful tendency to stick with a program too long. Abandonment option analysis not only provides an estimate of the value of optimal abandonment, but it also indicates when abandonment should be implemented. In merger and acquisition situations, abandonment is equivalent to being able to bail out of an investment at a floor price—the estimated exercise price of the abandonment option.

To illustrate the pricing of an abandonment option, let's pick some parameters to describe the stochastic process for the value of an underlying risky asset. Assume that its present value without flexibility is $1,000, that its up movement each time period is $u = 1.06184$ and that its down movement is $d = 1/u = .94176$, and that there are four time periods per year in our lattice. Assume the project pays no dividends. The continuous risk-free rate, r_f, is 5 percent per year, and the (continuous) cost of capital, k, for the project is 15 percent.[3] Exhibit 5.6 shows the value event tree for two time periods (6 months), which is the maturity date of the option. We assume that we can abandon the project by selling it for $900 at any point in time.

There is an implied triangularity between the current price of the underlying, the end-of-period expected payoffs (which are based on the volatility of the project), the cost of capital, and the objective probabilities of the up and down state. If we can observe everything else, we can calculate the objective probabilities. Take the first time period for example. The present value, $1,000, is equal to the expected end-of-period cash flows discounted at the project's cost of capital. Given continuous discounting, this may be written as

$$V_0 = puV_0e^{-kt} + (1-p)dV_0e^{-kt}$$
$$1,000 = p(1.06184)1000e^{-(.15/4)} + (1-p)(.9418)1,000e^{-(.15/4)}$$
$$1 = p(1.061840)(.9631944) + (1-p)(.9418)(.9631944)$$
$$1 = 1.022755p + .9071023 - .9071023p$$
$$p = .803246$$

In this way, we can estimate the *objective probabilities* that the market assigns to the end-of-period cash flows of the project.

Exhibit 5.6   Abandonment put, value of the underlying.

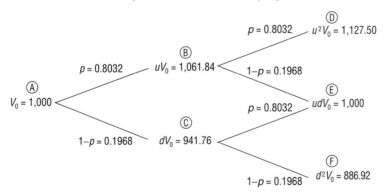

The solution for the value of the project with the added flexibility of being able to abandon it by selling out at $900 is shown in Exhibit 5.7. As always, we solve the problem by starting at the end of the decision tree for the optimal payoffs at the end nodes and then working backward through the tree. For example, the payoffs of the underlying asset at the end points exceed the exercise price of $900 in every state of nature except at "state F."

The payoff at each end node can be written as:

$$payoff = MAX[V_t, X]$$

Using the parameters of the example in Exhibit 5.7, the payoffs at the end nodes are:

Node	Payoff	Decision
D	$MAX[u^2V, X] = MAX[1,127.50, 900]$	Go
E	$MAX[udV, X] = MAX[1,000, 900]$	Go
F	$MAX[d^2V, X] = MAX[886.92, 900]$	Abandon

At node F, we would exercise our option to abandon because the market value of the underlying is less than the exercise price. The option is therefore valuable in state F.

Exhibit 5.7 Value of project with abandonment put.

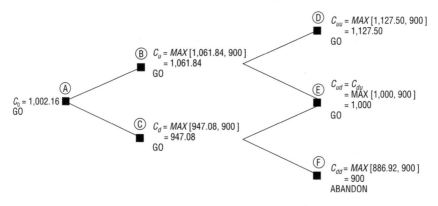

■ Decision Nodes

Next, we look at node C. Our payoff is the maximum of the value of the underlying risky asset (assuming optimal execution of the option in the last period) or the exercise price of the option, $900, whichever is greater. To decide what to do, we need to know the value of the asset if we choose not to exercise the option. We can solve for this value by using either the replicating portfolio approach or the risk-neutral probability approach. The portfolio that can be used to replicate the end-of-period payouts exactly is m units of the underlying plus B bonds, and its current value is

Replicating portfolio: $mdV_0 + B = $ Value of put at node C

The payoffs of the replicating portfolio in the up state (state E) and the down state (state F) must be equal to the payoffs of the put option in those states. The result is two equations and two unknowns, m and B:

$$\begin{array}{l} \textit{State E:} \quad m(duV_0) + (1 + r_f)B = 1{,}000 \\ \underline{\textit{State F:} \ -[m(d^2V_0) + (1 + r_f)B = 900]} \end{array}$$

$$mdV_0(u - d) = C_{du} - C_{dd} \qquad [5.1]$$

$$m = \frac{(C_{du} - C_{dd})}{dV_0(u - d)}$$

This is a general result that we shall use repeatedly. It says that the number of shares of the underlying asset in our replicating portfolio will be equal to the difference between the payoff of the option in the up state minus the payoff in the down state $(C_{du} - C_{dd})$, divided by the value of the underlying asset at the beginning of the period, dV_0, multiplied by the difference between the up and down movements $(u - d)$. Substituting in the numbers from our example at node C, we have,

$$m = \frac{(1{,}000 - 900)}{941.76(1.0618 - .9417)}$$

$$m = \frac{100}{113.08} = .88433$$

To solve for B, we can substitute the value of m into the first equation:

$$m(duV_0) + (1 + r_f)B = C_{du}$$

$$B = \frac{C_{du} - mduV_0}{(1 + r_f)}$$

Substituting the value of m from equation 1, we have

$$B = \left\{ C_{du} - \left[\frac{C_{du} - C_{dd}}{dV_0(u - d)} \right] duV_0 - \right\} \div (1 + r_f)$$

$$= \left[\frac{C_{du}(u - d) - (C_{du} - C_{dd})u}{u - d} \right] \div (1 + r_f) \qquad [5.2]$$

$$= \left[\frac{u C_{dd} - d C_{du}}{u - d} \right] \div (1 + r_f)$$

Again, this is a generalizable formula that we shall use repeatedly. Equation 5.2 says that the number of bonds that we need is equal to the up movement parameter, u, times the payout in the down state minus the down movement parameter, d, times the payout of the option in the up state; all divided by the difference between the up and down movements and by one plus the risk-free rate. Substituting in the values of the parameters, we find

$$B = \left\{ \frac{[1.06184(900) - .94176(1,000)]}{(1.06184 - .94170)} \right\} \div (1.01258)$$

$$= \left(\frac{13.896}{.12008} \right) \div 1.01258$$

$$= 115.72 \div 1.01258 = 114.28$$

Therefore, the replicating portfolio consists of .88433 units of the underlying asset plus a long position of 114.28 zero coupon bonds. Therefore, its present value at node C is

$$M(dV_0) + B = .88433(941.76) + 114.28 = 832.83 + 114.28 = 947.10$$

Because the value of the project with flexibility is $947.10 at node C and the value of the put if exercised is only $900, we would decide not to exercise our option to abandon at node C.

The following chart provides the numerical solutions for the number of units of the underlying risky asset, the number of zero coupon bonds, the value of the put option, and the optimal decision at each node in the decision tree:

Node	m = Units of the Underlying	B = No. of Bonds	Value	Decision
D	n/a	n/a	1,127.50	Go
E	n/a	n/a	1,000	Go
F	n/a	n/a	900	Abandon
B	1.0000	0.00	1,061.84	Go
C	0.8843	114.26	947.10	Go
A	0.9557	46.46	1,002.16	Go

The value at root node A, $1,002.16, is the value of the project with the flexibility of the abandonment option. Therefore, we can obtain the value of the option indirectly by subtracting the value of the project without flexibility from its value with flexibility:

$$Value\ of\ abandonment\ option = Value\ of\ project\ with\ flexibility$$
$$minus\ the\ value\ of\ project$$
$$without\ flexibility$$

$$Value\ of\ abandonment\ option = \$1,002.16 - \$1,000 = \$2.16$$

Exhibit 5.8   Risk-adjusted probabilities.

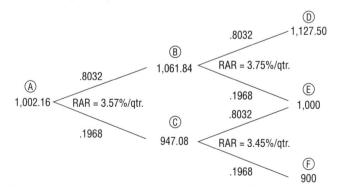

As a by-product of our analysis, we can derive the risk-adjusted discount rates (RARs) for each branch of the decision tree. The results are shown in Exhibit 5.8. Take node C as an example. We just finished calculating the value of the project with flexibility at node C as $947.08. The payoffs are $1,000 in the up state and $900 in the down state; and the objective probabilities (which were calculated earlier) are .8032 for the up state and .1968 for the down state. Using this information, we can solve for the risk-adjusted rate as follows:

$$Value\ at\ node\ C = \frac{\text{Expected payoffs}}{(1+RAR)}$$

$$947.08 = \frac{[8032(1,000)+(1-.8032)(900)]}{(1+RAR)}$$

$$947.08 = \frac{[803.2+177.12]}{(1+RAR)}$$

$$RAR = \frac{980.32}{947.08} - 1 = \frac{3.5097\%}{\text{quarter}}$$

The risk-adjusted rate of return (RAR) varies depending on where we are in the decision tree because the riskiness of outcomes changes as well. Recall that this is the major reason that decision-tree analysis does not work. DTA inappropriately assumes a constant discount rate.

VALUING ABANDONMENT OPTIONS DIRECTLY

Instead of inferring the value of the American put as the difference between the value of the project with the put minus the value of the project without the put, we can value the put directly. Its payoffs are

$$MAX[0, X-V]$$

Therefore, the decision tree looks like Exhibit 5.9. Using node C as an example, we can form a replicating portfolio to value the abandonment put. However, we can also take a different approach and form a hedge portfolio instead—one that is made up of m units of the underlying risky project

Exhibit 5.9   Decision tree with payoffs for the American put.

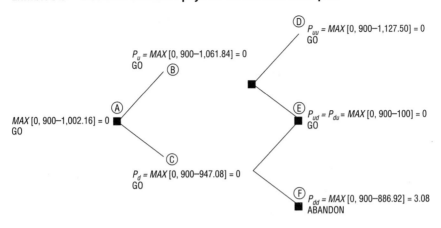

■ Decision Nodes

(without flexibility) and one unit of the American put option. If the hedge portfolio shown in Exhibit 5.10 is truly risk free, then its present value, multiplied by the risk-free rate will equal the end-of-period payoff of the hedge portfolio in either the up or the down state. In the following equation, the present value of the hedge portfolio is multiplied by one plus the risk-free rate and set equal to its payoff in the up state:

$$[m(dV_0) + P_d](1 + r_f) = m(udV_0) + P_{ud}$$

Exhibit 5.10   Payoffs on a hedge portfolio.

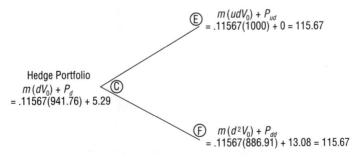

or the down state:

$$[m(dV_0) + P_d](1 + r_f) = m(d^2V_0) + P_{dd}$$

To solve for the hedge ratio, m, that guarantees this result, we equate the end-of-period payoffs of the hedge portfolio with each other and solve for m:

$$m(udV_0) + P_{ud} = m(d^2V_0) + P_{dd}$$

Solving for m, we have

$$m = \frac{P_{dd} - P_{du}}{dV_0(u - d)} = \frac{(13.08 - 0)}{[941.76(1.0618 - .9418)]} = \frac{13.08}{113.08} = .11567$$

Next, take the value of the hedge portfolio (which has zero default risk) and multiply it by the risk-free rate, then equate the result with the portfolio's end-of-period payoff (in either state of nature):

$$(mV_d + P_d)(1 + r_f) = muV_d + P_{ud}$$

$$(mdV_0 + P_d)(1 + r_f) = mduV_0 + P_{ud} \text{ since } V_d = dV_0$$

$$(mV_0 + P_0)(1 + r_f) = muV_0 + P_u \text{ since } P_d = dP_0 \text{ and } P_{ud} = dP_u$$

Substituting in the value of m and then solving for the put price, P_0, gives

$$P_0 = \frac{\left\{\left[\dfrac{u - (1 + r_f)}{u - d}\right]P_d + \left[\dfrac{(1 + r_f) - d}{u - d}\right]P_u\right\}}{(1 + r_f)}$$

We can interpret q and $(1 - q)$ as the probabilities that risk-adjust the payoffs so that they can be discounted at the risk-free rate:

$$q = \frac{u - (1 + r_f)}{u - d} = \frac{1.0618 - (1 + .012458)}{1.0618 - .9418} = \frac{.04926}{.12} = .4096,$$

$$1 - q = \frac{(1 + r_f) - d}{u - d} = 1 - .4906 = 0.5904$$

These are the same risk-neutral probabilities described in Chapter 3. Their values do not change as we move from node to node, so they have an advantage over the replicating portfolio method because m the hedge ratio, may be different at different nodes. Using the put equation that employs risk-neutral probabilities, we solve iteratively to value the American put directly. At node C, its value is

$$P_d = \frac{[qP_{dd} + (1 - q) P_{ud}]}{(1 + r_f)} = \frac{[.4096(13.08) + .5904(0)]}{(1.01258)} = \frac{5.357}{1.01258} = 5.29$$

$$P_u = \frac{[qP_{ud} + (1 - q) P_{uu}]}{(1 + r_f)} = \frac{[.4096(0) + (1 - .4096)(0)]}{(1 + .01258)} = 0$$

$$P_0 = \frac{[qP_d + (1 - q) P_u]}{(1 + r_f)} = \frac{[.4096(5.29) + .5904(0)]}{(1.01258)} = \frac{2.167}{1.01258} = 2.16$$

This is the same value obtained earlier with the replicating portfolio approach, but the calculations were somewhat easier because the risk-neutral probabilities remained constant.

VALUING THE OPTION TO CONTRACT (SHRINK) A PROJECT

The right to sell off some capacity, thereby shrinking the scale of operations, is an American put option that we call the *option to contract*. To illustrate the valuation of such an option, we keep the same underlying risky asset as before (see Exhibit 5.6) but introduce an option to contract the scale of operations (and therefore its value) by 50 percent by selling assets (plant and equipment) worth $450 after taxes. An alternative that is similar, would be to scale back operations and sublet equipment and facilities to another company.

Exhibit 5.11   Decision tree for the option to contract.

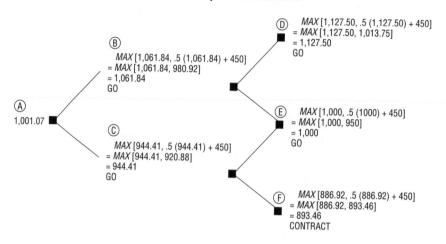

■ Decision Nodes

The decision tree that shows the payouts for the option to contract is illustrated in Exhibit 5.11. The decisions and payouts at the end nodes, are easy to calculate:

Node	Payoff	Decision
D	$MAX[1.127.5, 1,127.50/2 + 450] = 1,127.5$	Go
E	$MAX[1,000, 1,000/2 + 450] = 1,000$	Go
F	$MAX[886.92, 886.92 + 450] = 893.46$	Contract

We can use replicating portfolios at nodes B and C to solve for the value of the options at those nodes. At node C, the replicating portfolios for the end-of-period payouts can be written as follows:

$$\text{State E:} \quad mudV_0 - B(1 + r_f) = 1,000.00$$
$$\text{State F:} \quad -[md^2V_0 - B(1 + r_f) = 893.46]$$

$$m = \frac{106.54}{113.08} = .942165$$

Solving for the number of bonds, B, we have

$$mudV_0 - B(1 + r_f) = 1,000$$

$$.942165(1,000) - B(1 + .01258) = 1,000$$

$$B = \frac{(1,000 - 942.165)}{1.01258} = \frac{57.116}{1.01258} = 55.079$$

Therefore, the beginning of period value of the replicating portfolio is

$$mdV_0 - B = .942165(941.76) + 55.079 = 942.4$$

Using the replicating portfolio method again at node A, we find that $m = .99489$, $B = 5.17$, and the value of the replicating portfolio (and therefore the value of the project with the option to contract) is $1,001.07. As shown, the option in this example adds very little value.

VALUE OF THE OPTION TO EXPAND (WHEN THE UNDERLYING DOES NOT PAY DIVIDENDS)

If projects turn out better than expected, it is often desirable to invest in expanding them. The extra investment is the exercise price of an expansion option—an American call. The value tree for the underlying shifts upward to reflect the benefits of the expansion.

To illustrate the valuation of a simple expansion option, we keep the same underlying project event tree (Exhibit 5.6) and introduce the option to expand the scale of operations, at an expense of $100, for a benefit that increases the value of operations by 10 percent. Although the event tree remains the same, the new decision tree is shown in Exhibit 5.12. At the end nodes the payoffs are:

Node	Payoff	Decision
D	$MAX[1,127.50, 1.1(1,127.5) - 100] = 1,140.25$	Expand
E	$MAX[1,000, 1.1(1,000) - 100] = 1,000$	Expand = Go
F	$MAX[886.92, 1.1(886.92) - 100] = 886.92$	Go

Exhibit 5.12   Decision tree for the option to expand.

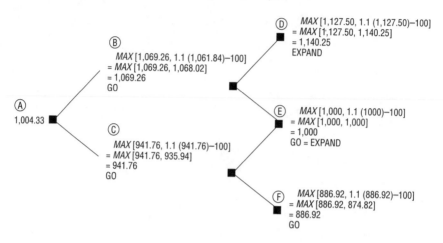

■ Decision Nodes

Next, we use the replicating portfolio method to calculate the value of the project with the flexibility to expand at the remaining nodes: B, C, and A. The number of units of the underlying, m, the number of bonds, B, the value of the project if the option is "kept alive" (i.e., if it is not exercised), its value if the option to expand is exercised, and the decision at each node are summarized in the following chart:

Node	m Units	B Bonds	Value if Kept Alive	Value if Exercised	Decision
B	1.100	98.76	1,069.26	1,068.02	Go
C	1.000	0.00	941.76	935.94	Go
A	1.062	57.69	1,004.31	1,000.00	Go

Note that in earlier nodes, the value of keeping the option alive is always greater than its value if the option is extinguished by exercising it before its maturity date. This is a general property of American call options on risky assets that do not pay dividends. The intuition is this: If you exercise the option, you get the value of the (expanded) project minus the exercise price. On the other hand, if you do not exercise, you get the present value of the project with the option to expand in the future minus the discounted present value of the exercise price (i.e., the value that the project with flexibility could be sold for in the open market). Thus, the value of keeping your option alive is always greater than exercising the option, as long as the underlying does not pay a dividend. If it does, and the exercise price of the option is not adjusted for the dividend, then it often pays to exercise early because the option value drops when the dividend payment decreases the value of the underlying. Later on, we describe the valuation of an expansion option on a project that pays out dividends.

VALUING COMBINATIONS OF SIMPLE OPTIONS

Next, consider the possibility of a project that allows any one of the three simple options to be exercised at each decision node:

1. An American put, the option to abandon for a salvage value of $900.
2. A contraction option, also an American put, to shrink the scale of operations by 50 percent by selling assets for $450.
3. The option to expand the scale of the project by 10 percent at a cost of $100, an American call.

The value tree for the underlying remains the same as before (see Exhibit 5.6). However, the decision tree, as shown in Exhibit 5.13, contains

Exhibit 5.13 Decision tree for a combination of options.

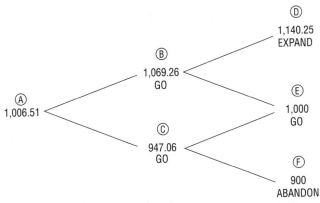

at each node all three possible options—to expand, to contract, and to abandon. Fortunately, they are mutually exclusive alternatives and exercising them does not make the tree path dependent. As usual, we begin to solve the valuation problem by starting with the optimal decisions and their corresponding payoffs at the end nodes:

Node	Payoff				Decision
D	MAX[1,127.50, 1.1(1,127.50) − 100, 1,127.50/2+ 450, 900] = 1,140.25				Expand
	MAX[1,127.50,	1,140.25,	1,013.75,	900]	
	Unexercised,	expand,	contract,	abandon	
E	MAX[1,000, 1.1(1,000) − 100, 1,000/2 + 450, 900] = 1,000				Go or
	MAX[1,000,	1,000,	950,	900]	expand
	Unexercised,	expand,	contract,	abandon	
F	MAX[886.92, 1.1(886.92) − 100, 886.92/2 + 450, 900] = 900				Abandon
	MAX[886.92,	875.61,	893.46,	900]	
	Unexercised,	expand,	contract,	abandon	

The payoffs from four mutually exclusive decisions are evaluated at each end node, and the decision that results in the highest payoff is chosen as optimal. Next, we work backward to nodes B and C. Once we have determined the optimal decisions at the end of the first period, we are then ready to work backward one final time to node A.

As usual, we apply the replicating portfolio approach and estimate the number of units of the underlying, m, and the number of risk-free bonds, B, that give us a replicating portfolio whose value is known because it is composed of two assets whose value we have already estimated, and whose value is equal to the project with flexibility. The only difference is that we must consider four mutually exclusive decisions at each node. To illustrate, we show the calculations for node B.

From Exhibit 5.13, we see that the end-of-period optimal payoffs from node B are $1,140.25 in the up state at node D where we would decide to expand, and $1,000 at node E, where we are indifferent between expanding and simply leaving our option unexercised. We form a replicating portfolio that will give us the identical end-of-period payoffs:

$$State\ D: \quad mu^2V_0 - B(1 + r_f) = 1,140.25$$
$$State\ E: \quad -[mud\ V_0 - B(1 + r_f) = 1,000.00]$$
$$\overline{\qquad\qquad muV_0(u - d) = C_u - C_d \qquad}$$

$$m = \frac{140.25}{(1,127.50 - 1,000)} = 1.1$$

And by substituting the value $m = 1.1$ into the equation for state D, and solving, we learn that $B = -\$98.76$. Therefore, the value of the project with flexibility at node B will be

$$muV_0 - B = 1.1(1,061.84) - 98.76 = \$1,069.26$$

Next, we compare the value of the project with flexibility with the payoffs from the mutually exclusive options to make a value-maximizing decision at node B:

$$MAX[1,069.26, 1.1(1,061.84) - 100, 1,061.84/2 + 450, 900]$$
$$= MAX[1,069.26, \qquad 1,068.02, \qquad 980.92, \qquad 900]$$
$$\qquad\quad [Unexercised, \quad expand, \qquad\qquad contract, \quad abandon]$$

Since the value is highest if we leave our options unexercised, that is what we decide to do. Next, a similar analysis is necessary at node C. When we formed the replicating portfolio, we calculated that it was worth $947.06, that $m = .8843$, and that $B = \$114.26$. We then looked at the optimal decision at node C:

$$MAX[947.06, 1.1(941.76) - 100, 941.76/2 + 450, 900]$$
$$MAX[947.06, \qquad 935.94, \qquad\qquad 920.00, \qquad 900]$$
$$MAX[Unexercised, expand, contract, abandon]$$

The value-maximizing decision was to leave the options unexercised because the value of the project with flexibility was higher.

The final step is to work back to node A. The end-of-period optimal payoffs are $1,069.26 at node B, and $947.06 at node C. Using the replicating portfolio method at node A, we calculated that $m = 1.0177$,

$B = -11.19$, and that the present value of the project with flexibility is $1,006.51. Furthermore, we would choose to leave all of our options open at node A.

The lattice approach makes it easy to evaluate a project with several simultaneous options on the underlying asset. The following values of the separate options and of the combined simultaneous options make it easy to draw conclusions:

Value of the option to abandon	$2.16
Value of the option to contract	$0.10
Value of the option to expand	$4.33
Value of the combination of options	$6.51

While it is true that the simple sum of the values of the three separate options is not equal to the value of their combination, we must look more carefully and note that the option to contract was never used in the combination—in other words it was valueless in the combination because it was dominated by the other two options. Therefore, the value of the combination, $6.51 is equal to the simple sum of the values of the (undominated) options, namely the abandonment option and the option to expand. The sum of their values is $6.49, within rounding error, the same as the value of the combination.

NET PRESENT VALUE AND REAL OPTIONS ANALYSIS HANDLE MUTUALLY EXCLUSIVE ALTERNATIVES DIFFERENTLY

Consider the decision tree illustrated in Exhibit 5.14. The cash flow of a project right now is $100. At the end of year 1, it goes up by 20 percent to $120 or down by 16.67 percent to $83.3 with similar percentage changes in year 2. At the end of the second year, the company has two mutually exclusive alternatives. In one branch of the decision tree, it can spend $700 to lock in its annual level of cash flows forever. In a mutually exclusive branch, it can spend an additional $120 to test-market a new version of the product (thereby forgoing a year of cash flows) to find out, as of year 4 that, with 50-50 probability, the perpetual cash flows will be either 50 percent higher, or 33⅓ percent lower. Then, in year 4, the

Exhibit 5.14   Tree of expected events.

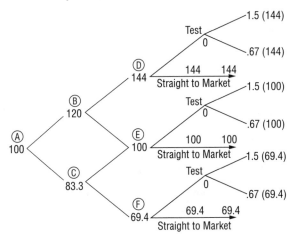

company can, at a cost of $700, lock in the perpetual cash flows or it can abandon the project. Additionally, the cost of capital is 10 percent, the risk-free rate is 5 percent, and the initial outlay required to commence the project is $400.

This example illustrates that the NPV approach treats the choice of whether to go straight to market or to conduct a test market as mutually exclusive alternatives at the beginning of the project, then chooses the one with the higher NPV. Real options analysis, on the other hand, works back in time from the end points of the decision tree, making the value-maximizing decision at each node, when the choice is actually available, contingent on the underlying state variable. The result is a single present value that is used to decide whether to start the project today.

Although we do not discuss it in detail here, the deferral decision is also a good example to illustrate the differences between NPV and ROA. If we use NPV, deferral must be treated as a large set of mutually exclusive deferral dates—defer for one year, defer for two years, and so forth. The real options approach tells us whether to start the project today and provides a value for the right to defer without saying when. It then gives value-maximizing rules of thumb for deciding when to defer.

We begin by solving for the NPVs of the two mutually exclusive alternatives—go straight to market or conduct a test market. Exhibit 5.15

Exhibit 5.15 Free cash flow tree for going straight to market.

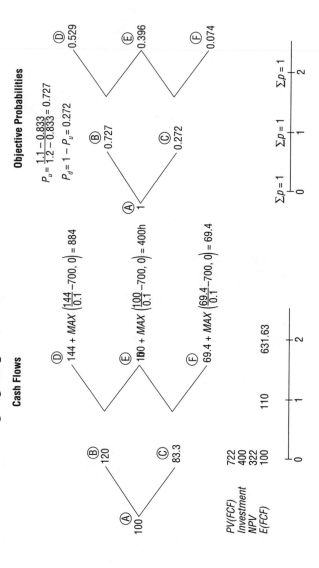

shows the cash flows and their objective probabilities for the first 2 years of the project and provides the calculations of the NPV assuming that the company decides to precommit to going straight to market. The NPV decision rule maximizes value given all of the information available at time zero. For example, the company has the foresight to know that if the project reaches node F, it will be abandoned. The present value of this alternative is estimated as:

$$PV = 100 + \frac{.727(120) + .272(83.3)}{1.1} + \frac{.529(884) + .396(400) + .074(69.4)}{(1.1)^2} = 722$$

$$NPV = PV - Investment = 722 - 400 = 322$$

Next, Exhibit 5.16 provides the NPV calculation assuming that the company precommits to conducting a market test. It will spend the $120 in all states of nature given the precommitment. This is the mutually exclusive alternative to going straight to market. We know today that we would abandon the project given the worst state of nature in year 4. The expected cash flow in year 3 is zero because the project provides no cash flow during the test year. Its expected cash flow in the other years is

$$E(CF, \text{year } 4) = .529(.5)1{,}676 + .529(.5)356 + (.396)(.5)950 + \\ .396(.5)33.3 + 0.74(.5)444.0$$

$$E(CF, \text{year } 4) = 749.2$$

$$E(CF, \text{year } 2) = .529(24) + .396(-20) + 0.74(-50.6) = 1.02$$

$$E(CF, \text{year } 1) = .727(120) + .272(83.3) = 110$$

Discounting these expected cash flows at 10 percent, adding the initial cash inflow of $100, and subtracting the initial investment of $400 results in an NPV of $312.55.

Because the NPV of going straight to market is $322 and the NPV of the test market is $312.55, we would decide today to precommit to go straight to market.

The real options analysis is given in Exhibits 5.17 and 5.18. The real options approach does not assume that we precommit. Rather, at the end of year 2, we decide whether it is better to go straight to market (nodes D

Exhibit 5.16   Free cash flow tree for the case with additional test.

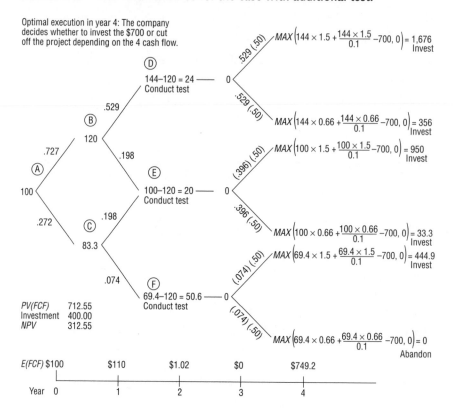

Optimal execution in year 4: The company decides whether to invest the $700 or cut off the project depending on the 4 cash flow.

$$MAX\left(144 \times 1.5 + \frac{144 \times 1.5}{0.1} - 700, 0\right) = 1{,}676$$ Invest

$$MAX\left(144 \times 0.66 + \frac{144 \times 0.66}{0.1} - 700, 0\right) = 356$$ Invest

$$MAX\left(100 \times 1.5 + \frac{100 \times 1.5}{0.1} - 700, 0\right) = 950$$ Invest

$$MAX\left(100 \times 0.66 + \frac{100 \times 0.66}{0.1} - 700, 0\right) = 33.3$$ Invest

$$MAX\left(69.4 \times 1.5 + \frac{69.4 \times 1.5}{0.1} - 700, 0\right) = 444.9$$ Invest

$$MAX\left(69.4 \times 0.66 + \frac{69.4 \times 0.66}{0.1} - 700, 0\right) = 0$$ Abandon

(D) 144–120 = 24 — 0 Conduct test
(E) 100–120 = 20 — 0 Conduct test
(F) 69.4–120 = 50.6 — 0 Conduct test

PV(FCF)   712.55
Investment 400.00
NPV   312.55

E(FCF) $100 $110 $1.02 $0 $749.2

Year   0   1   2   3   4

and E) or to conduct the test market (node F). If we take a closer look at node D, we see that if we go straight to market our payoff at the end of year 2 is $144 plus the present value of $144 forever, discounted at 10 percent minus the $700 investment (144 + 144/.1 – 700 = 844). In other words, we have a call option on the perpetual cash flow stream of $144 per year with an exercise price of $700.

If we consider the test-marketing alternative, our payoffs at the end of the fourth year are those shown in Exhibit 5.17. After the results of the test are known, we have the right, but not the obligation, to spend the $700 and lock in the cash flow forever. Here again, we have a call option whose exercise price is $700, this time in year 4. At the end of year 2, we have a call option between the two alternatives either to go straight to

Exhibit 5.17   ROA free cash flow tree.

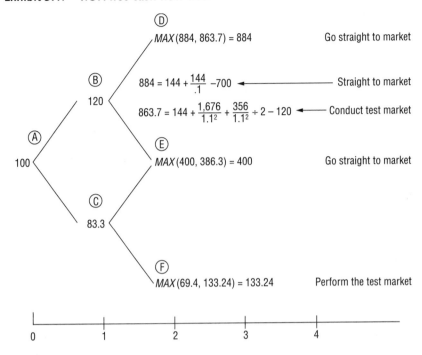

$$\frac{\left[\dfrac{1,676}{(1.1)^2} + \dfrac{356}{(1.1)^2}\right]}{2} + 144 - 120 = 863.7$$

market or to conduct a market test. The present value of the second alternative at node D is estimated as

Consequently, we would choose to go straight to market at point D, rather than attempting the test market.

Optionality changes the risk of our project payoffs, therefore we cannot use the 10 percent cost of capital. For example, let's analyze the value of the project at node C in Exhibit 5.18, using the replicating portfolio approach. We have the option of going straight to market or test marketing. Without the option, the value of the project at nodes E and F is either $400 or $69.40 and the project would be worth $281.70 at node C. With the option, as Exhibit 5.17 illustrates, we would elect to go

Exhibit 5.18   ROA analysis.

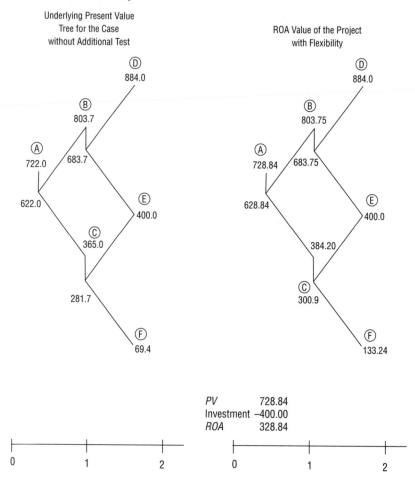

Underlying Present Value
Tree for the Case
without Additional Test

ROA Value of the Project
with Flexibility

PV   728.84
Investment −400.00
ROA   328.84

straight to market at node E and to test market at node F. These payoffs have different risks than the underlying; therefore, we build a replicating portfolio to value the flexibility:

$$Replicating\ portfolio\ value = mV + B$$

The end-of-period payoffs, as shown in exhibit 5.18, are

$$At\ node\ E:\ m\,400 + (1 + r_f)B = 400$$
$$At\ node\ F:\ m\,69.4 + (1 + r_f)B = 133.2$$

Solving the two equations for the two unknowns yields $m = 0.807$ and $B = -\$73.57$; therefore, the value of the replicating portfolio is

$$At\ node\ C:\ V = .807(440) - \$73.57 = \$300.9$$

Since the replicating portfolio has exactly the same end-of-year payoffs as the project with flexibility, its value is equal to the value of the project with the option at node C. Applying the same approach to the other node B, and then moving backward to node A, we can estimate the present value of the project with flexibility to be $728.84. Therefore, the NPV of the project with flexibility is

$$NPV\ with\ flexibility = \$728.84 - \$400 = \$328.84$$

There are several lessons learned from this example. First, the NPV approach must, of necessity, treat the alternatives of going straight to market and test marketing as mutually exclusive alternatives. The real options approach is able to reduce the choice between the alternatives to an option that has a single value—a value that captures the flexibility of choosing between the alternatives—conditional on the state of nature at a future date. As a result, the real options value of the project is greater than or equal to the value of either of the mutually exclusive NPVs without flexibility.

VALUING THE OPTION TO EXPAND WHEN THE UNDERLYING PAYS A DIVIDEND

As shown earlier, American call options, such as options to defer, to expand, or to extend a project, are always more valuable alive than exercised, assuming that the underlying does not pay a dividend or decline in value for any other reason. This section of the chapter shows how to value American call options on underlying assets that do pay dividends.

Suppose that we alter the value tree in Exhibit 5.6 by assuming the project will pay out half of its value in period 2. If so, the resulting value tree is Exhibit 5.19. This is a somewhat contrived example, because after the payout, the scale of the project going forward is also halved, thereby making future expansions anemic in comparison with the expansion that

Exhibit 5.19 Decision tree of an expansion option when the underlying pays a dividend.

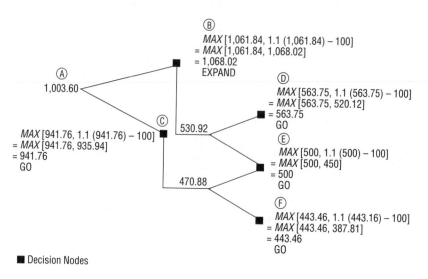

Ⓑ
MAX [1,061.84, 1.1 (1,061.84) – 100]
= *MAX* [1,061.84, 1,068.02]
= 1,068.02
EXPAND

Ⓐ
1,003.60

Ⓒ 530.92
MAX [941.76, 1.1 (941.76) – 100]
= *MAX* [941.76, 935.94]
= 941.76
GO

Ⓓ
MAX [563.75, 1.1 (563.75) – 100]
= *MAX* [563.75, 520.12]
= 563.75
GO

Ⓔ
MAX [500, 1.1 (500) – 100]
= *MAX* [500, 450]
= 500
GO

470.88

Ⓕ
MAX [443.46, 1.1 (443.16) – 100]
= *MAX* [443.46, 387.81]
= 443.46
GO

■ Decision Nodes

can take place in the second time period. Nevertheless, the example will serve its intended purpose. Having constructed the value tree, we start to price the expansion option by working out the payoffs and decisions at the end nodes. The results are as follows:

Node	Payoff	Decision
D	$MAX[563.75, 1.1(563.75) - 100] = MAX[563.75, 520.12]$	Go
E	$MAX[500, 1.1(500) - 100] = MAX[500, 450]$	Go
F	$MAX[443.46, 1.1(443.46) - 100] = MAX[443.46, 387.81]$	Go

Thus, the dividend has made it undesirable to exercise the expansion option in the third time period.

To continue the problem solution, we use a replicating portfolio to solve for the value of the project (ex dividend) at nodes B and C; and finally at node A. Starting at node B,[4] our payoff depends on whether we decide to exercise our expansion option. This decision is made before the dividend is paid. In fact, the dividend is larger if we make the right decision. If we leave the option unexercised we have the value of the underlying, $1,061.84. If we expand, we have 1.1($1,061.84) − 100 = $1,068.02. Since this is larger, we do exercise our option to expand. Then, in the next instant a 50 percent dividend of $530.92 is paid.

At node C, we get $941.76, the value of the underlying, which is bigger than our payout if we exercise our option, which is 1.1($941.76) − 100 = $935.94. Immediately, a 50 percent dividend of $470.88 is paid.

Note that once the option is exercised at node B, it cannot be exercised again along any of the paths that originate at node B. Therefore, there is no decision that can be made at node D, and a decision can be made at node E only if entered from node C. Therefore, the problem is path dependent. Note also that we did not use the replicating portfolio approach to obtain a MAD value at nodes B and C because the decision is made predividend, and the present values of the payouts ex dividend are not relevant in this case.

The final step is to use the replicating portfolio approach to determine the value of the project at node A:

$$\text{Node B:} \quad mu\,V_0 + (1 + r_f)B = 1{,}068.02$$
$$\underline{\text{Node C:} \quad -[md\,V_0 + (1 + r_f)B = 941.76]}$$
$$mV_0(u - d) = C_u - C_d$$
$$m1000(1.06184 - .4176) = 126.26$$
$$m = \frac{126.26}{120.08} = 1.0515$$

Substituting m into the equation for node B, we find that $B = -47.89$, and that the value of the project with flexibility is $1,003.6, a value that is only slightly less than the $1,004.33 that we estimated when the American call to expand was exercised in the third period.

WHAT IS THE UNDERLYING RISKY ASSET?

In some of the example problems, the event tree has been expressed in terms of cash flows, and elsewhere it has been the value of the project. Which should we use—cash flows or value?

Exhibit 5.20   Project expected value.

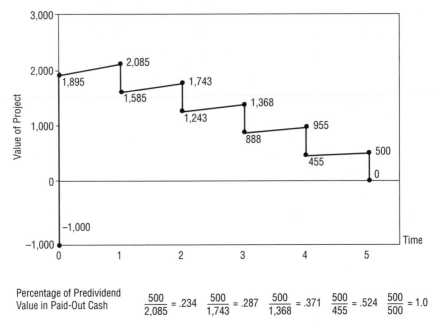

Percentage of Predividend
Value in Paid-Out Cash
$$\frac{500}{2,085} = .234 \quad \frac{500}{1,743} = .287 \quad \frac{500}{1,368} = .371 \quad \frac{500}{455} = .524 \quad \frac{500}{500} = 1.0$$

Unambiguously, the answer is that we should always use the value of the underlying risky asset to form the event tree or lattice that describes the uncertainty of the underlying. Conditional on the information at each decision node, our decisions (to abandon, expand, contract, or extend) should be based on the value of the underlying—not on its cash flow that period.

The evolution of the value of a project over time is quite different from the evolution of the value of a company. Projects are not replicable and have finite lives. A company is a sequence of projects that never end. Exhibit 5.20 shows the event tree for a project that requires an initial investment of $1,000 which produces expected annual cash flows of $500 each year for 5 years, but they could be higher or lower by 20 percent.

Given an assumed cost of capital of 10 percent, the NPV of this project is

$$NPV = -1,000 + \frac{500}{1.1} + \frac{500}{1.1^2} + \ldots + \frac{500}{1.1^5}$$
$$= -1,000 + 454.55 + 413.22 + 375.66 + 341.51 + 310.46$$
$$= -1,000 + 1,895.40 = 895.40$$

Notice that in Exhibit 5.20, the solid line shows the expected value of the project each year by discounting the expected cash flows from that year until the end of the project at the weighted average cost of capital. For example, if we assume that the cash flows occur at a single point in time (the last day of the year), then on the last day of the first year, the expected value is the sum of the present values of the stream of five payments of $500 each of free cash flow.

$$PV = 500 + \frac{500}{1.1} + \frac{500}{1.1^2} + \ldots + \frac{500}{1.1^4}$$
$$= 500 + 454.55 + 413.22 + 375.66 + 341.51$$
$$= 2,084.94$$

On the next day, the value drops by $500 down to $1,584.94 because that expected cash flow is no longer in the set of expected future cash flows. The value of the project continues to evolve in this sawtooth pattern, declining each period until it is expected to be zero at the end of the project.

The uncertainty regarding the evolution of the cash flows results in the binomial event tree illustrated in Exhibit 5.21. A critical assumption is that the reduction in value each period is proportional to the value realized that period. This guarantees the binomial event tree is recombining, and that the value as of the end of the project is zero regardless of the path taken.

Note also that once we model the present value and its up and down movements, we automatically set the objective probabilities of the up and down movements. For example, at time zero the present value of the project is $1,895, it can move up or down by 20 percent, its expected present value at the end of the first year is $2,085, and we have assumed

Exhibit 5.21   Project value-based event tree.

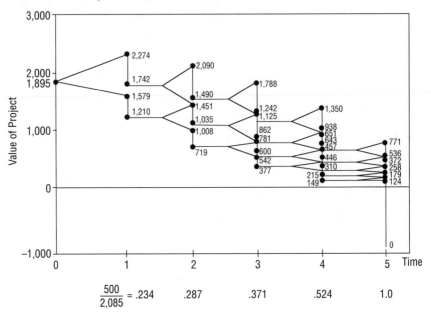

a 10 percent discount rate. Using these facts, we can solve for the objective probability of the up movement as follows:

$$PV_0 = \frac{E(PV_1)}{1+WACC} = \frac{p_u V_u + (1-p)V_d}{1+WACC}$$

$$1,895 = \frac{p(2,274) + (1-p)(1,579)}{1.1}$$

$$p = \frac{1.1(1,895) - 1,579}{2,274 - 1,579} = \frac{505.5}{695} = .727$$

Next, we examine the time pattern of value for an ongoing company. Suppose that instead of ending in 5 years, the annual cash flows of $500 continue forever. The value of the company will, at time zero, be equal to

$$PV_0 = \frac{\$500}{.10} = \$5,000$$

The value will gradually rise to $5,500 on the last day of the year. Then it falls back to $5,000 when a $500 cash flow is paid out. Exhibit 5.22 shows the present value of the company over time.

If we introduce uncertainty by assuming the value of the company goes up or down by 20 percent per year, the event tree looks like Exhibit 5.23. We assume that, as with the finite-lived project, the cash flows are proportional to the value of the company. Finally, in a fashion similar to our analysis of the project, we can estimate the objective probabilities of up and down movements. For example, in the first year:

$$PV_0 = \frac{p6,000 + (1-p)\ 4,167}{1.1} = 5,000$$

$$p = \frac{5,000(1.1) - 4,167}{6,000 - 4,167} = .727$$

This illustrates the relationship between the present value, the discount rate, the cash flows, and their probabilities. If you know any three, you can solve for the fourth.

Exhibit 5.22 Company expected value.

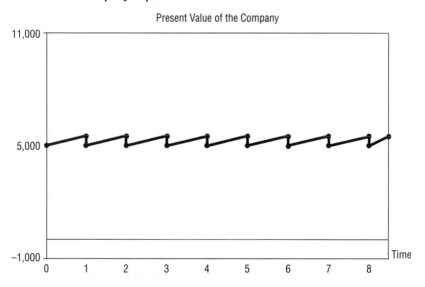

Exhibit 5.23 Event tree of company values.

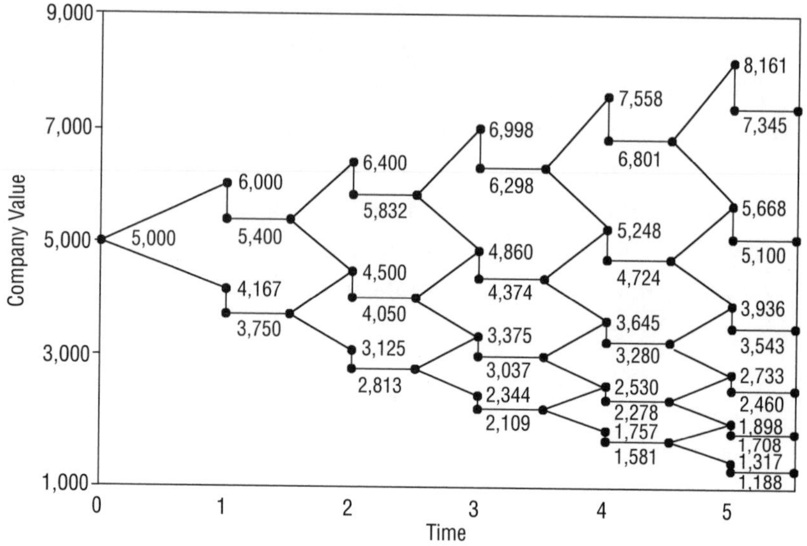

CONCLUSION

What have we learned in this chapter? The obvious content is the pricing of simple options such as abandonment, expansion, contraction, or combinations of them. We demonstrated that the solution methodology could use either the replicating portfolio method, which discounts expected cash flows at a risk-adjusted rate, or the risk-neutral probability method, which discounts certainty equivalent cash flows at a risk-adjusted rate. We discussed the important choice of modeling the uncertainty of the underlying risky asset as either a multiplicative or an additive process. In the limit, as the number of subintervals per year increases, the multiplicative process approaches a lognormal distribution (because values of the underlying cannot go negative), and the additive process, given 50-50 probabilities, approaches a normal distribution (which is symmetrical and can take negative values). We demonstrated that the NPV approach to decision making requires us to consider as mutually exclusive, decisions that really are not, while ROA provides a single value at the beginning of the project, a single go or no go decision, and decision rules for optimal behavior as uncertainty becomes resolved later on. Finally, we also learned that American call options (e.g., deferral, expansion, or extension) will not be exercised early unless the underlying declines in value (by paying a "dividend").

The next chapter extends our range of applications to include options on options, which are called compound options, and switching options.

QUESTIONS AND PROBLEMS

For solutions go to www.corpfinonline.com.

1. Using simple binomial trees, calculate the value of an abandonment option with the following characteristics:

    Underlying asset current value = 200.
    Abandonment value = 175.
    Up movement per period = 1.75.
    Risk-free rate = 10 percent.
    Time to expiration = 2 years.
    Number of time periods per year = 1.

    The steps you will need to follow include:

    Create the event tree for the underlying risky asset.
    Calculate whether to exercise the option on the end-nodes of the option valuation tree.
    Use replicating portfolio technique to value the option.

2. Using simple binomial trees, calculate the value of a call option with the following characteristics:

    Underlying asset current value = 1,000.
    Option exercise price = 1,250.
    Per-period dividends = 10 percent of asset value.
    Up movement per period = 1.5.
    Risk-free rate = 10 percent.
    Time to expiration = 2 years.
    Number of time periods per year = 1.

    The steps you will need to follow include:

    Create the event tree for the underlying risky asset.
    Calculate whether to exercise the option on the end-nodes of the option valuation tree.
    Use replicating portfolio technique to value the option.

3. Using simple binomial trees, calculate the value of a call option with the following characteristics:

    Underlying asset current value = 75.
    Option exercise price in period 1 = 100.
    Option exercise price in period 2 = 175.
    Up movement per period = 1.9.
    Risk-free rate = 10 percent.
    Time to expiration = 2 years.
    Number of time periods per year = 1.

The steps you will need to follow include:

    Create the event tree for the underlying risky asset.
    Calculate whether to exercise the option on the end-nodes of the option valuation tree.
    Use replicating portfolio technique to value the option.

4. Using simple binomial trees, calculate the value of a call option with the following characteristics:

    Underlying asset current value = 75.
    Option exercise price = 130.
    Up movement in period 1 = 1.5.
    Up movement in period 2 = 1.8.
    Risk-free rate = 10 percent.
    Time to expiration = 2 years.
    Number of time periods per year = 1.

The steps you will need to follow include:

    Create the event tree for the underlying risky asset.
    Calculate whether to exercise the option on the end-nodes of the option valuation tree.
    Use replicating portfolio technique to value the option.

5. Using simple binomial trees, calculate the value of a call option with the following characteristics:

    Underlying asset current value = 100.
    Option exercise price in period 1 = 110.
    Option exercise price in period 2 = 150.
    Up movement in period 1 = 1.2.
    Up movement in period 2 = 1.4.

Risk-free rate in period 1 = 10 percent.

Risk-free rate in period 2 = 8 percent.

Time to expiration = 2 years.

Number of time periods per year = 1.

The steps you will need to follow include:

Create the event tree for the underlying risky asset.

Calculate whether to exercise the option on the end-nodes of the option valuation tree.

Use replicating portfolio technique to value the option.

6. Using simple binomial trees, calculate the value of a combined call and put option with the following characteristics:

Underlying asset current value = 1,000.

Contraction option = 50 percent reduction in value.

Savings from contracting = 450.

Expansion option = 15 percent increase in value.

Exercise price to expand = 100.

Up movement per period = 1.15.

Risk-free rate = 10 percent.

Time to expiration = 2 years.

Number of time periods per year = 1.

The steps you will need to follow include:

Create the event tree for the underlying risky asset.

Calculate whether to exercise either option on the end-nodes of the option valuation tree.

Use replicating portfolio technique to value the option.

7. Using simple binomial trees, calculate the value of a call option with the following characteristics:

Underlying asset current value = 700.

Option exercise price = 750.

First period dividend = 10 percent.

Second period dividend = 15 percent.

Up movement per period = 1.5.

Risk-free rate = 10 percent.

Time to expiration = 3 years.

Number of time periods per year = 1.

8. A company's present value is 1,000 and follows a simple binomial model with an up movement per period of 1.5. The first year the company pays 10 percent of its value as a dividend. The second year it pays 15 percent of its value as a dividend. What is the present value of the dividends the company is expected to pay over the next 2 years?

The steps you will need to follow:

Build the event tree for the company's present value.

In a separate tree, write the dividend amount corresponding to each node.

Use replicating portfolio technique to find the present value of the dividends, assume the risk-free rate is 10 percent.

9. A company is considering a project with an expansion option. The present value of the project is $25 million with annual volatility of 20 percent. The required initial investment is $27 million. The project is expected to generate annual free cash flow equal to 15 percent of its value. There is a 2-year option to expand the future operations by 25 percent at any time with an additional investment of $16 million. Should the company undertake the project? What is the value of the expansion option? When and under what conditions should the expansion option be exercised? When would the expansion option be exercised if the project doesn't generate free cash flow for the first few years?

In that case, how would the project's ROA value change? Explain why.

10. A company wants to invest in new equipment. The risk-free rate is 10 percent. Management is considering four alternatives: Invest $10 million in a nonflexible technology with present value of $12 million and annual volatility of 15 percent. With additional investment of $0.2 million, the company can buy technology with the option to contract operation by 30 percent with savings of $4 million. Alternatively the company can invest $0.3 million and get broad application equipment. This would allow the company at any point to stop the project and

reemploy the facility with present value of $11 million. Finally, the company can spend an additional $0.4 million and acquire technology with both options. Which technology should the company choose?

REFERENCES

Following each reference is the type of option discussed in that article.

Abel, A., A. Dixit, J. Eberly, and R. Pindyck. 1996, August. "Options, the Value of Capital and Investment," *Quarterly Journal of Economics,* 753–777.

Berger, P., E. Ofek, and I. Swary. 1996, October. "Investor Valuation of the Abandonment Option," *Journal of Financial Economics 42,* 2, 257–287.

Bjerksund, P., and S. Ekern. 1990, Autumn. "Managing Investment Opportunities under Price Uncertainty: From Last Chance to Wait and See Strategies," *Financial Management,* 65–83.

Bonini, C. 1997, March. "Capital Investment under Uncertainty with Abandonment Options," *Journal of Financial and Quantitative Analysis,* 39–54.

Carr, P. 1988, December. "The Valuation of Sequential Exchange Opportunities," *Journal of Finance, 43,* 5, 1235–1256. (staged investment)

Kester, W. 1984, March–April. "Today's Options for Tomorrow's Growth," *Harvard Business Review, 62,* 2, 153–160. (growth options)

Kogut, B. 1991. "Joint Ventures and the Option to Acquire and to Expand," *Management Science, 37,* 1, 19–33.

MacDonald, R., and D. Siegle. 1985, June. "Investment and the Valuation of Firms When There Is an Option to Shut Down," *International Economic Review, 26,* 341–349. (abandonment option)

MacDonald, R., and D. Siegle. 1985. "Investment and the Valuation of Firms When There Is an Option to Shut Down," *International Economic Review, 28,* 2, 331–349.

MacDonald, R., and D. Siegle. 1986, November. "The Value of Waiting to Invest," *Quarterly Journal of Economics, 101,* 707–727. (option to defer)

Majd, S., and R. Pindyck. 1987. "Time to Build Option Value, and Investment Decisions," *Journal of Financial Economics, 18,* 7–27.

Margrabe, W. 1978, March. "The Value of an Option to Exchange One Asset for Another," *Journal of Finance, 33,* 1, 177–186. (switching options)

Myers, S., and S. Majd. 1991. "Abandonment Value and Project Life," *Advances in Futures and Options Research, 4,* 1–21. (abandonment option)

Pindyck, R. 1988, December. "Irreversible Investment, Capacity Choice, and the Value of the Firm," *American Economic Review, 78,* 5, 969–985. (switching option)

Titman, S. 1985, June. "Urban Land Prices under Uncertainty," *American Economic Review, 75,* 505–514. (option to defer)

Trigeorgis, L. 1988. "A Conceptual Options Framework for Capital Budgeting," *Advances in Futures and Options Research, 3,* 145–167. (growth options)

Trigeorgis, L. 1993, Autumn. "Real Options and Interactions with Flexibility," *Financial Management, 22,* 3, 202–224. (staged investment)

Trigeorgis, L. 1993. "The Nature of Options Interactions and the Valuation of Investments with Multiple Real Options," *Journal of Financial and Quantitative Analysis, 28,* 1, 1–20.

6 | Compound and Switching Options

Chapter 5 described simple options—to defer, expand, contract, and abandon an investment, as well as combinations of them; we now expand our reach to cover more complicated and more realistic types of real options. Compound options are options whose value is contingent on other options. Switching options allow the owner to start up and shut down operations, to switch from one mode of operation to another, or to enter and exit an industry.

VALUING COMPOUND OPTIONS

Compound options are options whose value is contingent on the value of other options. This is a very important and common set of problems. For example, Black and Scholes (1973) in their seminal paper recognized that the equity of a leveraged firm is an option on the value of the firm (a call option) whose exercise price is the face value of the firm's debt (D) and whose maturity is the maturity of the debt. A call option written on the equity of the firm as the underlying risky security is therefore an option on an option. The original solution for compound options can be found in Geske (1977). However, he used a closed form solution, while we will be solving the same problem using a lattice approach. This type of compounding is called a simultaneous compound option because the equity (an option on the value of the levered firm) and the call option on the equity are alive simultaneously.

Compound options can also be sequential. Any type of phased investment fits this category. For example, most factories can be constructed in several phases: a design phase, an engineering phase, and a construction phase. Product development programs are another example. Usually they have a development phase, a test market phase, and a full-scale product launch. Research and development programs usually have three laboratory phases before receiving FDA approval and these may be followed by discretionary research to prove out indications vis-à-vis other drugs. Exploration and development for natural resources (oil, natural gas, gold, copper, and coal) have multiple phases. Oil, for example, has sonic testing (2D and 3D), drilling, and development via construction of refineries, pipelines, and storage facilities.

The next two sections cover the lattice methodology for valuing both simultaneous and sequential compound options. The last section of the chapter covers the methodology for valuing switching options.

Methodology for Simultaneous Compound Options

The key feature of "simultaneous" compound options is that the underlying option and the option on it are simultaneously available. They are not sequential in time.

Suppose that we have a firm whose current value is $1,000 and that (given a multiplicative stochastic process) its value could go up by 12.75 percent or down by 11.31 percent—a standard deviation of 12 percent per annum. The risk-free rate is 8 percent. The equity of this firm is subordinate to debt that has a face value of $800 maturing in 3 years and that pays no coupons. What is the value of an American call option written on the equity if its exercise price is $400 and it matures in 3 years?

The solution proceeds in two steps. First, we value the equity as an American call on the value of the firm with its exercise price equal to the face value of debt. The result is an event tree that becomes the underlying for the call option. We start with the event tree for the value of the firm as illustrated in Exhibit 6.1. Next, we calculate the value of the equity at each of the four end nodes A, B, C, and D. The end node payoffs are:

A: $MAX[u^3 V_0 - X, 0] = MAX[1,433.34 - 800, 0] = MAX[633.34, 0] = 633.34$
B: $MAX[u^2 dV_0 - X, 0] = MAX[1,127.50 - 800, 0] = MAX[327.50, 0] = 327.50$

Exhibit 6.1   Firm value event tree.

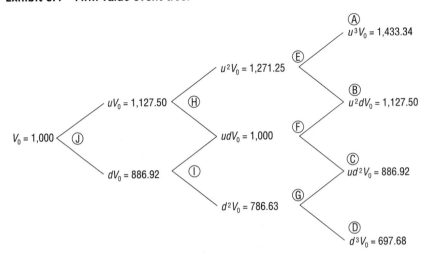

$V_0 = 1,000$ (J)

$uV_0 = 1,127.50$ (H)

$dV_0 = 886.92$ (I)

$u^2V_0 = 1,271.25$ (E)

$udV_0 = 1,000$ (F)

$d^2V_0 = 786.63$ (G)

(A) $u^3V_0 = 1,433.34$

(B) $u^2dV_0 = 1,127.50$

(C) $ud^2V_0 = 886.92$

(D) $d^3V_0 = 697.68$

C: $MAX[ud^2V_0 - X, 0] = MAX[886.92 - 800, 0] = MAX[86.92, 0] = 86.92$
D: $MAX[d^3V_0 - X, 0] = MAX[697.68 - 800, 0] = MAX[-102.32, 0] = 0$

Exhibit 6.2 shows the equity value tree with all of the results filled in. The calculations employ the replicating portfolio approach. At nodes E, F, and G, we have the following results for the equity (option) values:

| Node | End-of-Period Payoff | | Replicating Portfolio Parameters | | Option Value |
	Up State	Down State	m	B	
E	633.34	327.50	1.0000	−740.74	530.51
F	327.50	86.92	1.0000	−740.74	259.26
G	86.92	0	.4593	−296.71	64.58

Just for review, let's do the calculations for node G. The replicating portfolio consists of m units of the underlying plus B bonds. The portfolio payoffs at the end of the period are

$$mud^2V_0 + (1 + r_f)B = 86.92 \quad \textit{in the up state, and}$$
$$-[md^3V_0 + (1 + r_f)B = 0] \quad \textit{in the down state}$$
$$\overline{md^2V_0(u - d) = 86.92}$$

Exhibit 6.2   Equity value event tree.

Exercise Price = Face Value of Debt = $800

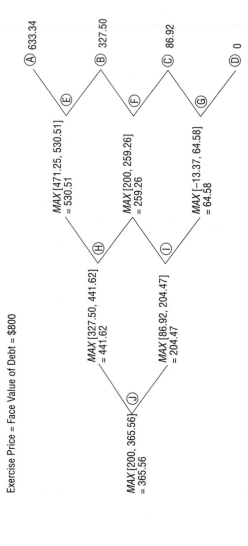

Solving for m and B, we have

$$m = \frac{86.92}{786.63\,(.2406)} = .4593$$

$$md^3 V_0 + (1 + r_f)B = 0$$

$$.4593\,(697.68) + 1.08\,B = 0$$

$$B = \frac{-320.44}{1.08} = -296.71$$

Therefore, the value of the call option (i.e., the value of the firm's equity) at node G is

$$md^2V_0 + B = .4593(786.63) - 296.71 = 64.58$$

Moving on to the remaining nodes, using the replicating portfolio approach, provides the following results:

Node	End-of-Period Payoff Up State	End-of-Period Payoff Down State	Replicating Portfolio Parameters m	Replicating Portfolio Parameters B	Option Value
H	530.51	259.26	1.0000	−685.87	441.62
I	259.26	64.58	0.0123	−604.67	204.47

And finally, at node J, we can solve for the present value of the firm's equity—once again, using the replicating portfolio approach:

$$muV_0 + (1 + r_f)B = 441.62 \quad \text{in the up state, node \textcircled{H} and}$$
$$-[mdV_0 + (1 + r_f)B = 204.47] \quad \text{in the down state, node \textcircled{I}}$$
$$\overline{mV_0(u - d) = 237.15}$$

$$m = \frac{237.15}{240.60} = .9857$$

Solving for B, we have

$$muV_0 + (1 + r_f)B = 441.62$$

$$.9857(1{,}127.50) + 1.08B = 441.62$$

$$B = \frac{(441.62 - 1111.38)}{1.08} = -620.15$$

Therefore, the value of the firm's equity is

$$mV_0 + B = .9857 \, (1000) - 620.15 = 365.56$$

Note that since the entity value of the firm was assumed to be $1,000, the market value of its risky debt must be $1,000 − $365.56 = $634.44. Since it matures in 3 years with a face value of $800, its yield to maturity is 8.03 percent.

Next, we value the compound option, an American call whose exercise price is $400, written on the firm's equity (itself a call option), having a 3-year maturity. The event tree that underlies this option is the equity value tree shown in Exhibit 6.2 which is replicated as Exhibit 6.3. The stock price does not follow the same lognormal distribution as the firm. However, since the payoffs for each node are known and are priced at the beginning of the node, we can use replicating portfolios to value the call that is written on the equity. Exhibit 6.4 shows the payoffs of the decision tree for the compound option.

Exhibit 6.3 Event tree underlying the compound option (equity values).

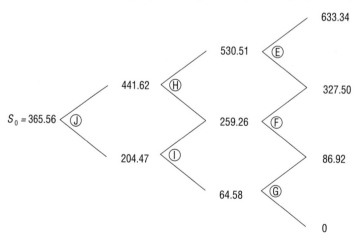

Exhibit 6.4 Compound option payout (American call on equity).

Exercise Price of Equity = Face Value of Debt = $800
Exercise Price of Call on Equity = $400

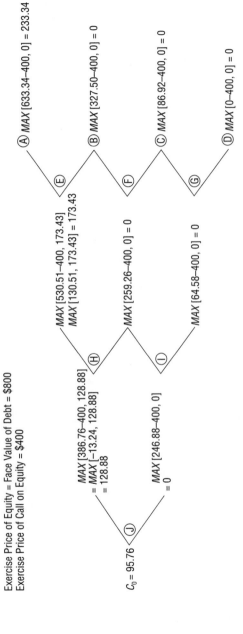

The End Node Payouts are:

Node A: $MAX [S_{3A} - X, 0] = MAX [233.34, 0] = 233.34$
Node B: $MAX [S_{3B} - X, 0] = MAX [-72.5, 0] = 0$
Node C: $MAX [S_{3C} - X, 0] = MAX [-313.08, 0] = 0$
Node D: $MAX [S_{3D} - X, 0] = MAX [-400, 0] = 0$

Notice that the end node payoffs are all zero except at node E. Using the replicating portfolio approach at node E, we can solve for m as follows:

$$
\begin{array}{ll}
mS_{2A} + (1 + r_f)B = 233.34 & \textit{in the up state, node \textcircled{A}} \\
-[mS_{2B} + (1 + r_f)B = \quad 0] & \textit{in the down state, node \textcircled{B}} \\
\hline
m(S_{2A} - S_{2B}) = 233.34
\end{array}
$$

$$
m = \frac{233.34}{633.34 - 327.50} = \frac{233.34}{305.84} = .7629
$$

Solving for B:

$$
mS_{2B} + (1 + r_f)B = 0
$$
$$
.7629(327.50) + (1.08)B = 0
$$
$$
B = \frac{-249.89}{1.08} = -231.38
$$

And solving for the value of the option at node E:

$$
mS_{2E} + B = .7629(530.51) - 231.38 = 173.43
$$

The solutions for nodes F and G are zero value because the payouts in either state are zero. Next, at node H, we have, solving for m:

$$
\begin{array}{ll}
mS_{2E} + (1 + r_f)B = 173.43 & \textit{in the up state, node \textcircled{E}} \\
-[mS_{2F} + (1 + r_f)B = \quad 0] & \textit{in the down state, node \textcircled{F}} \\
\hline
m(S_{2E} - S_{2F}) = 173.43
\end{array}
$$

$$
m(530.51 - 259.26) = 173.43
$$

$$
m = \frac{173.43}{271.25} = .6394
$$

Solving for B:

$$
mS_{2F} + (1 + r_f)B = 0
$$
$$
.6394(259.26) + 1.08B = 0
$$
$$
B = \frac{165.77}{108} = -153.49
$$

and the value of the American call at node H is

$$mS_{1H} + B = .6394(441.62) - 153.49 = 282.37 - 153.49 = 128.88$$

Finally at node J, we have, solving for m:

$$\begin{array}{ll} mS_{1H} + (1 + r_f)B = 128.88 & \textit{in the up state, node } ⓗ \\ -[mS_{1I} + (1 + r_f)B = \quad 0] & \textit{in the down state, node } ⓘ \\ \hline m(S_{1H} - S_{1I}) = 128.88 \end{array}$$

$$m = \frac{93.80}{441.62 - 204.47} = \frac{128.88}{237.15} = .5434$$

and solving for B:

$$mS_{1H} + (1 + r_f)B = 0$$
$$.5434(204.47) + 1.08B = 0$$
$$B = \frac{-111.11}{1.08} = -102.88$$

and the value of the American call at node J is

$$mS_0 + B = .5434(365.56) - 102.88 = 198.65 - 102.88 = 95.76$$

In this first section, we have shown how to use a lattice approach to value an American call that is contingent on the equity of the firm, which is in turn a call on the value of the firm. Since both options are alive during the same interval of time, the call contingent on the equity is a simultaneous compound option.

Methodology for Sequential Compound Options

Assume the same stochastic process for the value of the firm as before (it might be the present value of a project that has several investment phases). Now there are two call options in sequence. The first has an exercise price of $400, the investment required to move to the next phase at the end of year 1 when the option expires. It allows us to decide whether to abandon the project or to continue by making an additional investment. The second has an exercise price of $800 and expires at the end of year 3. As before, the firm value tree is the same as Exhibit 6.1. We will use this tree as the underlying risky asset.

If we turn the firm value event tree into a decision tree, it looks like Exhibit 6.5. At all end nodes, except for the node D, we choose to exercise the second option rather than to stop the project. The value of the project at nodes E, F, and G is as follows:

Node	End-of-Period Payoff		Replicating Portfolio Parameters		Option Value
	Up State	Down State	m	B	
E	633.34	327.50	1.0000	−740.74	530.51
F	327.50	86.92	1.0000	−740.74	259.26
G	86.92	0	.4593	−296.71	64.59

At all three nodes at the end of the second period, the value of the option unexercised is greater than its value if exercised.

At the end of the first time period, the first option expires. Therefore, it must be exercised at a cost of $400, or left unexercised (no cost). If it is exercised, the payouts are not directly dependent on the value of the underlying project, but on the value provided by the option to invest at the next stage. For example, at node H the end-of-product payouts are $530.51 in the up state and $259.26 in the down state if the company invests $400 at the beginning of the period to acquire the second phase option. Using as the underlying risky asset, the value of the market value of the second option at the end of the first period, we can solve for node H values as follows. First calculate the number of units, m, of the underlying:

$$\frac{\begin{array}{l} mu^2V_0 + (1 + r_f)B = 530.51 \quad \text{in the up state, node Ⓔ} \\ -[mudV_0 + (1 + r_f)B = 259.26] \quad \text{in the down state, node Ⓕ} \end{array}}{\begin{array}{l} muV_0(u - d) = 271.25 \\ m\,1{,}257.50\,(.2406) = 271.25 \end{array}}$$

$$m = \frac{271.25}{271.25} = 1$$

Exhibit 6.5 Sequential compound options.

Exercise price of first option = 400
Life of first option = 1 year
Exercise price of second option = $800
Life of second option = 2 years

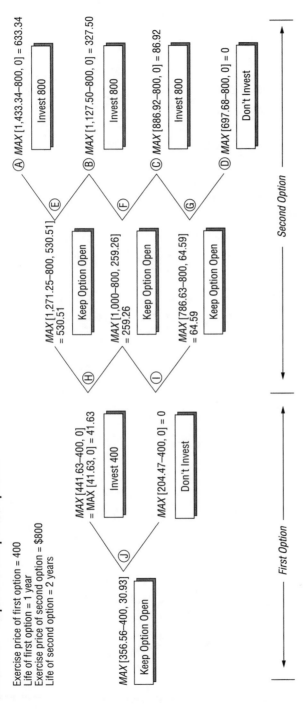

The end node payouts are:

Node A: $MAX[u^3V_0-X, 0] = MAX[1,433.34-800, 0] = 633.34$
Node B: $MAX[u^2dV_0-X, 0] = MAX[1,127.50-800, 0] = 327.50$
Node C: $MAX[ud^2V_0-X, 0] = MAX[886.92-800, 0] = 86.92$
Node D: $MAX[d^3V_0-X, 0] = MAX[697-800, 0] = 0$

173

Second, calculate the quantity of risk-free bonds, B:

$$mu^2V_0 + (1+r_f)B = 530.51$$
$$1(1,271.25) + 1.08B = 530.51$$
$$B = \frac{530.51 - 1,271.25}{1.08} = \frac{-740.74}{1.08} = -685.87$$

Finally, calculate the beginning of the period value of the replicating portfolio:

$$muV_0 + B = 1(1,127.50) - 685.87 = 441.63$$

In the up state at the end of the first period, the value of the second option, $441.63, is greater than the exercise price of $400, therefore the firm will invest.

At node I, the down state, the value of the second option is determined as follows.[1] The number of units of the underlying asset in a replicating portfolio is

$$
\begin{array}{ll}
mudV_0 + (1+r_f)B = 259.26 & \text{in the up state, node \textcircled{F}} \\
-[md^2V_0 + (1+r_f)B = 64.59] & \text{in the down state, node \textcircled{G}} \\
\hline
m\, dV_0(u-d) = 194.67 & \\
m\, 886.92\,(.2406) = 194.67 &
\end{array}
$$

$$m = \frac{194.67}{213.39} = .9123$$

The quantity of risk-free bonds in the replicating portfolio is

$$m\, d^2V_0 + (1+r_f)B = 0$$
$$.9123(786.63) + 1.08B = 64.59$$
$$B = \frac{-653.05}{1.08} = -604.68$$

The beginning-of-period value of the replicating portfolio is

$$m\, dV_0 + B = .9123(886.92) - 604.7 = 809.17 - 604.7 = 204.47$$

Since $204.47 is less than the $400 investment cost, we would not invest at node I.

Standing at time zero, node J, we can estimate the present value of the compound option by recognizing that we can either keep the first option open or we can exercise it at a cost of $400. If exercised at time zero, the first option starts the second option immediately. (uncovers it).

Therefore, we proceed by valuing the second option at time zero. To avoid confusion, Exhibit 6.6 shows the value tree for the second option for all 4 points in time, even though it is "alive" only from the end of the first time period. The value of the second option at time zero (node J) is determined via the replicating portfolio method by calculating the number of units, m, of the underlying risky asset:

$$
\frac{\begin{array}{ll} m u V_0 + (1 + r_f)B = 441.63 & \textit{in the up state, node } Ⓗ \\ -[m d V_0 + (1 + r_f)B = 204.47] & \textit{in the down state, node } Ⓘ \end{array}}{m\,V_0(u - d) = 237.16}
$$

$$
m = \frac{237.16}{240.60} = 0.4858
$$

And by calculating the quantity of risk-free bonds:

$$
mu V_0 + (1 + r_f)B = 441.63
$$

$$
0.9858(1,127.50) + (1.08)B = 441.63
$$

$$
B = \frac{441.63 - 1,111.47}{1.08} = -\frac{669.85}{1.08} = -620.23
$$

Finally, the present value of the replicating portfolio at node J is

$$
m\,V_0 + B = 0.9858(1000) - 620.23 = 365.56
$$

Again, for clarity, Exhibit 6.7 shows the value tree for the first option that has an exercise price of $400 and expires at the end of the first period. If exercised, its payoff is the value of the second option. The actual value of the first option at time zero is determined as follows. Define C_u

Exhibit 6.6 Value tree for second option.

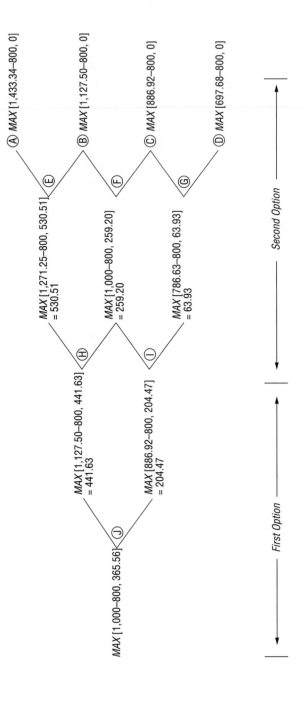

Exhibit 6.7   Value tree for first option.

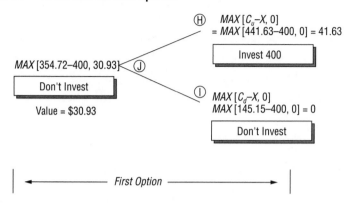

H $MAX[C_u-X, 0]$
$= MAX[441.63-400, 0] = 41.63$

Invest 400

$MAX[354.72-400, 30.93]$ J

Don't Invest

Value = $30.93

I $MAX[C_d-X, 0]$
$MAX[145.15-400, 0] = 0$

Don't Invest

First Option

and C_d as the payouts of the second option at the end of the first year, nodes H and I:

$$
\begin{aligned}
m\,C_u + (1 + r_f)B &= 41.63 \qquad \textit{in the up state, node } H \\
-[m\,C_d + (1 + r_f)B &= 0] \qquad \textit{in the down state, node } I
\end{aligned}
$$

$$m(C_u - C_d) = 41.63$$

$$m(441.63 - 145.15) = 41.63$$

$$m = \frac{41.63}{296.48} = .1404$$

Solving for the quantity of default-free bonds, B, we have

$$mC_u + (1 + r_f)B = 41.63$$

$$.1404(441.63) + (1.08)B = 41.63$$

$$B = \frac{41.63 - 62.00}{1.08} = -18.87$$

Finally, the value of the replicating portfolio is the present value of the first option:

$$m\,C_0 + B = .1404\,(354.72) - 18.87 = 49.80 - 18.87 = 30.93$$

We can interpret $30.93 as the net present value of a project that has present value of $1,000 today, whose value has a standard deviation of 12 percent per year, and requires completing two investments —$400 for the first stage (perhaps a design phase), and $800 for a construction phase that must start by the end of the third year. If the start-up cost (if any) is greater than $30.93, the project would be rejected; otherwise it would be accepted.

Review of Compound Options

We have covered two types of compound options—loosely described as options on options. The first type is called *simultaneous compound options.* An example is a Chicago Board of Options Exchange (CBOE) call option on the equity of a levered firm. The first option is the equity on the levered firm. Its life is longer than (or equal to) the life of the second option, the CBOE option written on it. During the life of the second option, both options are alive simultaneously. In our numerical example, both options were alive for 3 years. The value of the underlying risky asset for the first option, the equity, was the value of the firm itself, and the exercise price was the face value of debt, $800. The underlying risky asset for the second option, the CBOE call, was the value of the equity, and the exercise price was $400. The second option—the compound option—was worth $95.76.

The second type is called a sequential compound option because the second option is created only when the first option is exercised. In a sense, the first option chronologically is the right to buy the second option. Our example was a multiphase construction project. The first option, chronologically, the design phase, had a life of one year and an exercise price of $400. The underlying risky asset was the payoffs provided by a construction phase. The underlying risky asset for the construction phase was the payoffs of the project/firm itself. Thus, from an economics point of view the second option chronologically is the first option. It has an exercise price of $800 in our example and its underlying risky asset is the value of the project. It follows that the first chronological option is the second option from an economics point of view because it will be exercised contingent on the value of construction phase. Thus, with sequential compound options the order of economic priority is the opposite of the time sequence. In our example, the compound option was worth $30.93.

VALUING SWITCHING OPTIONS

Switching options give their owner the right to switch between two modes of operation at a fixed cost. The option to exit and then reenter an industry, the option to switch between two modes of operation, and the option to start up and shut down a facility (e.g., an automobile assembly plant) are all switching options. Enron has been quoted as saying that they have used switching options to price peak load power generation facilities. In many areas of the world, peak load capacity is gas-fired turbines that are turned on when intraday spot prices of energy rise rapidly due to excess demand, usually driven by extreme weather conditions. The turbines are then turned off when spot prices return to normal levels.

To illustrate the economics of switching options, consider a gold mining operation. Assume that the average extraction cost is $250 per ounce, that the mine is in operation, and that the world price of gold is currently $300 per ounce. Traditional microeconomic theory says that if the average revenue—the price—falls below $250 per ounce, the mine should be shut down. But there are fixed costs of shutting down. There are safety requirements, severance wages for workers, extra maintenance and pumping charges. Since the price of gold is uncertain, we could shut down today only to find that the price of gold has moved back up overnight to higher than $250 per ounce and that we should bear the additional fixed costs of opening the mine again. The optimal rule in a world of certainty, or when the costs of shutting down and reopening are zero, is to shut down when average revenue falls below average cost. With uncertainty and fixed costs of shutting down and starting up, the answer changes. We will shut down when the present value of expected losses from remaining in operation are larger than the cost of shutting down. This rule depends on the amount of fixed cost, the volatility of prices (and extraction costs), and the amount of mineral in the ground. It implies that if we are currently in operation, we will optimally stay in operation, losing money, until the price of gold falls far enough below the extraction average cost that we can expect to recoup the fixed cost of shutting down. If we are shut down, the price will have to rise well above our average cost of extraction before we optimally open up again. Of course, this is exactly the behavior that we actually observe of mining operations. Moel and Tufano (2000) studied the opening and closing of mines, and found that the real options model is a useful descriptor of the opening and closing of mines.

Switching options are among the more complicated option problems because they are path dependent. If there are two modes of operation, for example, the optimal action in a future state of nature depends on the price of the commodity, but it also depends on the mode of operation that we were in when we entered the state of nature—were we open or closed? Path dependency means that we use a backward dynamic programming process—one that is both backward and forward looking.

We use an example to demonstrate the application of switching options. Assume that a company already has a manufacturing facility operating that uses technology X. Due to increased demand, we are considering a new factory with the following options: to use technology X again, to use alternative technology Y, or to invest in a flexible technology Z that allows us to switch from X to Y for $15 and from Y to X for $10. These switching costs are designated C_{xy} and C_{yx} respectively.

Technology X, because of a higher fixed costs has higher volatility. The two event trees in Exhibit 6.8 represent the free cash flows of the two modes of operation, each defined at the same states of nature. Unlike the value event trees we developed in other examples, here every node of the tree represents not the value of the project but the free cash flow it will generate given the mode of operation in that state of nature. Both modes of operation generate the same free cash flow at time zero (at node A) but the first mode of operation is better in favorable states of nature, whereas the second mode of operation is better in unfavorable states of nature. The initial investment required to build a factory with technology X or Y is $100. The flexible technology Z requires a higher investment of $110.

The first question we have to answer is, given a choice only between the two inflexible technologies X and Y, which one should we choose? As always, we have to make a choice based on the NPV each technology pro-

Exhibit 6.8   Cash flows from modes of operation.

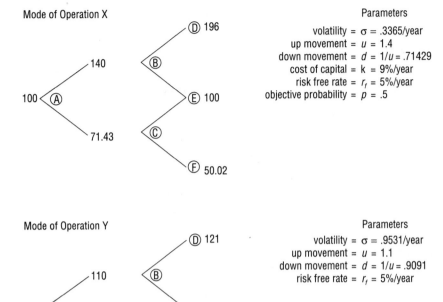

Mode of Operation X

Parameters

volatility = σ = .3365/year
up movement = *u* = 1.4
down movement = *d* = 1/*u* = .71429
cost of capital = k = 9%/year
risk free rate = r_f = 5%/year
objective probability = *p* = .5

Mode of Operation Y

Parameters

volatility = σ = .9531/year
up movement = *u* = 1.1
down movement = *d* = 1/*u* = .9091
risk free rate = r_f = 5%/year

vides. A brief note on the parameters given in Exhibit 6.8 is advisable at this point. We assume a geometric stochastic process, where the up movement is *u* = *exp*[*sigma*(*sqrt T*)]. [Note: *sigma* = *volatility* = σ, *exp* means e^x.]*

Therefore, if *u* = 1.4, then *sigma* = ln(1.4) = .3365. Next, *k* is defined as the risk-adjusted rate of return that is required if we are in a given mode of operation. For technology X, from the analysis of our current operation we assume that its cost of capital is *k*(X) = 9%. The risk-free rate of

---

* Generalized versions of switching options [e.g., Margrabe (1978)] have two correlated sources of uncertainty, each one driving a separate mode. Our example implicitly assumes perfectly correlated uncertainties, thereby reducing the problem to a single uncertainty.

return is 5 percent. Finally, we assume that the objective probability for up movement on every step is 50 percent.

Given this information, we can discount the expected cash flow along the event tree for X and to get a corresponding tree with the present values (PV_{Xt}), as shown in Exhibit 6.9. For example, we calculate the present value at point B in the following way:

$$PV_{XB} = \frac{p \times PV_{XD} + (1-p)PV_{XE}}{(1 + WACC_X)} + FCF_{XB}$$

$$= \frac{0.5 \times 196 + (1-0.5)100}{(1+0.09)} + 140 = 135.27 + 140 = 275.27$$

As can be seen, the present value of the factory at each possible stage of nature is equal to the expected value the factory has in the future discounted at a risk-adjusted discount rate plus the free cash flow (FCF_{XB}) from the operations in the current period. The present value (PV_X) of the new factory with technology X is equal to 289.96. Subtracting the investment required (I_X) we get a net present value (NPV_X) of 189.96:

$$NPV_X = PV_X - I_X = 289.96 - 100 = 189.96$$

Exhibit 6.9 PV event tree with technology X.

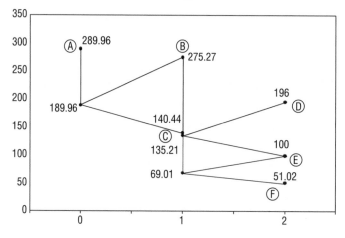

Now that we have the present value tree for technology X, we can develop the corresponding present value tree for technology Y. The cash flow that Y provides for every state of nature is sufficient to find its present value using the value tree of X to form a nonarbitrage replicating portfolio for each state. To solve for the value of Y, without flexibility, we use the replicating portfolio approach, forming a portfolio of *m* units of asset X and B units of the risk-free bond. The results are given in Exhibit 6.10. For technology Y, the replicating portfolios are

$$mPV_{XD} + (1 + r_f)B = PV_{YD}$$
$$mPV_{XB} + (1 + r_f)B = PV_{YB}$$

and the solution for *m*, *B*, and the present value at point B (PV_{YB}) are

$$m = \frac{PV_{YD} - PV_{YE}}{PV_{XD} - PV_{XE}} = \frac{121 - 100}{196.01 - 100} = 0.2187$$

$$B = \frac{PV_{YD} - nPV_{XD}}{1 + r_f} = \frac{121 - 0.2187 \times 196.01}{1.05} = 74.41$$

$$PV_{YB} = mPV_{XB} + B + FCF_{YB} = 0.2187 \times 135.27 + 74.41 + 110 = 103.99 + 110 = 213.99$$

Exhibit 6.10   PV event tree with technology Y.

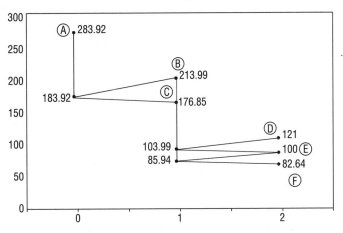

The net present value (NPV_Y) for the new factory with technology Y is equal to its present value (PV_Y) minus the investment required (I_Y):

$$NPV_Y = PV_Y - I_Y = 283.92 - 100 = 183.92$$

Similar calculations produce the net present value of the new factory with technology X:

$$NPV_X = PV_X - I_X = 289.96 - 100 = 189.96$$

Given a choice between technology X and Y without flexibility, we choose X because of its higher net present value:

$$NPV_X = 189.96 > NPV_Y = 183.92$$

Next, we examine the choice between precommitment to technology X versus investing in the flexible technology Z. To find the present value of Z, we have to identify the optimal switching behavior to pursue for each possible sequence of states of nature. As discussed, because of the cost associated with switching between technologies, the optimal mode of operation at a given state depends on the mode we were in at the previous state and on the optimal modes in the possible following states. At the beginning of the project, we could be ether in mode X or Y, therefore we have to develop two sets of optimal switching strategy and their corresponding decision trees for each of those possibilities. Having the flexibility to switch means that, if we are currently in mode X, we have the European call option to buy the present value provided by mode Y for an exercise price equal to the switching cost from X to Y and vice versa. As with the analysis of other options, we start at the end of the decision tree; but for each node, we ask the same question twice:

- Assuming we have been in mode X at the previous state, would we stay in X or would we switch to Y and pay the switching cost?
- Assuming we have been in mode Y at the previous state, would we stay in Y or would we switch to X and pay the switching cost?

Applying these questions to state (D), we get the following optimal decisions:

$$S_{XD} = MAX\left(PV_{XD}, PV_{YD} - C_{XY}\right) = MAX\left(196, 121-15\right) = 196 \Rightarrow \textit{Stay in X}$$
$$S_{YD} = MAX\left(PV_{YD}, PV_{XD} - C_{YX}\right) = MAX\left(121, 196-10\right) = 186 \Rightarrow \textit{Switch to X}$$

After we have identified an optimal switching for the end-of-period states in both decision trees, we move backward to analyze the states at the previous period. The first step is to find the present value for the two decision trees. This is illustrated in Exhibit 6.11. For node B, current mode X, we see that if we start in X we are not going to switch in any of the possible follow-up states D and E. The present value is the same as the corresponding node in the inflexible X value tree (275.27). For node B, current

Exhibit 6.11   Present values for technology X and Y in state B.

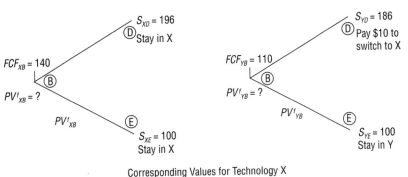

Future Values and Current Cash Flow for Mode X   Future Values and Current Cash Flow for Mode Y

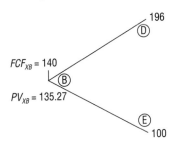

Corresponding Values for Technology X

Exhibit 6.12   ROA valuation of flexible technology Z.

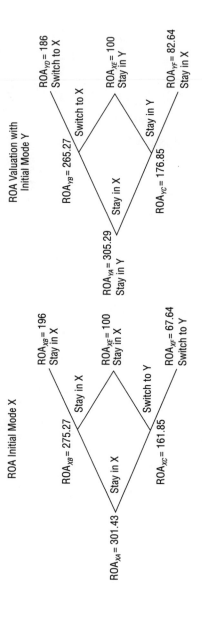

ROA Initial Mode X

ROA Valuation with
Initial Mode Y

ROA$_{XB}$ = 275.27
Stay in X

ROA$_{XB}$ = 196
Stay in X

ROA$_{XE}$ = 100
Stay in X

ROA$_{XA}$ = 301.43
Stay in X

ROA$_{XC}$ = 161.85
Switch to Y

ROA$_{XF}$ = 67.64
Switch to Y

ROA$_{YB}$ = 265.27
Switch to X

ROA$_{YD}$ = 186
Switch to X

ROA$_{XE}$ = 100
Stay in Y

ROA$_{YA}$ = 305.29
Stay in Y

ROA$_{YC}$ = 176.85
Stay in Y

ROA$_{YF}$ = 82.64
Stay in X

Stay in X

mode Y, next period in state D we will have to switch to X. We find the flexible present value PV^f_{YB} using the present value tree of technology X (we could use Y as well):

$$m = \frac{S_{YD} - S_{YE}}{PV_{XD} - PV_{XE}} = \frac{186 - 100}{196 - 100} = 0.8958$$

$$B = \frac{S_{YD} - mPV_{XD}}{1 + r_f} = \frac{186 - 0.8958 \times 196}{1.05} = 9.92$$

$$PV^f_{YB} = mPV_{XB} + B + FCF_{YB} = 0.8958 \times 135.27 + 9.92 + 110 = 241.10$$

Now for both decision trees, we have to check to see whether it is optimal to stay in their corresponding modes or to switch. For point B mode X, the choice is between staying in X and getting the present value of (275.27) or switching to Y at the cost of \$15 and receiving the corresponding present value for mode Y which is PV^f_{YB} of 241.10:

$$S_{XB} = MAX(PV^f_{XB}, PV^f_{YB} - C_{XY}) = MAX(275.27, 241.10 - 15) = 275.27 \Rightarrow \textit{Stay in X}$$

Reversing the test for decision tree Y, we get

$$S_{YB} = MAX(PV^f_{YB}, PV^f_{XB} - C_{YX}) = MAX(241.10, 275.27 - 10) = 265.27 \Rightarrow \textit{Switch to X}$$

Following the same process backward all the way to the beginning, as shown in Exhibit 6.12, we have developed two real options valuations ($ROA_{XA} = 301.43$, $ROA_{YA} = 305.29$) of the flexible technology Z, depending on the starting mode:

$$ROA_{AY} > ROA_{AX} > PV_{XA}$$

As shown, the ROA value of technology Z is higher than the present value of either of the two technologies without flexibility. This means that if available and optimally utilized, the flexibility provided by technology Z would be valuable. The question we have to answer is whether this additional value is sufficient to justify the additional investment required to build the new factory with technology Z:

$$ROA_{ZX} = ROA_{XA} - I_Z = 301.43 - 110 = 191.43$$
$$ROA_{ZY} = ROA_{YA} - I_Z = 305.29 - 110 = 195.29$$
$$ROA_{ZY} > ROA_{ZX} > NPV_X$$

Building the new factory with the flexible technology Z is the superior choice, no matter which initial mode of operating is selected. If a choice for selecting the initial mode is available, then we should start in mode Y as shown in Exhibit 6.13.

As with the other real option analysis, the final result is not only the correct valuation of the project with flexibility but an optimal contingent plan for executing the available options. In our simple example, it doesn't matter in which mode of operation we are at state E, as in both modes we generate the free cash flow of $100. In more complicated examples however, frequently operations are caught in a mode that generates smaller free cash flow than an alternative mode. Companies stay in foreign markets even when they lose money or they don't switch to alternative suppliers even when the quality and the prices are better. The application of real options provides an interesting insight to why many times this behavior is actually optimal given high switching cost.

Exhibit 6.13 Optimal execution of the switching options.

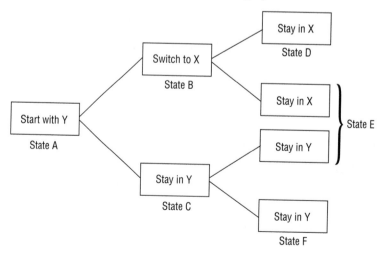

One of the many extensions of the switching problem is to consider what happens when the underlying asset is an exhaustible resource like an oil reserve and there are two modes of operation—fast pumping and slow pumping. Another example is the harvesting of trees. In this case, the resource is replicable at constant scale, because an acre of trees can be replanted over and over again. Suppose the price of oil or lumber goes up? Should one pump faster or slower, and how does the optimal harvest rate change—should trees be harvested faster or slower?

CONCLUSION

We have built up our basic set of skills in this chapter to include not only simple options such as abandonment, contraction, expansion, extension, and deferral; but also compound options and switching options. While more complicated than their cousins of Chapter 5, compound and switching options are quite common and are almost necessary to apply real options to many real-world situations. Also, compound and switching options are much more versatile than the simple Black-Scholes model— and they give much better answers. Not only are they more accurate than Black-Scholes, but they also tell us when to take action; for example, the price points to optimally switch between modes of operation. Typically, when management is confronted with losses of continuing operations versus the cost of shutting down, the shutdown decision is delayed too long. And at the inception of a project, the value of flexibility is underestimated.

QUESTIONS AND PROBLEMS

For solutions go to www.corpfinonline.com.

1. Suppose that the cost of switching changes over time. For example, it might be easy to switch between courses of action early in the life of a strategy, but very costly to switch later on. Rework the switching example illustrated in Exhibits 6.8 to 6.13 given the assumption that the cost of switching from mode X to Y time periods 1 through 3 is $10, $15, and $20 respectively, and the cost of switching from Y to X is $20, $10, and $5 respectively.

2. The value of a mineral extraction project depends on the inventory in the ground (12,000 tons), the price in the spot market (currently $20 per ton), the cost of capital (12%), the risk-free rate (5% per year), the rate of extraction (4,000 tons per year), and the extraction cost ($22 per ton). Additionally, there is a 50/50 chance the price can go up by 50 percent or down by 33⅓ percent in a year. The cost of opening up is $20,000 while the cost of shutting down is $30,000. If the mine is currently open, what is the optimal rule for shutting it down? What is its value? How does the answer change if the price of the mineral is currently $26 per ton?

3. Rework question 2 assuming that there are three modes of operation: producing 4,000 tons per year, 2,000 tons per year, or shutting down. The cost of going from 4,000 to 2,000 tons is zero in either direction. The cost of going from 2,000 tons to zero is $30,000, and the cost of reopening is $20,000.

4. Suppose that we have a simultaneous compound option where the volatility of the underlying risky asset decreases over time. Rework the example illustrated in Exhibits 6.1 through 6.4 but assume that the volatility of the firm decreases from an up movement of 12.75 percent in the first year to 8 percent in the second, and 4 percent in the third year. (Note: This will produce a nonrecombining tree.)

5. Combine a deferral option with a sequential compound option. Use the example illustrated in Exhibits 6.5 through 6.7, but assume the second phase of the project can be deferred for one year at a cost of $65.

(Solve this problem only after reading Chapter 7.)

6. A company has a license to operate the project in a foreign market for two more years.

For the venture the company applies a 12 percent WACC.

It is facing the following uncertainty for its cash flow and present value.

The company considers exiting the market next year if its cash flow and present value of the project turn negative. If the company exits the market at the end of the first year, it would require additional $20 million to reenter the market in the last year. Should the

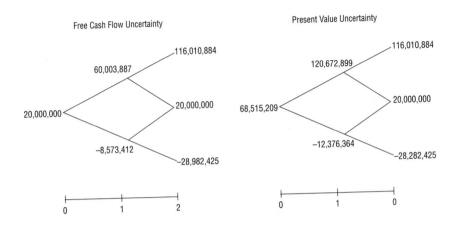

company exit the market next year if its cash flow and present value turn negative? Will your answer change if the cost of reentering the market in the second year is $10 million?

7. (Solve this problem only after reading Chapter 7.) Build your own spreadsheet for two periods to value a project with switching flexibility between two modes of operation.

Mode A:
—Initial Free Cash Flow, $10.
—Period Volatility of Free Cash Flow 35 percent.
—Upward probability, 0.5.

Mode B:
—Initial Free Cash Flow, $10.
—Period Volatility of Free Cash Flow 15 percent.
—Upward probability, 0.5.

Cost of switching:
—From mode A to mode B is $2.
—From mode B to mode A is $1.

The risk-free rate is 5 percent, and WACC is 12 percent.

What is the value of the project starting with mode A? What is the value of the project starting with mode B? If the switching costs are zero, would it matter in which mode we start?

REFERENCES

Baldwin, C.Y. 1982, June. "Optimal Sequential Investment when Capital Is Not Readily Reversible," *Journal of Finance, 37,* 3, 763–782.

Black, F., and M. Scholes. 1973, May–June. "The Pricing of Options and Corporate Liabilities," *Journal of Political Economy,* 637–659.

Brennan, M., and E. Schwartz. 1985, April. "Evaluating Natural Resource Investments," *Journal of Business,* 135–157.

Carr, P. 1988, December. "The Valuation of Sequential Exchange Opportunities," *Journal of Finance, 43,* 5, 1235–1256.

Cortazar, G., and E. Schwartz. 1993. "A Compound Option Model of Production and Intermediate Inventories," *Journal of Business, 66,* 4, 517–540.

Dixit, A. 1989. "Entry and Exit Decisions Under Uncertainty," *Journal of Political Economy, 97,* 3, 620–638.

Geske, R. 1977, November. "The Valuation of Corporate Liabilities as Compound Options," *Journal of Financial and Quantitative Analysis,* 541–552.

Kaslow, T., and R. Pindyck. 1994, March. "Valuing Flexibility in Utility Planning," *The Electricity Journal, 7,* 60–65.

Kulatilaka, N. 1993, Autumn. "The Value of Flexibility: The Case of a Dual-Fuel Industrial Steam Boiler," *Financial Management,* 271–280.

Margrabe, W. 1978, March. "The Value of an Option to Exchange One Asset for Another," *Journal of Finance, 33,* 1, 177–186.

Moel, A., and P. Tufano. 2000. "When are real options exercised? An empirical study of mine closings," working paper, Harvard Business School, forthcoming in *Review of Financial Studies.*

Morck, R., E. Schwartz, and D. Strangeland. "The Valuation of Forestry Resources under Stochastic Prices and Inventories," *Journal of Financial and Quantitative Analysis, 24,* 473–487.

Pindyck, R. 1988, December. "Irreversible Investment, Capacity Choice, and the Value of the Firm," *American Economic Review, 78,* 5, 969–985.

Zinkham, F. 1991. "Option Pricing and Timberland's Land-Use Conversion Option," *Land Economics, 67,* 317–325.

7 | Going from One Step per Time Period to Many

This chapter focuses on how to make the lattice solutions to real options more accurate by dividing the span of annual time intervals in the simple lattices that we have discussed thus far into many smaller intervals so that, in the limit, our results approach a continuous time solution. It also shows how to build Excel spreadsheet models for using binomial lattices for valuing basic types of options. While important for the mechanics of lattice solutions, and therefore important to those of us who do the programming and check the models, this chapter can be skipped by senior executives who are reading this book for the intuition it provides.

Lattices are, broadly speaking, more versatile than stochastic calculus solutions to option pricing problems, but are less elegant. Our objective in this chapter is to review the work of Cox, Ross, and Rubinstein (1979). They use probability theory to develop a binomial lattice approach to option pricing that employs discrete mathematics to achieve isomorphic results to the Itô calculus used by Black-Scholes (1973) and others. From a practitioner's point of view, the advantage is that discrete mathematics is algebraic in nature and simpler to understand than are stochastic differential equations.

The chapter is organized as follows. We first review Pascal's triangle because it is the foundation of the combinatorial mathematics used in binomial probability theory. Then we derive the binomial option pricing model, and we show how the binomial model approaches Black-Scholes in the limit. Finally, we provide instructions for building simple spreadsheet models to value basic types of European and American options. In Chapter 8, we show that almost all real option problems can be solved using binomial lattices because the present value of real assets follows a geometric Brownian process as modeled by binomial lattices.

PASCAL'S TRIANGLE—A BUILDING BLOCK

To understand a binomial decision tree, which is the most common lattice that we will work with, we begin with Pascal's triangle—a simple aid to counting the distribution of outcomes of binomial trials such as the flip of a coin that has only two possible outcomes, heads or tails. Exhibit 7.1 illustrates Pascal's triangle. Without any flips of the coin (row zero), the coin shows either heads or tails with certainty, so there is only one outcome. With one trial (a single flip of the coin) there are two equally likely outcomes, heads or tails as shown in the first row ($T + 1$) of the exhibit. With two trials, there are three outcomes: two heads, one head and one tail, or two tails. Pascal's triangle adds the numbers in the row above to obtain the numbers in the next row. We find that in row two, there is only

Exhibit 7.1 Pascal's triangle.

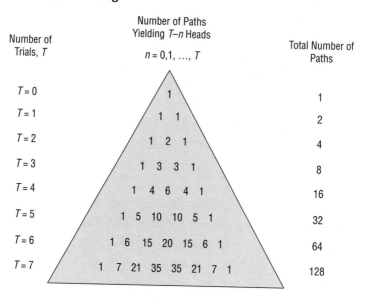

Number of Trials, T	Number of Paths Yielding $T-n$ Heads, $n = 0,1, ..., T$	Total Number of Paths
$T = 0$	1	1
$T = 1$	1 1	2
$T = 2$	1 2 1	4
$T = 3$	1 3 3 1	8
$T = 4$	1 4 6 4 1	16
$T = 5$	1 5 10 10 5 1	32
$T = 6$	1 6 15 20 15 6 1	64
$T = 7$	1 7 21 35 35 21 7 1	128

one way to get two heads (HH), but there are two ways of getting one head and one tail (HT and TH), and there is only one way of getting two tails (TT). A quick look at row three ($T = 3$) shows how Pascal's triangle cascades down. There is one way to get three heads, three ways of getting two heads and one tail (e.g., HHT, HTH, and THH), three ways of getting two tails and one head (e.g., HTT, HTH, and TTH), and one way of getting three tails. The probability of each combination is ½.

In general, the probability of observing n heads given T trials is

$$Pr(n \mid T) = coef.\ p^n (1-p)^{T-n}$$

where *coef.* is the coefficient taken from Pascal's triangle. For example, the probability of observing two heads and one tail out of three trials is

$$Pr(2 \mid 3) = 3\left(\frac{1}{2}\right)^2 \left(1 - \frac{1}{2}\right)^{3-2} = 3\left(\frac{1}{2}\right)^2 \left(\frac{1}{2}\right) = \frac{3}{8}$$

Another way to calculate the value of coef. is to use combinatorial notation:

$$Coef. = \binom{T}{n} = \frac{T!}{(T-n)!\,n!}$$

Read $T!$ as *T-factorial*, where *factorial* means T times $T-1$ times $T-2$, and so on down to one. Also, read the term T over n as "T things taken n at a time." In this example, it is three things (i.e., three trials) taken 2 at a time (i.e., two heads out of three trials). Finally, remember from basic algebra that zero factorial, $0!$, is defined as being equal to one. If we use combinatorial notation to figure out the number of combinations of two heads out of three coin flips (instead of using Pascal's triangle), it would be

$$Coef. = \binom{3}{2} = \frac{3!}{(3-2)!\,2!} = \frac{3 \times 2 \times 1}{(1 \times 2 \times 1)} = 3$$

Using combinatorial notation, the binomial probability of observing n heads out of T trials, given that the probability of a head is p, we have

$$B(n, | T, p) = \binom{T}{n} p^n (1-p)^{T-n}$$

For example, the binomial probability of three heads out of the seven trials for the binomial lattice illustrated in Exhibit 7.2 is calculated as

$$B(3 \text{ heads}, | 7 \text{ trials}, p = .5) = \binom{7}{3} .5^3 .5^{7-3} = \frac{7!}{(7-3)!3!} .5^7$$

$$= \frac{7 \times 6 \times 5 \times 4 \times 3 \times 2 \times 1}{(4 \times 3 \times 2 \times 1)(3 \times 2 \times 1)} .0078125$$

$$= 7 \times 5 \times .0078125 = 35 \times .0078125 = .2734375$$

Exhibit 7.2   Binomial probabilities for seven trials.

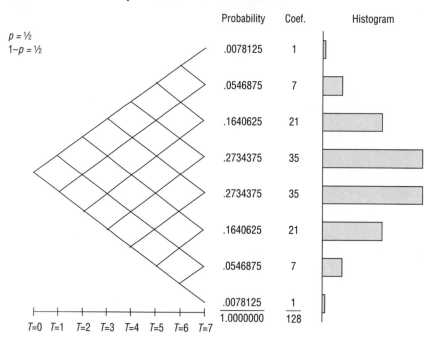

The derivation of the expected number of heads and the variance are beyond the scope of this book (see Feller, 1968). However, the expected number of heads is

$$E(T \mid n) = Tp$$

And the variance is

$$VAR(n \mid T, p) = Tp(1 - p)$$

Given that the up and down movements of value in a binomial tree are multiplicative (geometric) and the starting value is positive, the discrete payouts at the branches of the tree are bounded by zero at the bottom and approach infinity as the number of periods grows. The probability distribution approaches a lognormal distribution as the number of branches becomes infinite, as illustrated in Exhibit 7.3.

Furthermore, if the up and down movements in a binomial tree are additive (with $p = \frac{1}{2}$), the payoffs at the ends of the branches of the tree are not bounded and approach plus or minus infinity as the number of periods grows as shown in Exhibit 7.4. Both the multiplicative and additive models approach their respective limit either if we add more time periods or if we subdivide each period into smaller increments of time.

Exhibit 7.3 Multiplicative binomial lattice.

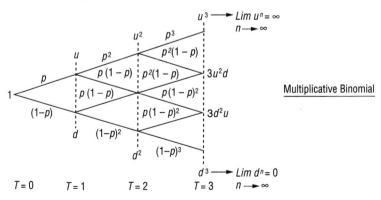

Exhibit 7.4   Additive binomial lattice.

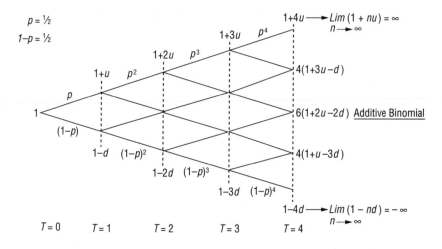

DERIVATION OF THE BINOMIAL OPTION PRICING EQUATION—TWO PERIODS

We begin with a review. In Chapter 4, we derived a simple one-period model for a call option (equation 4.2) that was written as follows:

$$C = [pC_u + (1-p)C_d] \div (1+r_f)$$
$$p = \frac{(1+r_f) - d}{u - d}$$
$$1 - p = \frac{u - (1+r_f)}{u - d}$$

The value of the call option, C, is equal to the end-of-period payouts, C_u and C_d, multiplied by their risk-neutral (or risk-adjusted) probabilities, p and $(1 - p)$ respectively, and then discounted at the risk-free rate, r_f. The end-of-period payouts depend on the value of the underlying risky asset contingent on the state of nature that we are in (up or down) and on the exercise price of the option, X. Therefore, $C_u = MAX[uV_0 - X, 0]$ and $C_d = MAX[dV_0 - X, 0]$. Note that the value of the call option does not depend on investors' subjective estimates of the probabilities of the up and down states, because the market-aggregated probability of each state is contained in the value of the underlying risky asset, V_0.

We now extend this model to many time periods. We first assume that the up and down movements are multiplicative: $u = 1/d$ the underlying risky asset pays no dividends, the risk-free rate is constant (a flat term structure) and the exercise price on the option, X, is fixed. Exhibit 7.5 shows a two-period extension of the model, assuming that $V_0 = \$20$, that $u = 1.2$, that $X = \$21$, and that the risk-free rate equals 10 percent. The left panel shows the underlying risky asset and the right panel shows the option written on it.

We can solve for C_u and C_d by applying the one-period option-pricing formula as follows:

$$C_u = [pC_{uu} + (1-p)C_{ud}] \div (1+r_f)$$
$$C_d = [pC_{ud} + (1-p)C_{dd}] \div (1+r_f)$$

As before, we can construct a riskless hedge during the first period. The result provides the following equation for the value of the call:

$$C_0 = [pC_u + (1-p)C_d] \div (1+r_f)$$

Substituting in the values of C_u and C_d we have the result:

$$C_0 = [p^2C_{uu} + p(1-p)C_{ud} + (1-p)pC_{du} + (1-p)^2 C_{dd}] \div (1+r_f)^2$$

where: $C_{uu} = MAX[0, u^2V_0 - X]$
$C_{du} = C_{ud} = MAX[0, udV_0 - X]$
$C_{dd} = MAX[0, d^2V_0 - X]$

Substituting the numbers of Exhibit 7.5 into the formula yields

$$p = \frac{(1+r_f)-d}{u-d} = \frac{(1+.1) - \dfrac{1}{1.2}}{1.2 - \dfrac{1}{1.2}} = .7273$$

$$1 - p = .2727$$

$$C_0 = \frac{.7273^2(7.80)}{1.1^2} = \$3.41$$

Exhibit 7.5   Two-period binomial example.

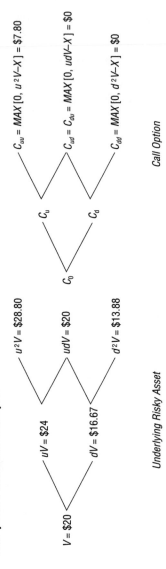

$C_{uu} = MAX[0, u^2V-X] = \$7.80$

$C_{ud} = C_{du} = MAX[0, udV-X] = \$0$

$C_{dd} = MAX[0, d^2V-X] = \$0$

C_u

C_d

C_0

Call Option

$u^2V = \$28.80$

$udV = \$20$

$d^2V = \$13.88$

$uV = \$24$

$dV = \$16.67$

$V = \$20$

Underlying Risky Asset

EXTENDING THE BINOMIAL APPROACH
TO MANY TIME PERIODS

Continuing with our assumption of a multiplicative process, the general form of the payoff function, where T is the total number of periods, and n is the number of upward movements in the value of the underlying risky asset, may be written as

$$MAX[0, u^n d^{T-n} V_0 - X]$$

Using the expression for binomial probabilities that was developed earlier, the probability of each payoff is:

$$B(n|T, p) = \frac{T!}{(T-n)!n!} p^n (1-p)^{T-n}$$

Multiplying the payoffs by the probabilities and summing across all possible payoffs, we have

$$C_0 = \left\{ \sum_{n=0}^{T} \frac{T!}{(T-n)!n!} p^n (1-p)^{T-n} MAX[0, u^n d^{T-n} V_0 - X] \right\} \div (1+r_f)^T$$

Although this formula will suffice, we want to compare it with the Black-Scholes formula. To do so, we extend the analysis.

First, we note that many of the final payoffs will be zero because the option finishes out-of-the-money in many states of nature. Denote a as the positive integer that bounds those states of nature where the option has a nonnegative value. Then we can rewrite the general form of the binomial equation as follows:

$$C_0 = \left\{ \sum_{n=a}^{T} \frac{T!}{(T-n)!n!} p^n (1-p)^{T-n} [u^n d^{T-n} V_0 - X] \right\} \div (1+r_f)^T$$

All of the states of nature where $n < a$ have zero payoffs because the call option will not be exercised. Next, we separate the equation into two parts:

$$C_0 = V_0 \left[\sum_{n=a}^{T} \frac{T!}{(T-n)!n!} p^n (1-p)^{T-n} \frac{u^n d^{T-n}}{(1+r_f)^T} \right] - X(1+r_f)^{-T} \left[\sum_{n=a}^{T} \frac{T!}{(T-n)!n!} p^n (1-p)^{T-n} \right]$$

The second bracketed expression is the discounted exercise price, $X(1 + r_f)^{-T}$, multiplied by what is called the complementary binomial distribution, $B(n \geq a \mid T, p)$. It is the cumulative probability of having an in-the-money option (i.e. where $n \geq a$) where the probabilities are the certainty-equivalent probabilities determined by the risk-free hedge portfolio. For example, if we go back to Exhibit 7.2 as a starting point, and let V_0 equal $100, let $u = 1.5$ (i.e., 150% per year), the exercise price be $250, the life of the option be seven periods, and the annual risk-free rate equal 10 percent, we have the parameters of Exhibit 7.6. There are eight end states. The number of up movements ranges from zero to seven. Given an exercise price of $250, the option is in the money only for the three uppermost states where n, the number of up movements, is 5, 6, or 7. Therefore, the value of the border state, state a, is 5. The risk-neutral probability is $p = (1.1 - .667)/(1.5 - .667) = .52$. The complementary binomial probability is the cumulative probability (based on risk-neutral probabilities) of finishing in-the-money, namely 26 percent. This is the probability that the exercise price will be paid. Therefore, the value of the second term in the binomial formula is

$$X(1+r_f)^{-T} B\left(n \geq a \mid T, p\right) = 250(1.10)^{-7}(.260668) = \$33.44$$

The first term in the binomial option pricing model is the current value of the underlying risky asset, $V_0 = \$100$, multiplied by another complementary binomial probability that is equal to one over the hedge ratio of options to the underlying that is necessary to form a riskless portfolio consisting of one unit of the underlying and m call options. To estimate the complementary probability to be used in the first term, we let

$$p' \equiv \left[\frac{u}{(1+r_f)} \right] p$$

Exhibit 7.6 Seven-period binomial example.

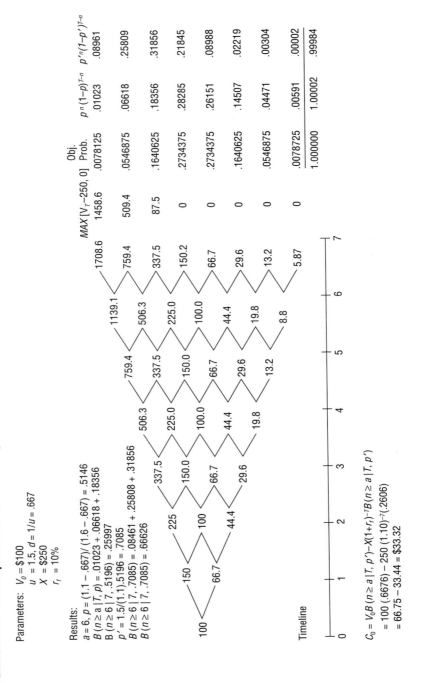

and

$$1 - p' \equiv \left[\frac{d}{(1 + r_f)} \right] (1 - p)$$

We then can reduce the probability function in the first term as follows:

$$p^n (1-p)^{T-n} \frac{u^n d^{T-n}}{(1+r_f)^T} = \left[\frac{u}{(1+r_f)} p \right]^n \left[\frac{d}{(1+r_f)} (1-p) \right]^{T-n} = (p')^n (1 - p')^{T-n}$$

Having made this transition, the binomial model for pricing a European call option (with a multiplicative stochastic process) can be summarized as follows:

$$C_0 = V_0 B \left(n \geq a \,\middle|\, T, p' \right) - X(1 + r_f) B \left(n \geq a \,\middle|\, T, p \right)$$

where

$$p \equiv \frac{(1 + r_f) - d}{u - d}$$

$$p' = \left[\frac{u}{1 + r_f} \right] p$$

$a \equiv$ *The smallest nonnegative integer greater than* $\ln(X/V_0 d^n)/\ln(u/d)$
$B(n \geq a \,|\, T, p) =$ *The complementary binomial probability that* $n \geq a$

Now we can finish the numerical example in Exhibit 7.6 by calculating the complementary binomial probability in the first term of the equation:

$$p' = \left[\frac{u}{1 + r_f} \right] p = \left(\frac{1.5}{1.1} \right) .52 = .7091$$

and

$$1 - p' = \left[\frac{d}{(1 + r_f)} \right] (1 - p) = \left(\frac{.667}{1.1} \right) (1 - .52) = .2909$$

The last column in Exhibit 7.6 shows the distribution of probabilities in the seventh time period. The value of the complementary binomial probability $B(n \geq 6 \mid 7, .7091)$ is .6676. Therefore, the value of the option, using a binomial approach for 7 time periods is

$$C_0 = V_0\, B\left(n \geq a \mid T,\ p'\right) - X(1 + r_f)^{-T}\, B\left(n \geq a \mid T,\ p\right) = \$100(.6676) - \$250(1.1)^{-7}\,(.2606)$$
$$= \$66.75 - \$33.44 = \$33.32$$

In the next section, we divide each annual time period into an infinite number of subintervals and show that the result equals the Black-Scholes formula.

THE LIMIT OF THE BINOMIAL OPTION PRICING MODEL IS THE BLACK-SCHOLES FORMULA

The binomial formula can be extended to a continuous time form by dividing its life, T years, into more and more subintervals, n, until n approaches infinity. Both models are written below for the purpose of comparison. First, the Black-Scholes model:

$$C_0 = V_0 N(d_1) - Xe^{-r_f T} N(d_2)$$

where

$$d_1 = \frac{\ln\left(\dfrac{V_0}{X}\right) + r_f T}{\sigma\sqrt{T}} + \frac{1}{2}\sigma\sqrt{T}$$
$$d_2 = d_1 - \sigma\sqrt{T}$$

And then the binomial model:

$$C_0 = V_0 B\left(n \geq a \mid T, p\right) - X(1 + r_f) B\left(n \geq a \mid T, p'\right)$$

where

$$p = \frac{(1 + r_f - d)}{u - d}$$
$$p' = \frac{u}{1 + r_f} p$$

The correspondence between discrete and continuous compounding of the risk-free rate is fairly straightforward. If we define r_f as the annual rate of return and j as the rate that is compounded n times in interval T, defined as the number of years to maturity then

$$\underset{N \to \infty}{Lim}(1+\frac{j}{n/T})^{n/T} = e^j = (1+r_f)$$

Cox, Ross, and Rubinstein (1979) derive a relationship that allows us to convert between the up and down movements in a binomial lattice and the annual instantaneous standard deviation of the rate of return on the underlying risky asset. Their results are

$$u = e^{\sigma\sqrt{T/n}}$$
$$d = e^{-\sigma\sqrt{T/n}}$$

Next, if we compare the binomial and Black-Scholes models, we need to compare the cumulative normal probability terms with the complementary binomial probability terms. The terms converge in the limit, as the number of lattice nodes per time period becomes large. Mathematically:

$$B(n \geq a | T, \ p') \to N(d_1)$$
$$B(n \geq a | T, \ p) \to N(d_2)$$

Thus, in the limit, the binomial model approaches the Black-Scholes model. We will demonstrate this result in the next section as we build an Excel spreadsheet using the binomial model, and allow the number of steps per year to become larger and larger. However, first we find the value of the same call option using the Black-Scholes formula as applied to the seven-period example in Exhibit 7.6. First, we need to find the standard deviation, σ, that corresponds to the up and down movements in our binomial tree. Our example has 7 years ($T = 7$) and seven subintervals ($n = 7$), therefore,

$$u = e^{\sigma\sqrt{T/n}}$$

$$\ln(u) = \sigma\sqrt{\frac{T}{n}} = \sigma\sqrt{7 \div 7}$$

$$\sigma = \ln(u) = \ln(1.5) = .4055$$

The Black-Scholes formula calls for a continuously compounded risk-free rate. The conversion is

$$1 + r_f = e^j$$

$$\ln(1.1) = j$$

$$j = .0953$$

Next we estimate the unit normal values, d_1 and d_2, as well as the cumulative normal densities $N(d_1)$ and $N(d_2)$:

$$d_1 = \frac{\ln\left(\frac{V}{X}\right) + r_f T}{\sigma\sqrt{T}} + \frac{1}{2}\sigma\sqrt{T}$$

$$= \frac{\ln\left(\frac{100}{250}\right) + .0953(7)}{.4055\sqrt{7}} + \frac{1}{2}.04055\sqrt{7}$$

$$= \frac{-.9163 + .6672}{.4055(2.646)} + .5(.53638)$$

$$= \frac{-.2491}{1.0728} + .53638 = .3042$$

$$N(d_1) = .5 - .1195 = .6195$$

$$d_2 = d_1 - \sigma\sqrt{T} = -.3042 - .4055\sqrt{7} = -.7686$$

$$N(d_2) = .5 - .27894 = .22106$$

Finally, substituting these values into the Black-Scholes model, we find the value of the option:

$$C_0 = VN(d_1) - Xe^{r_fT}N(d_2) = 100(.61950) - 250e^{.0953(7)}(.22106)$$
$$= 61.95 - 250(.5132)(.22106) = 61.95 - 28.36 = 33.59$$

The value obtained using the binomial model was $33.32, an error of only seven cents, or 0.2 percent. In the next section, we show that by increasing the number of periods per year we can reduce the error to zero.

BUILDING A SPREADSHEET MODEL OF A BINOMIAL TREE (EVENT TREE)

Now let's build a binomial tree on an Excel spreadsheet. There will be three sections to the spreadsheet. Input data and model parameters calculated from it compose the first section. We need to know the current value of the underlying (the present value of the project without flexibility), the exercise price, the life of the option in years, the annual risk-free rate, and the number of steps per year. From these, we calculate the up and down movements per step, the risk-free rate per step, and the risk-neutral probabilities (which, strictly speaking, are not needed for the event tree). Exhibit 7.7 provides some values for these parameters that we will use in a numerical example.

Exhibit 7.7   Input and calculated parameters.

Input Parameters		Calculated Parameters
Present value of the underlying	$100	up $u = \exp\left(\sigma\sqrt{T}\right) = \exp(.4055)\sqrt{1/1} = 1.5$
Exercise price	$250	down $d = 1/u = .6667$
Life of the option (in years)	7	
Annual risk-free rate	0.10	risk-neutral prob. $= (1 + r_f - d)/(u - d) = 0.52$
Standard deviation of return	40.55%	down state risk-neutral prob. $1 - p = 0.48$
Number of steps per year	1	

The second part of the spreadsheet is a diagonal matrix that represents the values that the underlying risky asset will take in a binomial tree. Normally, this matrix is illustrated as a branching tree. For example, see Exhibit 7.6. On an Excel spreadsheet, however, it is much easier to rotate the tree 45 degrees so that it becomes a diagonal matrix like Exhibit 7.8. Notice that the pattern of exponents of the up and down movements is quite regular. If we number the columns and rows starting at zero, then each cell can be written algebraically as

$$\text{For the nth row and the mth column } V_{n,m} = V_0 u^{m-n} d^n$$

For example, if we look at the third column, third row (cell E15), we see that $V_{3,3} = V_0 u^0 d^3 = 29.63$. Without using macros, we can quickly build a spreadsheet. Referring to Exhibit 7.8, step 1 is to define border cells for our matrix. Columns are numbered 0 to 7 in cells B11 through I11. Rows are numbered 0 to 7 in cells A12 to A19. Next, cell B12 is set up as a "seed" cell with $V_0 u^0 d^0 = \$D\$3*(\$I\$2^B\$11)*(\$I\$3^\$A12)$. By copying this cell to the right up to and including cell I12, we produce the initial value multiplied by u^m. Finally, notice that the C13 cell is the B12 cell multiplied by d, that the D13 cell is the C12 cell multiplied by d,

Exhibit 7.8 Excel spreadsheet for the value of the underlying.

	A	B	C	D	E	F	G	H	I
1	Input Parameters					Calculated Parameters			
2	1. Annual risk-free rate			10%		1. Up movement per step			1.5000
3	2. Current value of underlying, V_0			100		2. Down movement per step			0.6666
4	3. Exercise price, X			250		3. Risk free rate			0.1
5	4. Life of option in years			7		4. Risk neutral prob. (up)			0.519981
6	5. Annual standard deviation			0.4055		5. Risk neutral prob. (down)			0.480019
7	6. Number of steps per year			1					
8									
9									
10	Event tree for the underlying								
11		0	1	2	3	4	5	6	7
12	0	100	150.0052	225.0157	337.5353	506.3207	759.5075	1139.301	1709.011
13	1		66.66434	100	150.0052	225.0157	337.5353	506.3207	759.5075
14	2	0	0	44.44134	66.66434	100	150.0052	225.0157	337.5353
15	3	0	0	0	29.62653	44.44134	66.66434	100	150.0052
16	4	0	0	0	0	19.75033	29.62653	44.44134	66.66434
17	5	0	0	0	0	0	13.15543	19.75033	29.62653
18	6	0	0	0	0	0	0	8.777312	13.16643
19	7	0	0	0	0	0	0	0	5.851337

Exhibit 7.9 Logic used to create the event tree for the value of the underlying.

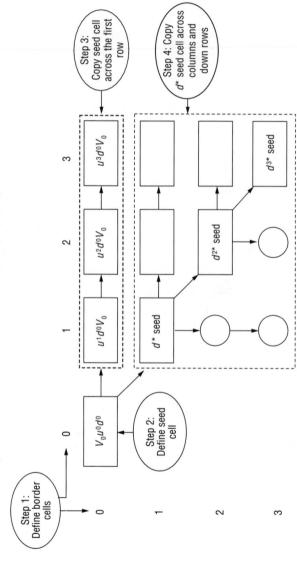

and so forth all the way across row 13. Furthermore, the D14 cell is the C13 cell multiplied by *d*, and so forth all the way across row 14. Therefore, in step 4 we define cell C13 as I2*B12, and copy it across from cell C13 to I13 and down to I19.

The result is a diagonal matrix with the state contingent values of the underlying risky project. Exhibit 7.9 shows the logic that was used to create Exhibit 7.8.

USING YOUR SPREADSHEET TO MODEL SIMPLE OPTIONS

Having completed the input section of our spreadsheet (Exhibit 7.7), and the event tree for the values of the underlying risky asset (a diagonal matrix as shown in Exhibit 7.8), the third and final step is to value the option(s) on the underlying. Let's start with an American call—the right to buy the asset for a fixed exercise price, $250, anytime during the next 7 years. Exhibit 7.10 shows the spreadsheet and Exhibit 7.11 shows the logic that was used to construct it.

Exhibit 7.10 Excel spreadsheet for American call.

	A	B	C	D	E	F	G	H	I
21	Input Parameters					Calculated Parameters			
22	1. Annual risk-free rate			10%		1. Up movement per step			1.5000
23	2. Current value of underlying, V_0			100		2. Down movement per step			0.6666
24	3. Exercise price, X			250		3. One plus nominal rate/step			1.1
25	4. Life of option in years			7		4. Nominal risk-free rate/step			0.1
26	5. Annual standard deviation			0.81		4. Risk-neutral probability (up)			0.519981
27	6. Number of steps per year			1		5. Risk-neutral probability (down)			0.480019
28	7. One plus annual risk-free rate			1.1					
29									
30	Event tree for the underlying								
31		0	1	2	3	4	5	6	7
32	0	33.32	60.25	107.55	189.14	326.8	552.9	912.03	1459.01
33	1		11.09	21.56	41.58	79.43	149.97	279.05	509.51
34	2			2.07	4.37	9.25	19.56	41.38	87.54
35	3					0.00	0.00	0.00	0.00
36	4					0.00	0.00	0.00	0.00
37	5						0.00	0.00	0.00
38	6							0.00	0.00
39	7								0.00

Exhibit 7.11 Spreadsheet logic used to value options.

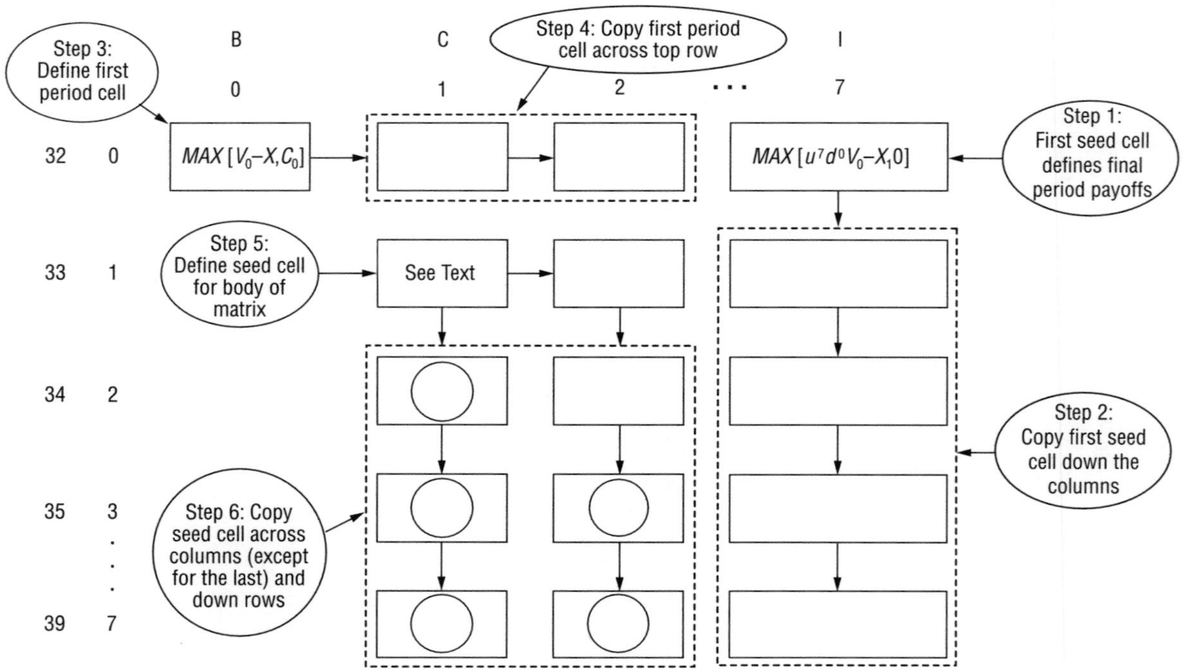

Starting with the end nodes, the payoffs are defined as the maximum of the value of the underlying or zero, $MAX[V_0 u^{m-n}d^n, 0]$. Step 1 defines the uppermost ending branch of the tree, the first of two seed cells. The last column of the spreadsheet in the first row defines the cell I32, which is coded as $MAX[(I12 - \$D\$24), 0]$ where I12 is the value of the underlying in the uppermost state of period 7 (see Exhibit 7.10) and $\$D\$24$ is the exercise price. Step 2 copies this cell down column I from cell I32 to cell I39. Step 3 is the coding of the first cell, B32 as the value of the option if exercised, $V_0 - X$, (i.e., C13 − $\$D\$24$) or its value if alive which is $C_0 = [pC_u + (1-p)C_d]/(1 + r_f)$, [i.e., ($\$I\$26*C32 + \$I\$27*$ C33)/$\$I\$24$], whichever is larger. Step 4 is to copy the cell across the first row up to but not including the last column (up to cell I 31).

Step 5 defines a second seed cell, C33. It is coded as an "if statement." If the neighboring cell, diagonally one row up and one column to the left in the event tree of the underlying (see cell B12 in Exhibit 7.8) is blank, then this cell is also blank. If this root cell, B12, is not blank then choose the maximum of either the value of the option if exercised, or its value if alive. In our example the coding of seed cell C33 is

$$\boxed{C33} \rightarrow IF(B12 = \text{" "}, \text{" "}, MAX((C13 - \$D\$24),$$
$$((\$I\$26*D33 + \$I\$27*D34)/\$I\$240)))$$

Cell B13 is not blank in this case, therefore, we chose between the value if exercised $C13 - \$D\$24 = 66.66 - 110 = -33.34$, or its value if kept alive, which is calculated using the risk-neutral probability approach:

$$\$I\$26*D33 + \$I27*D34 / \$I\$24 = \frac{[.51998(21.56) + .48001(2.07)]}{1.1} = 11.09$$

Step 6 copies cell C33 across the columns up to and including cell H33, then down the rows to row H36.

These six steps complete the coding of a simple Excel model to value a 3-year American call on a nondividend-paying underlying risky asset. In this example, assuming one step per year for 7 years, the estimated call value is $33.32.

Comparing the Spreadsheet Results with Black-Scholes

The Black-Scholes value for this option is calculated as follows:

$$C = VN(d_1) - Xe^{-r_f T} N(d_2)$$

$$d_1 = \frac{\ln\left(\dfrac{V}{X}\right) + r_f T}{\sigma\sqrt{T}} + \frac{1}{2}\sigma\sqrt{T}$$

$$d_2 = d_1 - \sigma\sqrt{T}$$

To substitute the parameter values into the expression for d_1, we start by calculating the continuously compounded risk-free rate:

$$\ln(1.10) = j$$
$$j = 9.53\%$$

Next, we calculate d_1 and d_2, the values of the unit normal variables:

$$d_1 = \frac{\ln\left(\dfrac{100}{250}\right) + .0953(7)}{.4055\sqrt{7}} + .5(.4055)\sqrt{7}$$

$$= \frac{-.9163 + .6671}{1.0729} + .5364 = -.2323 + .5364 = .3041$$

$$d_2 = .3041 - .4055\sqrt{7} = .3041 - 1.0729 = -.7687$$

The cumulative normal probabilities are

$$N(d_1) = .5 + .1195 = .6195$$
$$N(d_2) = .5 - .279 = .2210$$

Substituting these into the Black-Scholes formula, we have

$$C = 100(.6195) - 250e^{-.0953(7)}(.2210) = 61.95 - 250(.5132)(.2210)$$
$$= 61.95 - 28.35 = 33.60$$

CONVERGENCE OF BINOMIAL TREE TO BLACK-SCHOLES

Once the Excel spreadsheet has been constructed, it is easy to model the binomial tree with more steps per year. Remember that with one step per year, the binomial tree gave us an estimate of $33.32 for our 7-year call option and the Black-Scholes formula gave an answer of $33.60. This is a difference of only $.28 or 0.8 percent.

Exhibit 7.12 shows how the binomial approach converges to Black-Scholes. What jumps out immediately is that the rate of convergence is not smooth. With one step per year, the error is 28 cents; with two steps per year, it drops to 11 cents; then to 6 cents with three steps. With four steps per year, however, it increases to 24 cents.

The intuition behind the inconstant convergence is that the branches at the end of the binomial tree do not smoothly match up with the boundary condition (the exercise price) of the Black-Scholes formula. Binomial trees with more branches inevitably become more accurate in modeling the boundary, but the error does not vanish smoothly. Consequently, the

Exhibit 7.12   Lattice versus Black-Scholes as a function of the number of steps per year (for a 7-year option).

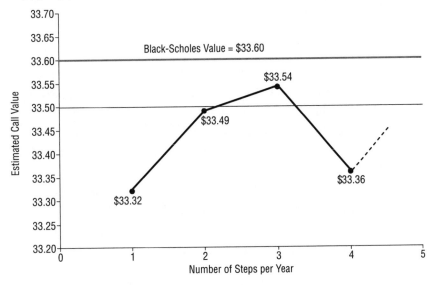

binomial model will produce errors that sometimes overshoot and sometimes undershoot the Black-Scholes result, but converge to it on average as the number of steps per year increase.

CONCLUSION

This chapter has shown how a binomial lattice can be used to value options on underlying assets that follow either a multiplicative or additive stochastic process. If the binomial lattice is multiplicative, then options valued by using it approach the Black-Scholes formula as the number of subintervals per year becomes large. We also showed how to use an Excel spreadsheet to build a binomial lattice for the underlying risky asset and how to value call options on it. This same approach can easily be used to value European and American puts, and compound options.

It is not difficult for a practitioner to construct an Excel spreadsheet to model compound options. The process starts with a binomial lattice for the value of the underlying risky asset, then builds a lattice for the first option (with payoffs contingent on the underlying), then builds a third lattice for the second option (with payoffs contingent on the first option).

QUESTIONS AND PROBLEMS

For solutions go to www.corpfinonline.com.

1. Build your own Excel spreadsheet to use the binomial approach to value an American call option, using the methodology described in Exhibits 7.7 through 7.11. Then use it to value a call with 18 months to maturity and an exercise price of $40 written on a stock worth $35 per share and annual standard deviation of returns of 50 percent. The stock pays no dividends, and the annual risk-free rate is 6 percent. Use 1, 4, 12, and 52 subintervals per year, then plot the option value as a function of the number of subintervals.

2. Take the spreadsheet that you built for question 1 and modify it to value European and American put options. Change the exercise

price to $30 but keep everything else the same. Plot the value of both the European and American put as a function of the number of subintervals.

3. Modify your spreadsheet again to handle simultaneous call and put options at each node. Value the portfolio of one call with an exercise price of $40 and one American put with an exercise price of $30.

4. Now go back to question 1 and change your spreadsheet to handle the case where the underlying risky asset pays quarterly dividends (with certainty) of 3 percent.

5. Extend your spreadsheet to handle simultaneous compound options. Use the same facts as those given for question 1, but now assume that there is a second call option, whose payout is contingent on the first option, with an exercise price of $5 and 18 months to maturity. What is the present value of this second option?

6. Modify your spreadsheet to handle sequential compound options. Using an underlying like the stock described in question 1, but with a 5-year time frame, estimate the value of two sequential options. The first expires in two years and has an exercise price of $30. The second can be exercised only if the first is, and has a 5-year life with an exercise price of $50.

7. Use your spreadsheet to value an option with a changing exercise price. Suppose the underlying is the same stock as in problem 1, but the exercise price is $40 for the first year, then $50 for the second year, and then $60 for a third year. What is the value of a 3-year American call with these characteristics?

8. Suppose the call option that you are valuing can be exercised at some points in time but not others. Use the parameters of problem 2 but assume the American put can be exercised only during the first 3 months, then again for months 12 to 15, and once again on the 18-month maturity date.

9. Suppose that your management team provides forecasts that are not conveniently broken down into up-and-down movements as required by a binomial tree. Instead, they provide the following table for a 2-year investment.

Medium	Year 1		Year 2 Given High		Year 2 Given Medium		Year 2 Given Low	
	Prob.	Value	Prob.	Value	Prob.	Value	Prob.	Value
High	.2	150	.3	225	.3	150	.3	100
Medium	.6	100	.4	150	.4	100	.4	67
Low	.2	67	.3	100	.3	67	.3	44

How would you use a binomial approach to approximate a solution to the problem?

10. Rewrite the spreadsheets that you developed to answer question 1 to use risk-neutral probabilities, instead of the replicating portfolio approach. (Draw a binomial tree.)

REFERENCES

Black, F., and M. Scholes. 1973. "The Pricing of Options and Corporate Liabilities," *Journal of Political Economy, 3,* 639–654.

Cox, J., S. Ross, and M. Rubinstein. 1979, September. "Option Pricing: A Simplified Approach," *Journal of Financial Economics, 7,* 3, 229–264.

Feller, W. 1968. *An Introduction to Probability Theory and Its Applications,* Vol. I, 3rd edition. New York: John Wiley & Sons.

Omberg, E. 1987. "A Note on the Convergence of the Binomial Pricing and Compound Option Models," *Journal of Finance, 42,* 2, 463–469.

Rubinstein, M. 1994. "Implied Binomial Trees," *Journal of Finance, 69,* 3, 771–818.

8 | A Four-Step Process for Valuing Real Options

With this chapter, we describe the four-step process that we use in nearly all of our client applications. The examples described earlier in the book have been sketches or cartoons—oversimplified (if that is possible) illustrations of the fieldwork that must be done to capture the reality of a complex decision. So far, we have assumed that the parameters needed for valuation were readily available. Now we discuss the difficulties of estimating them. How, for example, do we go about estimating the volatility of a project from real-world data? How do we build decision trees? How do we actually build spreadsheet models that reflect the complexity of the decision at hand without overcomplicating or oversimplifying the problem?

This chapter also discusses a theoretical keystone that simplifies the process of applying real options methodology in real-world settings. It allows us to reduce many sources of uncertainty to only one. It is very difficult (if not downright impossible) to analyze a lattice that is driven by more than two sources of uncertainty. To avoid this complexity, we use two assumptions. The first is the MAD (marketed asset disclaimer) that uses the present value of the underlying risky asset without flexibility as if it were a marketed security. The second, is that properly anticipated prices (or cash flows) fluctuate randomly. The implication is that regardless of the pattern of cash flows that a project is expected to have, the changes in its present value will follow a random walk. This theorem, attributable to Paul Samuelson (1965), allows us to combine any number of uncertainties into a spreadsheet by using Monte Carlo techniques, and to produce an estimate of the present value of a project conditional on the set of random variables drawn from their underlying distributions. Thousands of iterations produce an estimate of the standard deviation of shareholder returns that is then used for the up and down movements in a binomial lattice. We provide several numerical examples to illustrate the logic of Samuelson's theorem and empirical evidence consistent with it. The last section of the chapter describes some common errors that we have encountered in the application of real options. All of this is discussed in the second half of the chapter.

A Four-Step Process

Exhibit 8.1 shows the four-step process that we use. Step 1 is a standard net present value analysis of the project using traditional techniques. We forecast the entity-free cash flows over the life of the project; or if the investment is an acquisition, we value the target company whose cash flows are expected to last indefinitely. Later on, we will double-check to be sure that our option-pricing solution reduces, under the assumption of no flexibility, to equal the NPV result.

The second step is to build an event tree, based on the set of combined uncertainties that drive the volatility of the project. An event tree

Exhibit 8.1 Overall approach: A four-step process.

	Step 1	Step 2	Step 3	Step 4
	Compute base case present value without flexibility using DCF valuation model	Model the uncertainty using event trees	Identify and incorporate managerial flexibilities creating a decision tree	Conduct Real Options Analysis (ROA)
Objectives	Compute base case present value without flexibility at $t = 0$.	Understand how the present value develops over time.	Analyze the event tree to identify and incorporate managerial flexibility to respond to new information.	Value the total project using a simple algebraic methodology and an Excel spreadsheet.
Comments	Traditional present value without flexibility.	Still no flexibiliy; this value should equal the value from Step 1. Estimate uncertainty using either historical data or management estimates as input.	Flexibility is incorporated into event trees, which transforms them into decision trees. The flexibility has altered the risk characteristics of the project, therefore, the cost of capital has changed.	ROA will include the base case present value without flexibility plus the option (flexibility) value. Under high uncertainty and managerial flexibility, option value will be substantial.

* Event trees map out the cash flows explicity and use objective probabilities and the WACC to calculate the project value without flexibility.
** This value should equal the present value calculated by the valuation model.

does not have any decisions built into it. Instead, it is intended to model the uncertainty that drives the value of the underlying risky asset through time. We assume that in most cases, the multiple uncertainties that drive the value of a project can be combined, via a Monte Carlo analysis, into a single uncertainty: the distribution of returns on the project. This single estimate of volatility is all we need to build an event tree—a binomial tree of the type described in Chapter 7.

When we combine all uncertainties into the single uncertainty of the value of the project, we call this the *consolidated approach* for dealing with uncertainty. The details of the consolidated approach for estimating the volatility of the value of the project are described in Chapter 9. In some cases, however, it will not be useful to combine uncertainties. For example, when decisions must be tied to a particular uncertainty, then combining them into the value of the project will not help. Instead, we have to use a *separated approach,* where two or more sources of uncertainty must be estimated separately. Separated approaches are discussed in Chapter 10.

Options with multiple explicit sources of uncertainty are called rainbow options. An interesting, common example is a type of compound rainbow options called learning options. A phased investment decision often has both economic and technological uncertainty. For example, a pharmaceuticals research and development project has both. Technological uncertainty is large at the start of the project, but is diminished as the company invests to learn more. Economic uncertainty (e.g., the price of a cure), grows more diffuse through time. Thus, there are two (independent) sources of uncertainty—one increasing through time and the other decreasing (as investments are made). Other examples of learning options include, but are not limited to, exploration and development and new product development decisions. These are also discussed in Chapter 10.

The third step in the process of estimating the option value of a project is putting the decisions that management may make into the nodes of the event tree to turn it into a decision tree. The event tree models the set of values that the underlying risky asset may take through time. The decision tree, shows the payoffs from optimal decisions, conditional on the state of nature. Therefore, its payoffs are those that would result from the option or options that we are trying to value.

The fourth and final step illustrated in Exhibit 8.1 is the valuation of the payoffs in the decision tree using either the method of replicating portfolios, or risk-neutral probabilities. This topic has already been covered in depth earlier in the book; therefore, we have nothing to add.

SAMUELSON'S PROOF THAT PROPERLY ANTICIPATED PRICES FLUCTUATE RANDOMLY

In 1965, Paul Samuelson, the first Nobel Laureate in economics, proved the following theorem. The rate of return on any security will be a random walk regardless of the pattern of cash flows that it is expected to generate in the future as long as investors have complete information about those cash flows. This fundamental insight implies that the returns will not be cyclical on companies that have cyclical cash flows. The intuition is that all of the information about the expected future cash flows is already baked into the current stock price in such a way that if expectations are met, investors will earn exactly their expected cost of capital. Therefore, if the cycle evolves as expected, investors receive their required return—exactly. Only deviations from the expected cycle will keep the stock price from changing as expected. But these deviations are caused by random events. Consequently, deviations from the expected rate of return are also random.

Proof that properly anticipated prices fluctuate randomly is extremely useful for the valuation of real options. It means that multiple, correlated sources of uncertainty, some of them with mean reversion (i.e., autoregressive behavior) can be combined into a single multiplicative binomial process. Mean reversion is a common phenomenon. For example, suppose that a baseball player achieves a batting average of .500 for the first half of the season, while the average player bats .250. Mean reversion in batting averages means that his high average is more likely to be lower during the remainder of the season (i.e., closer to the mean) than it is likely to increase. Mean reverting variables are more likely to move toward the mean than to stay at their current levels. High batting averages are likely to come down and low averages are likely to go up.

Applying the idea of properly anticipated prices to the volatility of the cash flows of a company starts with price uncertainty, cost uncertainty, and uncertainty about the quantity sold and about the amount of capital that will be invested. Any of these risky variables may be correlated with itself through time. Furthermore, they are usually correlated with each other at a given point of time. If we can reduce them to a single uncertainty—the return on the project—and if this return is a random walk, then we can use a binomial lattice as our event tree.

Samuelson starts his proof by assuming that the spot price of an asset, S_{t+1}, follows a stationary autoregressive scheme, assuming that the coefficient of adjustment, a, is less than one and that the error term is distributed normally with mean zero and standard deviation sigma (σ). For simplicity, he also assumes that interest rates are zero. He then picks a simple example to illustrate, by setting the adjustment coefficient a equal to ½, the initial spot price equal to $80, the standard deviation equal to a constant, σ_ε, and the covariance between the error term and the spot price to be zero, $COV(S_t, \varepsilon_t) = 0$. Exhibit 8.2 shows how the spot price is expected to decline over time.

Exhibit 8.2   The expected spot price falls.

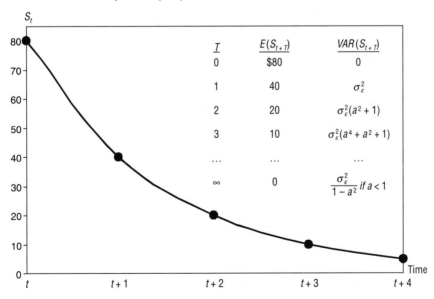

I	$E(S_{t+T})$	$VAR(S_{t+T})$
0	$80	0
1	40	σ_ε^2
2	20	$\sigma_\varepsilon^2(a^2 + 1)$
3	10	$\sigma_\varepsilon^2(a^4 + a^2 + 1)$
...	...	...
∞	0	$\dfrac{\sigma_\varepsilon^2}{1 - a^2}$ if $a < 1$

We now proceed to show that even the expected spot price declines over time, our rate of return will equal the market rate, which in this case is assumed to be zero.

The argument starts by looking at the expected spot prices and their variance. Today's spot price is a constant, with no variance:

$$E(S_t) = S_t$$
$$VAR(S_t) = 0$$

Next period's spot price, however, is a random variable:

$$S_{t+1} = aS_t + \varepsilon_t$$

Its mean and variance are, respectively,

$$E(S_{t+1}) = aE(S_t), \text{ since } E(\varepsilon_t) = 0$$
$$VAR(S_{t+1}) = E[aS_t + \varepsilon_t - aE(S_t)]^2 = E(\varepsilon_t)^2 = \sigma_\varepsilon^2$$

The mean and the variance of the spot price two periods hence can be derived by substituting the one-period price into the expression for the two-period price as follows:

$$\begin{aligned} S_{t+2} &= aS_{t+1} + \varepsilon_t \\ &= a(aS_t + \varepsilon_t) + \varepsilon_{t+1} \\ &= a^2 S_t + a\varepsilon_t + \varepsilon_{t+1} \end{aligned}$$

From this result, the mean and the variance of the spot price two periods hence can be written as:

$$E(S_{t+2}) = a^2 E(S_t), \text{ since } E(\varepsilon_{t+1}) = E(\varepsilon_t) = 0$$

$$\begin{aligned} VAR(S_{t+2}) &= E[a^2 S_t + a\varepsilon_t + \varepsilon_{t+1} - a^2 E(S_t)]^2 \\ &= E[a^2\varepsilon_t^2 + 2a\varepsilon_t\varepsilon_{t-1} + \varepsilon_{t+1}^2] \\ &= a^2\sigma_\varepsilon^2 + \sigma_\varepsilon^2 \\ &= \sigma_\varepsilon^2(a^2 + 1) \end{aligned}$$

The preceding equation follows from the fact that the expected covariance between error terms of adjacent time periods is zero (i.e., $E(\varepsilon_t, \varepsilon_{t+1})$ $= COV(\varepsilon_t, \varepsilon_{t+1}) = 0$). Also, the squared error terms from one time period are equal to those of the next period, therefore, $E(\varepsilon_t)^2 = E(\varepsilon_{t+1})^2 = \sigma^2_\varepsilon$. Exhibit 8.3 summarizes the progression of expected spot prices and their variances.

The expected spot price declines through time and the expected variance increases in our example because we have assumed that the adjustment coefficient is $a = \frac{1}{2}$. If we argue, instead, that it is $a = 1$, then the expected stock price is the same each time period:

$$S_t = E(S_{t+1}) = E(S_{t+2}) = \cdots = E(S_{t+T})$$

And the variance is equal to

$$VAR(S_{t+T}) = T\sigma^2_\varepsilon$$

In other words, the standard deviation of the spot price is $\sigma_\varepsilon \sqrt{T}$. These are the standard assumptions of the Gauss-Wiener process that describes

Exhibit 8.3 The progression of expected spot prices and their variances.

T	$E(S_{t+T})$	$\sigma^2_\varepsilon(S_{t+T})$
0	S_t	0
1	$aE(S_t)$	σ^2_ε
2	$a^2E(S_t)$	$\sigma^2_\varepsilon(a^2+1)$
3	$a^3E(S_t)$	$\sigma^2_\varepsilon(a^4+a^2+1)$
$\vdots$	$\vdots$	$\vdots$
∞	$a^T E(S_t)$	$\left(\dfrac{\sigma^2_\varepsilon}{1-a^2}\right)$ if $a<1$

the stochastic process that we assume for the underlying risky asset in the Black-Scholes formula.

Next, Samuelson proves that expected prices of futures contracts do not change through time. For us, the important thing about this is that we can think of a futures contract as a promise to pay one dollar of cash at time t. If we can prove that the price of a futures contract for delivery of one dollar does not change through time (in a world with zero interest rates and no carrying costs), then the value of a project which is the sum of the values of T futures contracts, will remain constant through time if we remember to add back the value of the contract that expires this time period. The crucial implication is that so long as we add back dividends paid each period, the value of a project through time will be a random walk, *regardless of the pattern of cash flows.*

The proof starts with the price of a futures contract as of time t for the delivery of one dollar at time T. Given the assumption of a zero interest rate and no cost of carry, the price of the futures contract at time t will be equal to the expected spot price:

$$_t F_T = E_t(S_t)$$

For example, if the delivery is three periods hence,

$$_t F_3 = E_t(S_{t+3})$$
$$= E_t(a^3 S_t + a^2 \varepsilon_{t+1} + a\varepsilon_{t+2} + \varepsilon_{t+3})$$
$$= a^3 S_t, \text{ since } E_t(a^2 \varepsilon_{t+1}) = E_t(a\varepsilon_{t+2}) = E_t(\varepsilon_{t+3}) = 0$$

The futures price in the following period will be

$$_{t+1} F_3 = E_{t+1}(a^3 S_t + a^2 \varepsilon_{t+1} + a\varepsilon_{t+2} + \varepsilon_{t+3})$$
$$= a^3 S_t + a^2 \varepsilon_{t+1}, \text{ since } E_{t+1}(a\varepsilon_{t+2}) = E_{t+1}(\varepsilon_{t+3}) = 0$$

Notice that the expectation, taken at $t+1$, of the error term at $t+1$ does not vanish because the error already exists at $t=1$.

To complete the proof that the expected futures price does not change from one time period until the next, write down the change in the futures price:

$$_tF_3 - _{t+1}F_3 = a^3 S_t - a^3 S_t - a^2 \varepsilon_{t+1}$$

Therefore, the expected change in the futures price, evaluated at time t is zero because $E_t(a^2 \varepsilon_{t+1}) = 0$. Even though the spot prices change in a known fashion, the futures price is not expected to change. The intuition is quite simple. Futures contracts are written to deliver cash (in this case) at a single point in time. The futures price tracks the expectation of one dollar paid at one point in time therefore the pattern of cash flows is irrelevant. If individual futures contract prices do not change, their sum doesn't change either. The only thing that happens to the sum is that it is diminished by the cash paid out during period t when we move to period $t+1$. Thus, if we add back the current period cash payoff to the sum, it remains constant through time.

Going back to Exhibit 8.2 for a moment, we see that the futures price for delivery of cash in period $t+2$ is \$20 even though the spot price of today's cash is \$80. Since expected information about the spot price at maturity is random and unbiased, $E(\varepsilon_{t+T}) = 0$, the futures price is a random walk with zero drift (in the case where interest rates and carrying costs are zero).

In our numerical example where $a < 1$, the change in the variance of futures price from period t to period $t+1$ is

$$VAR[_{t+1}F_3 - _tF_3] = E_{t+1}[(a^2 \varepsilon_{t+1})^2] = a^4 \sigma_\varepsilon^2$$

And, in general, the changes in the variance of the futures prices are

$$VAR[_{t+1}F_3 - _tF_3] = a^4 \sigma_\varepsilon^2$$
$$VAR[_{t+2}F_3 - _{t+1}F_3] = a^2 \sigma_\varepsilon^2$$
$$VAR[_{t+3}F_3 - _{t+2}F_3] = \sigma_\varepsilon^2$$

Note that with $a < 1$, the variance increases as one gets closer to maturity. But if $a = 1$, the futures price (and the expected spot price) is a random walk with zero drift and with a standard deviation of $\sigma_\varepsilon \sqrt{T}$, constant across time.

NUMERICAL EXAMPLES TO DEMONSTRATE SAMUELSON'S PROOF

The following examples demonstrate that it is also true that the rate of return on properly anticipated streams of cash flow fluctuates randomly in a world with positive discount rates, regardless of the pattern that the cash flows follow through time.

Start with a very simple case. A project pays $1,000 of cash flow at the end of each year for 5 years, and investors require a 20 percent rate of return on the investment. Exhibit 8.4 illustrates the cash flows and the change in the market price over time. As one would expect, the market price falls each period until it reaches zero after the last payment is completed at the end of year 5. But an investor's return is the change in total wealth, not just the change in the market price. As can be seen in Exhibit 8.5, wealth is calculated by adding back and reinvesting the cash

Exhibit 8.4   Constant return, declining value.

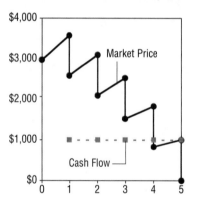 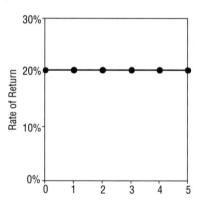

T	CF_t	Price	Wealth	Percent Change in Wealth
0	0	2,990.61	2,990.61	
1	1,000	2,588.73	3,588.73	20%
2	1,000	2,106.48	4,306.48	20
3	1,000	1,527.78	5,167.78	20
4	1,000	833.33	6,201.33	20
5	1,000	0	7,441.60	20

Exhibit 8.5 Investor's wealth calculations.

Year	Cash Flow	Investor Wealth
0	0	$PV_a(\$1{,}000, 5 \text{ yrs.}, 20\%) = \$2{,}990.61$
1	$1,000	$D_1 + PV_a(\$1{,}000, 4 \text{ yrs.}, 20\%) = \$1{,}000 + \$2{,}588.73$ $= \$3{,}588.73$
2	$1,000	$D_1(1.2) + D_2 + PV_a(\$1{,}000, 3 \text{ yrs.}, 20\%) = \$1{,}200$ $+ \$1{,}000 + \$2{,}106.48 = \$4{,}306.48$
3	$1,000	$D_1(1.2)^2 + D_2(1.2) + D_3 + PV_a(\$1{,}000, 2\text{yrs.}, 20\%)$ $= \$1{,}440 + \$1{,}200 + \$1{,}000 + \$1{,}527.78$ $= \$5{,}167.78$
4	$1,000	$D_1(1.2)^3 + D_2(1.2)^2 + D_3(1.2) + D_4$ $+ PV_a(\$1{,}000, 1\text{yr.}, 20\%) = \$1{,}728 + \$1{,}440$ $+ \$1{,}200 + \$1{,}000 + \$833.33 = \$6{,}201.33$
5	$1,000	$D_1(1.2)^4 + D_2(1.2)^3 + D_3(1.2)^2 + D_4(1.2) + D_5$ $= \$2{,}073.60 + \$1{,}728 + \$1{,}440 + \$1{,}200 + \$1{,}000$ $= \$7{,}441.60$

outflows of the project. For example, the investor's wealth at $t = 2$ is the sum of cash flow received (dividends) from the project at the end of the first period, D_1, which is reinvested for 1 year at 20 percent, plus cash flow received at the end of period two, D_2, plus the present value of an annuity of three payments of $1,000 at the end of each period for 3 years $PV_a(\$1{,}000, 3\text{yr.}, 20\%)$. Shown in the third line of the table, this sum is $1,200 + $1,000 + $2,106.48 = $4,306.48. The percent change in wealth between periods one and two is ($4,306.48 − $3,588.73)/ $3,588.73 = 20%. The important result is that the rate of return is constant when it is measured as the percent change in wealth.

Our next example is a cyclical pattern of cash flows with $100 received every odd year and $200 every even year for 5 years. Exhibit 8.6 shows the market price of the project which declines over time; the cyclical cash flows; and the rate of return, which is constant. As before, investor returns are measured by adding reinvested cash flows (dividends) to the current market price (i.e., to the present value of the project) that period. Exhibit 8.7 shows the calculations. The rate of return between any

Exhibit 8.6 Constant return, finite cyclical cash flows.

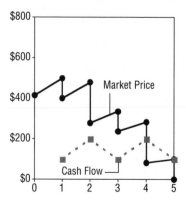 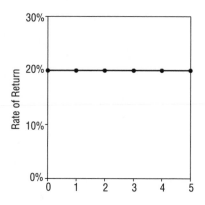

T	CF_t	Price	Wealth	Percent Change in Wealth
0	0	416.73	416.73	
1	100	400.08	500.08	20%
2	200	280.09	600.03	20
3	100	236.11	720.11	20
4	200	83.33	864.13	20
5	100	0	1,036.96	20

Exhibit 8.7 Investor wealth calculations: Five years of cyclical cash flows.

Year	Cash Flow	Investor Wealth
0	0	$PV(5 \text{ yrs. } CF, 20\%) = \$416.73$
1	$100	$D_1 + PV(4 \text{ yrs. } CF, 20\%) = \$100 + \$400.08$ $= \$500.08$
2	$200	$D_1(1.2) + D_2 + PV(3 \text{ yrs. } CF, 20\%) = \$120 + \$200$ $+ \$280.09 = \$600.09$
3	$100	$D_1(1.2)^2 + D_2(1.2) + D_3 + PV(2 \text{ yrs. } CF, 20\%)$ $= \$144 + \$240 + \$100 + \$236.11 = \$720.11$
4	$200	$D_1(1.2)^3 + D_2(1.2)^2 + D_3(1.2) + D_4 + PV(1 \text{ yr. } CF,$ $20\%) = \$172.80 + \$288 + \$120 + \$200 + \$83.33$ $= \$864.13$
5	$100	$D_1(1.2)^4 + D_2(1.2)^3 + D_3(1.2)^2 + D_4(1.2) + D_5$ $= \$207.36 + \$345.60 + \$144 + \$240 + \$100$ $= \$1,036.96$

two consecutive years of wealth is 20 percent. The cyclicality of annual cash flows has no impact on the pattern of total return to shareholders.

Before showing that Samuelson's proof is valid for real equity returns, let's look at one last example, which is the most realistic of the three. Assume the same cash flow pattern as in the second example with $100 of cash in odd years and $200 of cash in even years, but assume that the cash flows go on forever. Exhibit 8.8 shows the cyclical cash flows and price of the project. Note that the amplitude of the price cycle is less than the amplitude of the annual cash flows. This happens because the present values are discounted averages of an infinite number of full cycles, therefore, the full impact of the cash flow cycle gets averaged out in the present value results. Notice also, that the rate of return is a constant 20 percent. Once again, cyclicality in the cash flows is irrelevant, if they are properly anticipated. Exhibit 8.9 has the results of the investor wealth calculations. The initial wealth estimate is the sum of two annuities. The first is the present

Exhibit 8.8   Constant return, infinite cyclical cash flows.

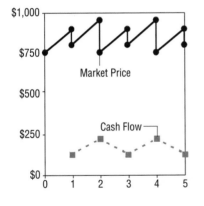 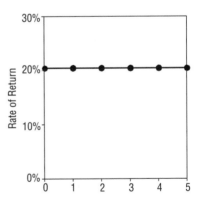

T	CF$_t$	Price	Wealth	Percent Change in Wealth
0	0	727.13	727.13	
1	100	772.57	872.57	20%
2	200	727.13	1,047.13	20
3	100	772.57	1,256.57	20
4	200	727.13	1,507.93	20
5	100	772.57	1,809.53	20

Exhibit 8.9 Investor wealth calculations: Infinite cyclical cash flows.

Year	Cash Flow	Investor Wealth
0	0	PV(infinite CF, odd yr. First, 20%) = $727.13
1	100	D_1 + PV(infinite CF, even yr. First, 20%) = $100 + $772.57 = $872.57
2	200	$D_1(1.2) + D_2$ + PV(infinite CF, odd yr. First, 20%) = $100(1.2) + $200 + $727.13 = $1,047.13
3	100	$D_1(1.2)^2 + D_2(1.2) + D_3$ + PV(infinite CF, even yr. First, 20%) = $100(1.2)^2 + $200(1.2) + $100 + $772.57 = $1,256.57
4	200	$D_1(1.2)^3 + D_2(1.2)^2 + D_3(1.2) + D_4$ + PV(infinite CF, odd yr. First, 20%) = $172.8 + $288 + $120 + $200 + $727.13 = $1,507.93
5	100	$D_1(1.2)^4 + D_2(1.2)^3 + D_3(1.2)^2 + D_4(1.2) + D_5$ + PV(infinite CF, even yr. First, 20%) = $207.36 + $345.6 + $144 + $240 + $100 + $772.57 = $1,809.53

value of an infinite series of $100 payments received every odd-numbered year $(1, 3, 5 \ldots, N)$. The second is the present value of an infinite series of $200 payments received at the end of every even numbered year $(2, 4, 6 \ldots, N+1)$. The annuity formulas are derived in the footnotes.[1] The results are as follows:

$$PV(odd) = \frac{bu}{1-u^2}$$

We define b as the biannual annuity payment, which is $100 in odd years, and u as $1/(1 + r)$, where r is the 20 percent discount rate. The formula for the present value of the annuity of payments in the even years is

$$PV(even) = \frac{bu^2}{1-u^2}$$

The value of investor's wealth at time zero is the sum of the present values of the odd and even biannual annuities:

$$PV(odd) + PV(even) = \frac{bu}{1-u^2} + \frac{bu^2}{1-u^2} = \frac{\$100\left(\frac{1}{1.2}\right)}{1-\left(\frac{1}{1.2}\right)^2} + \frac{\$200\left(\frac{1}{1.2}\right)^2}{1-\left(\frac{1}{1.2}\right)^2}$$

$$= \$272.68 + \$454.45 = \$727.13$$

This is written in Table 8.9 as PV(infinite CF, odd yr. First, 20%). Moving on to calculate investors' wealth at time one, we assume that their wealth is equal to the $100 payment at the end of year zero (i.e., at time one), plus the present value of the infinite stream of cyclical cash flows, which now starts with $200 at the end of year one. This is calculated as follows:

$$D_1 + 1.2PV(even) + \frac{PV(odd)}{1.2} = \$100 + 1.2(\$454.45) + \$272.68 = \$872.57$$

Repeating this line of reasoning from period to period produces the numbers in Table 8.9. As before, when based on investor wealth—the value of the project in the current period plus reinvested dividends—the year-to-year rates of return are constant at 20 percent.

EMPIRICAL EVIDENCE IN SUPPORT OF SAMUELSON'S PROOF

To test Samuelson's proof, we studied three cyclical industries: steel, commodity chemicals, and forest products. There are many ways of measuring their cycles. We chose two. Illustrated in Exhibit 8.10 are industry aggregate return on invested capital (ROIC) and cash flow to equity. The latter is calculated as net income, plus depreciation, admittedly a crude measure. There are obvious cycles in every graph. It is interesting that cash flow peaks occurred simultaneously in all three industries in 1988–1989 and in 1995, and they experienced a trough in 1996–1997.

Exhibit 8.10   Cyclicality of cash flows and ROIC for three industries (1981–1999).

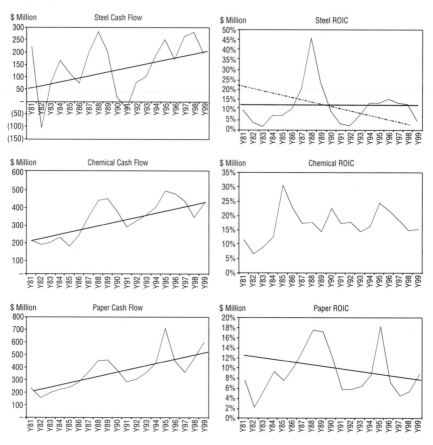

To provide statistical tests of significant cyclicality, we ran two types of time series regressions. The first tests for autoregressive behavior with one- and two-year lags. The form of the equation was

$$X_t = a + bX_{t-1} + cX_{t-2} + \varepsilon_t$$

The other test looked for mean reversion:

$$X_t = a + b(\overline{X} - X_t) + \varepsilon_t$$

Exhibit 8.11 Evidence of cyclicality of cash flows and ROIC in three industries.

Industry/Variable	Autoregression Tests		Mean Reversion Tests	
	r-squared	Significance	r-squared	Significance
Steel/Cash	.380	.040†	.119	.162
Steel/ROIC	.414	.024†	.286	.022†
Chemicals/Cash	.688	.000†	.666	.000†
Chemicals/ROIC	.172	.266	.148	.115
Paper/Cash	.412	.024†	.425	.003†
Paper/ROIC	.330	.061*	.228	.045†

* Significant at the 5% confidence level.

† Significant at the 10% confidence level.

The idea is that next period's value of X will adjust back to the long-term mean, X-bar, at a rate equal to b percent per year. The results of our tests for cyclicality of cash flows and of ROIC are found in Exhibit 8.11. We used annual data from 1981 through 1999. In every industry, there is statistically significant evidence of cyclicality. The only insignificant result was the time series of ROIC in chemicals.

If Samuelson's theorem is correct, there should be no evidence of cyclicality in the time series of the total return to shareholders, even when cash flows or ROIC are cyclical. The results of our tests for the cyclicality of total return to shareholders are shown in Exhibit 8.12. At the 10 percent confidence level, none of the tests are significant—a result that is

Exhibit 8.12 No evidence of cyclicality in total returns to shareholders.

Industry	Autoregression		Mean Reversion	
	r-squared	Significance	r-squared	Significance
Steel	.157	.301	.146	.117
Chemicals	.106	.456	.001	.922
Paper	.211	.191	.085	.240

consistent with Samuelson's proof that properly anticipated prices fluctuate randomly.

Academic papers, using more sophisticated and more powerful tests have found evidence of statistically significant time dependency in the total return to shareholders. But few if any have found evidence of dependencies that are economically significant after deducting transactions costs and risk-adjusting the returns. Therefore, we take the stance that Samuelson's proof is a valid enough assumption to use in practice.

COMMON MISTAKES

As important as the prescription for what to do when implementing real options is the list of things that are commonly done wrong. First among them is the incorrect assumption that the volatility of the underlying risky asset is the same as the volatility of one of its components. This problem is illustrated in Exhibit 8.13. Suppose that we are interested in estimating the volatility of project A (e.g., a gold mine). How shall we estimate its volatility? Remember, the underlying risky asset for our analysis will be the value of the gold mine without flexibility. The first mistake would be to use the volatility of the price of gold as a proxy for the volatility of the value of the gold mine. After all, many other things affect the volatility of the value of the mine. A partial list includes uncertainty about the quantity of gold in the mine, about the cost of extraction, and about interest rates. Furthermore, the mine has fixed costs that affect the volatility of its value. Another mistake would be to use the volatility of the equity in the company as a proxy for the volatility of the gold mine. Going in that direction would imply deleveraging the company's volatility, removing the effects of hedging, and untangling the diversification among the firm's multiple projects. In Chapter 9, we describe how to use Monte Carlo analysis to estimate the volatility of a project starting with many source uncertainties such as price and quantity.

The next problem is the temptation to overcomplicate the analysis with either too many uncertainties or too many options. Usually, most of the volatility can be traced to two or three sources of uncertainty.

Exhibit 8.13 Difficulty of estimating the volatility of a project.

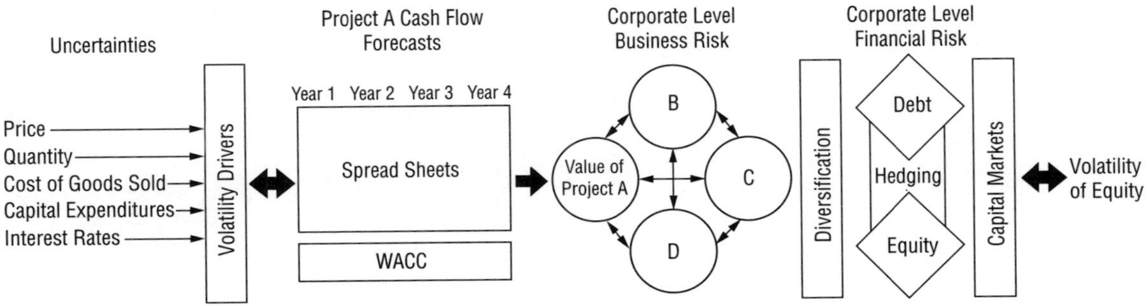

Furthermore, the set of realistic options can be reduced, at least in the near term, to a few.

In Chapter 2, we talked about the change process and the necessity of thinking carefully about how to effectively speed the acceptance of important new ideas such as real options. The new idea should be superior to the one that it is replacing, and it should be compatible, have low complexity, be triable, and observable. A common mistake of implementation is failure to recognize and plan out all of these aspects. Complexity is the biggest stumbling block. Practitioners need to be skilled in drawing decision trees and estimating volatility—two of the less practiced skills of developing a real options analysis. Also, there should be a deliberate effort to avoid using higher mathematics, because the problem solution becomes a "black box" from the user's point of view.

Finally, many practitioners make the mistake of trying to use the Black-Scholes formula as an approximation for more general models. Remember that the Black-Scholes model is the simplest and makes some very restrictive assumptions. It is a European option that can be exercised only at maturity. It assumes a single source of uncertainty that remains stationary through time—a constant variance. It cannot handle compound option situations, or underlying assets that pay a dividend (e.g., a project that throws off cash flows during its finite life). And it assumes a constant exercise price. Most real-world applications violate one or more of these restrictive assumptions.

Consider an approach that tries to use Black-Scholes at every branch of a decision tree. At the end points of the branch, the option must either be exercised or abandoned. This ignores the possibility of keeping the option open if that value exceeds the value if exercised. Consequently, the option is undervalued. Additionally, we lose valuable information about when the option should be optimally exercised—results that are particularly important in research and development programs with abandonment options (American puts).

Another common mistake is to use a decision tree approach without the final necessary step of solving, using the replicating portfolio approach to ensure that there are no arbitrage opportunities. The incorrect approach usually uses a market risk-adjusted rate for market-related risks and a risk-free rate for risks independent of the market. The problem is that market-related risks are not constant throughout the lattice—an important fact that was demonstrated in Chapter 5.

The question often arises about how far out in time to extend the lattice for a real option. The answer arises from the fact that options are riskier than the underlying risky asset on which they depend. Consequently, the present value of their (optimally executed) expected cash flows that are reasonably far out in time, is discounted by a present value factor that rapidly diminishes toward zero. A rule of thumb worth considering is to ignore options beyond about 15 years out (unless the future cash flows are heavily weighted toward the longer term end of the spectrum).

CONCLUSION

Even the most complex set of uncertainties that may affect the cash flows of a real options project can be reduced to a single uncertainty—the variability of the value of the project through time. Samuelson's proof that properly anticipated prices fluctuate randomly implies that no matter how strange or irregular the stochastic pattern of future cash flows may be, the value (wealth relative) of the project will follow a normal random walk through time with constant volatility.

This means that most real options problems can be solved with a four-step process that starts with the traditional discounted cash flow estimate of the value of the underlying risky asset (without flexibility). The second step uses Monte Carlo analysis to inject our assumptions about the causal uncertainties (e.g., price, quantity, and variable cost per unit) into a valuation spreadsheet for estimation of the volatility of the returns that result from changes in value. The source uncertainties may be autocorrelated through time and may be cross-correlated with each other. These relevant relationships can be captured in the Monte Carlo simulation. The end product of this second step is a value-based event tree—a binomial lattice that models the stochastic process of the value of the underlying as a normal random walk.

The third step is to add decision nodes to the event tree. Each node captures the flexibility available to the decision maker at that point in time (i.e., his or her option or options). No options may be available at a node, or there may be one, or many.

The fourth and final step is to value the payoffs of the decision tree by working backward in time, from node to node, using the replicating portfolio method (or risk-neutral probabilities).

Chapters 9 and 10 focus on the problem of estimating uncertainties and valuing the option. Chapter 9 assumes that all uncertainties are combined into a single binomial lattice, thereby completing our understanding of the four-step approach. Chapter 10 assumes that one of the uncertainties is kept separate from the others for decision-making purposes, and introduces a quadranomial approach for valuing the options.

QUESTIONS AND PROBLEMS

For solutions go to www.corpfinonline.com.

1. Explain in your own words, the intuition behind Samuelson's proof that properly anticipated prices fluctuate randomly.

2. Why can stock prices show predictable patterns when the total return to shareholders does not?

3. The following chart provides the expected free cash flows of a project. The weighted average cost of capital is assumed to be 10 percent, and constant through time. Plot the cash flows, the value of the project, the wealth of shareholders, and their expected return through time.

Time Period	Free Cash Flow
0	−10,000
1	1,000
2	−2,000
3	5,000
4	3,000
5	9,000

4. Go back to the cash flow tree of problem 6 in Chapter 7. Assuming an upward objective probability of 0.6 and expected rate of return of 13 percent, turn the cash flows into a value tree.

5. The marketed asset disclaimer (MAD) and Samuelson's proof that properly anticipated prices fluctuate randomly are cornerstones of the four-step process for valuing real options.

   (a) Explain in your own words how these two propositions enable us to use the four-step process.

   (b) What limitations or applicability would be imposed if we believe these two propositions to be false?

6. What are the problems that arise when we try to use the Black-Scholes equation to solve real options problems?

7. In the text of Chapter 7, we assert that decision tree analysis (DTA) fails to correctly value real options because it uses a constant discount rate throughout the event tree, but that risk changes depending on where one is in the tree. Let's use a numerical example to illustrate. The value-based event tree for the underlying is graphed below.

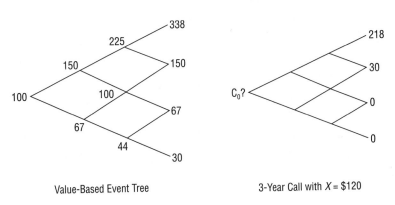

Value-Based Event Tree   3-Year Call with X = $120

   The risk-free rate is 5 percent, the asset pays no dividends, and $u = 1.5$ (therefore $d = .67$). We want to value a call option that expires in 3 years and has an exercise price of $120.

   Value the call options using a DTA approach that discounts the payoff at the company's weighted average cost of capital, 10 percent. Next, use ROA two ways: the replicating portfolio approach and the risk-neutral probability approach (they should give the same answer).

   (a) What is the difference between DTA and ROA?

   (b) What are the implied risk-adjusted discount rates at each node?

8. Near the end of the chapter we raise the issue of how far into the future we should extend the lattice. To get a start on further analysis of this issue, consider the two projects whose cash flows are given below. Note that both can be (and will be) replicated forever at constant scale. The cost of capital is 10 percent.

Project Cash Flows

	Project A	Project B
Year 0	−10.00	−10.00
Year 1	6.00	4.00
Year 2	6.00	4.00
Year 3		4.75

NPV (A) = $0.41
NPV (B) = $0.50

This simple comparison of NPVs is incorrect because the projects have different lives. To compare them, textbooks [e.g., Copeland and Weston (1992)] suggest replicating them forever at constant scale. The math results in estimates of NPV (N, ∞) where an N year project is replicated forever. The calculations are given below:

$$NPV(2, \infty) = NPV(2)\left[\frac{(1+K)^N}{(1+K)^{N-1}}\right] = 41\text{¢}\left[\frac{(1.10)^2}{(1.10)^{2-1}}\right] = 41\text{¢}\left[\frac{1.21}{.21}\right] = \$2.36$$

$$NPV(3, \infty) = NPV(3)\left[\frac{(1.1)^3}{(1.1)^{3-1}}\right] = 50\text{¢}\left[\frac{1.32}{.32}\right] = \$2.06$$

NPV-based analysis indicates that, if replicated forever, the 3-year project is better than the 2-year project.

Now, suppose the projects have flexibility—for example, an abandonment option with an exercise price of $8.00 that becomes available after the initial investment has been made. Furthermore, assume that the up and down movements in *value* are $u = 1.5$ and $d = .67$.

(a) The abandonment option should add more value to NPV(3) than to NPV(2). Calculate the values of the two projects with flexibility.

(b) Assume that the projects will be replicated (i.e., no flexibility). How much are the replicated projects worth, for example, what are ROA(2, ∞) and ROA (3, ∞)?

9. Suppose that the price of gold varies over a one-year period as follows:

Price of Gold

Today		End-of-Year	
Prob.	Price	Prob.	Price
1.0	$200/oz.	.2	$330/oz.
		.6	$220/oz.
		.2	$147/oz.

(a) What is the annual standard deviation of the gold price?

(b) Suppose that a gold mine is worth 10 times its end-of-year EBIT. It is expected to produce 10 million ounces of gold at an extraction cost of $140 an ounce and has fixed costs of $50 million. What is the annual standard deviation of the value of the mine and of the return on the value?

REFERENCES

Copeland, T., and J.F. Weston. 1992. *Financial Theory and Corporate Policy,* 3rd edition, Reading, MA: Addison-Wesley.

Samuelson, P. 1965, Spring. "Proof That Properly Anticipated Prices Fluctuate Randomly," *Industrial Management Review,"* 41–49.

9 | Estimating Volatility: Consolidated Approach

This chapter, along with Chapter 10, focus on estimating the volatility of the underlying risky asset and how to use it to build an event tree. Not much has been written elsewhere on the problems of estimation, except that we pointed out in the previous chapter that the volatility of a project is not the same as the volatility of any of the input variables (e.g., the price or the quantity of the product), nor is it equal to the volatility of the company's equity.

The first part of the chapter shows how to use a Monte Carlo approach to value a project, assuming that we have already estimated the stochastic properties of the variables that drive volatility. Monte Carlo tools are fairly simple to use and can model the cross correlations among various inputs such as price and quantity, as well as time series properties such as mean reversion. Once we have discussed the use of Monte Carlo analysis, we return to the problem of estimating volatility.

Two approaches for estimating a consolidated measure of the volatility of a value-based event tree are discussed later in this chapter. We call them the historical and the subjective approaches. We use the term "consolidated" because the output is a single estimate of volatility, built up from the many uncertainties (e.g., price, quantity, and variable costs) that contribute to it. Estimates of these separate uncertainties are taken either from historical data, or from the subjective estimates of management. We shall also provide some empirical evidence that validates our approach.

In Chapter 10, we will study what we must do when we want to keep the sources of uncertainty separate for purposes of decision making. This will be particularly relevant when we introduce a class of compound rainbow options called learning options. Examples of learning options are compound options with two independent sources of uncertainty, technological uncertainty, and product-market uncertainty. They are kept separate so that changes in value that are tied to technological uncertainty can be linked directly to the outcome of an experiment, test marketing, or drilling.

MONTE CARLO ANALYSIS FOR COMBINING UNCERTAINTIES

This section describes how to perform a Monte Carlo simulation, estimate the project's volatility, and build an event tree, assuming we have all the necessary input information.

Exhibit 9.1 illustrates the way that we use Monte Carlo programs (e.g., Crystal Ball or At Risk) to combine many uncertainties into one by running them through a spreadsheet. Each sampling of a set of parameters generates an estimate of the present value of a project (or a company), PV_t. The volatility that we need for the binomial tree, however, is the volatility of the rate of return, and Samuelson's proof (discussed in Chapter 8) is also based on rates of return. Therefore, we convert values

Exhibit 9.1   Using Monte Carlo methods to construct an event tree.

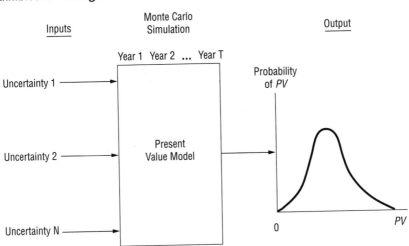

produced by the spreadsheet into rates of return by using the following relationship:

$$PV_t = PV_0 e^{rt}$$

$$\ln \frac{PV_t}{PV_0} = rt$$

For $t = 1$, this is a simple transformation that helps to convert between consecutive random draws of present value estimates in a Monte Carlo program and the standard deviation of the rate of return (project volatility, σ_r).

Exhibit 9.2 describes the process that we shall follow to construct an event tree—one where all uncertainties driving the present value have been combined into one. We start with a present value spreadsheet, model the variable uncertainties, use the Monte Carlo simulation to estimate the standard deviation of rates of return (based on the distribution of present values), and then construct the event tree binomial lattice.

We use a simple, but realistic 7-year project to illustrate the process. Its life is assumed to be nonstochastic and there are no options to extend its life. There is uncertainty about three input parameters:

1. Price per unit (which is autocorrelated with itself through time).
2. Quantity of output (which is positively correlated with price).
3. Variable cost per unit (which is positively correlated with quantity).

Exhibit 9.2 Monte Carlo process for building a value-based event tree.

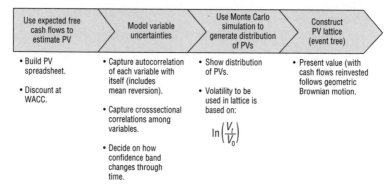

At first, we model only the price uncertainty using the Crystal Ball Monte Carlo program, then we complicate the problem by adding in the other sources of uncertainty.

Exhibit 9.3 shows the spreadsheet of expected cash flows over the life of the project. It captures not only the numbers, but also the functional relationships that forecast the cash flows. If the weighted average cost of capital is 12 percent, the present value is $1,507.63; and if the investment outlay is $1,600, the net present value is −$92.37. Without flexibility, the project would be rejected. The expected price per unit starts out at $10, but declines over time due to anticipated competitive pressure. The expected quantity sold grows at 20 percent in the year after the product is released, but despite price cuts, growth slows to 5.8 percent in the last year of the forecast. The variable cost per unit is expected to decline from $6.00 in the first year of operation to $3.56 per unit in the last year.

Exhibit 9.3   Spreadsheet used to estimate project present value.

	0	1	2	3	4	5	6	7
Price/unit		10	10	9.5	9	8	7	6
Quantity		100	120	139	154	173	189	200
Variable cost/unit		6.0	6.0	5.7	5.4	4.8	4.2	3.6
Revenue		1,000	1,200	1,321	1,386	1,384	1,323	1,200
− Variable cash costs		−600	−720	−792	−832	−832	−790	−711
− Fixed cash costs		−20	−20	−20	−20	−20	−20	−20
− Depreciation		−229	−229	−229	−229	−229	−229	−229
EBIT		151	231	280	305	303	284	240
− Cash taxes		−61	−93	−112	−122	− 121	−114	−96
+ Depreciation		229	229	229	229	229	229	229
− CAPEX	−1,600	0	0	0	0	0	0	0
− Increase in working capital		−200	−40	−24	−13	0	13	24
Free cash flow		119	327	373	399	411	412	397
WACC		0.12	0.12	0.12	0.12	0.12	0.12	0.12
Discount factor		0.893	0.797	0.712	0.636	0.567	0.507	0.452
PV of free cash flow		107	261	265	253	233	209	180
PV of project	1,507.63							
Investment	−1,600.00							
NPV of project	−92.37							

Next, we assume that there is uncertainty in the price estimates. There are many ways to think about the confidence band of estimated prices; however, there are two extremes. Either we believe that there is a constant confidence band, or that the confidence band increases over time. We illustrate both, starting with the assumption that the confidence band is constant. There are an infinite number of other possibilities. For example, forecasters might believe that the confidence band is proportional to the predicted price level. No matter how we decide to model the period-by-period confidence bands, the Monte Carlo program allows us to capture them. Suppose that forecasters at the company believe that they have estimated the expected price each year with a standard deviation of 10 percent. Furthermore, they believe that their errors of estimation will be highly positively correlated through time (autocorrelation of 90%), implying that if they underestimate the price that is achievable in one year, they are highly likely to have underestimated it the next year as well. This time dependence is called autocorrelation, and if it is negative, implying that a high value is more likely to be followed by a low value (and vice versa), then it is called mean reversion.

Now let's discuss Monte Carlo analysis using the Crystal Ball program overlaid on an Excel spreadsheet to build this price uncertainty into our model. To randomize the input prices, we first click on the cell in our Excel spreadsheet that we want to select as a random variable (e.g., the price in year one).

1. *Define Assumptions.* Next, we click on the "define assumption" icon, which looks like this. The program responds by asking us to choose a probability distribution. There are many choices such as the binomial uniform, normal, and lognormal distributions. We'll select the lognormal distribution, because we believe that prices will never go negative, and because combinations of lognormal distributions are themselves lognormal. Next, we set the mean and the standard deviation for the price in year 1—the mean is $10 and the standard deviation is 10 percent (i.e., $1.00). The Crystal Ball program assumes that the value in the cell is the mean for the distribution. We then move the cursor to the second-year price forecast and repeat the selection of the lognormal distribution, set

the mean equal to the expected price (still $10) and the standard deviation equal to 10 percent (again $1.00).

2. *Set Autocorrelations.* At this point, we also want to model the autocorrelation between prices in the first two time periods. To do so, we click on the "correlate" icon. When asked by Crystal Ball to "select an assumption," we choose the variable that we want the second period price to be correlated with. We choose the first period price. Next, we are asked for the magnitude of the *r*-squared between them. Rather than going off onto a tangent at this point, let's just say for now that the *r*-squared is the same as the autocorrelation coefficient. We will provide more details and a proof in the next section. Since the *r*-squared is the same as the autocorrelation coefficient, we set the *r*-squared equal to 90 percent. This means that high positive errors in price in the first time period are very likely to be followed by positive errors in the second time period as well. We repeat this procedure by defining the assumptions for all 7 years of price forecasts. The Crystal Ball program highlights the selected price forecast cells in green.

3. *Define Forecast Variable.* We now want to define the forecast variable whose distribution will be simulated by the Monte Carlo program. The "define forecast" icon looks like this . Remember that the standard deviation that we want to use to build our event tree is the standard deviation of the percent changes in the value of the project from one time period to the next, therefore the variable of interest is

$$z = \ln\left(\frac{PV_1 + FCF_1}{PV_0}\right)$$

This value is computed using the PV_0 (present value at time zero) for the project in the denominator, and the present value at time 1:

$$PV_1 = \sum_{t=2}^{7} \frac{FCF_t}{(1+WACC)^{t-1}}$$

plus the cash flow at time 1, FCF_1, in the numerator. To do so, we create a new cell on our spreadsheet that contains the formula for "z," then click on the "define forecast" icon in Crystal Ball. This will be the cell that the Monte Carlo program uses to produce an output for each random draw.

4. *Run the Simulation.* To run the simulation, click on the "run" icon that looks like this ▶. Next, "reset" the program so that it is initialized. Use the "run preferences" command to set the maximum number of trials (we usually choose 1,000), then click on the "run" icon and the Monte Carlo simulation will start.

After 1,000 iterations using the parameters that we chose, the mean return was 13 percent (remember the cost of capital was 12 percent), and the annual standard deviation was 21 percent. If you are following along on your personal computer or laptop, you should get similar results, but they will not be exactly the same because, after all, it is a simulation based on 1,000 randomly chosen sets of numbers (focusing on the price uncertainty in the model). Exhibit 9.4 shows the frequency distribution of the annual rates of return that is produced as an output of the Crystal Ball program. Note, in particular, that the standard deviation of prices was equal to 10 percent, but the standard deviation of the rate of return on the project is 21 percent. This serves to reinforce the point that the volatility

Exhibit 9.4   Return distribution frequency chart.

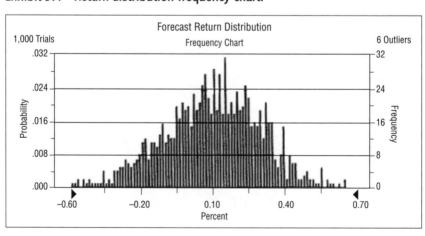

of the input variables that drive uncertainty is not the same as the volatility of the project.

Building the Event Tree

Now that we have the present value of the project, an estimate of the volatility of returns (based on Monte Carlo analysis), and the expected cash flows, we can construct a value-based event tree. It is graphed in Exhibit 9.5.

Note that the event tree is recombining because we assume that the free cash flows generated at the end of each period are a constant proportion of the value at the end of the period. As an example, look at the end of the second period. The up and down movements in the tree are annual in this example; therefore the length of time between nodes is $T = 1$; therefore, $u = e^{\sigma\sqrt{T}} = e^{.21} = 1.2337$ and $d = 1/u = .8106$. The present value of the project, after the free cash flows have been paid out at the end of the first time period, is $1,569.12 as shown in Exhibit 9.6. By the end of the second time period, we can see from Exhibit 9.7 that the value can be either $1,935.79 or $1,271.90. The present value of the expected free

Exhibit 9.5   Present value event tree.

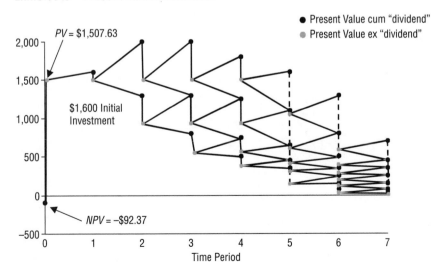

Exhibit 9.6 Present values ex dividends.

0	1	2	3	4	5	6	7
1,507.63	1,569.12	1,575.13	1,491.21	1,306.66	1,007.52	574.52	0
		1,034.93	979.80	858.54	661.99	377.46	0
			643.77	564.10	434.96	248.03	0
				370.64	285.79	162.96	0
					187.77	107.08	0
						70.35	0
							0

cash flow that period is $261 and the expected present value at that point in time is

$$PV_2 = \sum_{t=3}^{7} \frac{FCF_t}{(1+WACC)^t} = \$261 + \$265 + \$253 + \$233 + \$209 + \$180 = \$1,401.$$

The ratio is $261/$1,401 = .1863$. Multiplying this ratio times the up state value, $1,935.79 yields the up state dividend, namely $360.66. The down state dividend is the same ratio multiplied by the down state value, namely $236.95. These proportional dividends are subtracted from the value of the project "cum dividend" to get the starting values "ex dividend" for the third time period of our binomial tree.

Exhibit 9.7 Present values before dividends.

0	1	2	3	4	5	6	7
-92.37	1,688.55	1,935.79	1,943.20	1,839.67	1,612.00	1,242.95	708.77
		1,271.90	1,276.77	1,208.75	1,059.16	816.68	465.70
			838.90	794.21	695.92	536.59	305.98
				521.83	457.25	352.57	201.05
					300.43	231.65	132.10
						152.21	86.79
							57.03

The event tree provides the values of the underlying project without flexibility. The next step would be to place option decisions into the nodes of the tree to turn it into a decision tree. This is the third step of the process for valuing options that was described in Chapter 8. The final step would be to use replicating portfolios (or risk-neutral probabilities) to value the decisions embedded in the decision tree to obtain the value of the project with flexibility.

More on Autocorrelation

Before going on, let's take a side journey into the realm of time series analysis to discuss autocorrelated time series. Many natural phenomena exhibit autocorrelated behavior. Perhaps the most common is mean reversion. When an outlier is observed (e.g., a very high early season baseball batting average, say .500), it will tend, in later observations, to regress toward the mean (let's say .250). Thus, very tall parents tend to have shorter children, a Wall Street analyst with an outstanding performance record will tend to have average performance thereafter (if luck and not skill was the overarching consideration), and profit margins in the commodity chemical industry will be more likely to widen if they are currently narrow. A mathematical description of one-period mean reversion can be written as

$$\begin{aligned} X_{t+1} &= X_t - b[X_t - E(X)] + \varepsilon_t \\ &= bE(X) + (1-b)X_t + \varepsilon_t \\ &= \alpha + \beta X_t + \varepsilon_t \end{aligned}$$

Define $E(X)$ as the long-run expected value of the random variable X, and b as the speed of adjustment—the percentage of the departure from the long-run average that is eliminated each time period. You can see from the equation that if this period's value, X_t, is above the long-term mean, then the next observation is likely to be lower. Exhibit 9.8 graphs a mean-reverting time series for $E(X) = \$100$ and $b = .5$. The initial value of X is 150, and the random error terms for each of 10 years are given in the exhibit.

Exhibit 9.8   Example of a mean-reverting time series.

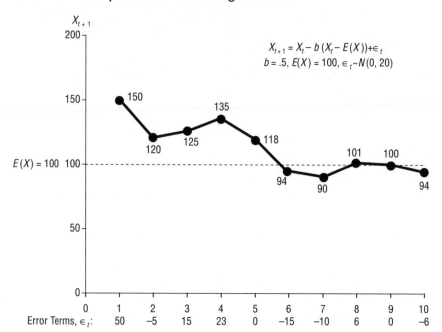

The Crystal Ball program only allows us to enter the r-squared between adjacent time periods. How can we make this fit the mean-reverting behavior just described? First, write down the definition of r-squared between the values of random variables in adjacent periods:

$$X_{t+1} = \alpha + \beta X_t + \varepsilon_{t+1}$$
$$r^2 = \frac{COV(X_t, X_{t+1})}{\sigma_t \sigma_{t+1}}$$

Next, the slope of the equation, β, is defined as follows:[1]

$$\beta = \frac{COV(X_t, X_{t+1})}{VAR(X_t)}$$

Because the time series of the random variable, X_t, is stationary, we can take advantage of the fact that

$$\sigma^2(X_t) = \sigma^2(X_{t+1})$$

And therefore $\sigma_t = \sigma_{t+1}$

Consequently $\sigma_t \sigma_{t+1} = \sigma_t^2 = VAR(X_t)$

This implies that the r-squared and the beta coefficient are identical, that is, $r^2 = \beta$. Therefore, it does not matter that the Crystal Ball program only allows us to enter the r-squared. Note also that beta is equal to one minus the speed of adjustment, $1 - b$, and that the intercept of a linear regression of X_{t+1} on X_t is equal to $bE(X)$. Thus, where simple first order autocorrelation is a reasonable assumption, we can use the parameters of a linear regression to provide the inputs for the Monte Carlo program.

In the example of the 7-year project that we have been using, we modeled positive autocorrelation. In general, positive autocorrelation will result in greater volatility than assuming independence (i.e., zero autocorrelation) across time. Negative autocorrelation, with the simple mean reversion that we have been describing, assumes that positive error terms are followed by negative errors. To illustrate the effect, we reran the 7-year project three ways with the results that are given in Exhibit 9.9. Note that positive autocorrelation increases the standard deviation of project returns and negative autocorrelation decreases it.

Multiple Correlated Variables

To complete our example, we keep to the assumption that the confidence band for prices remains constant with a 10 percent standard deviation

Exhibit 9.9 **The standard deviation of returns with three different autocorrelations.**

	Standard Deviation of Project Returns
Positive correlation between intervals = .9	.21
No correlation	.09
Negative correlation between intervals = −.9	.03

and that prices have a positive autocorrelation of 90 percent. However, we add to these assumptions our belief that quantity is negatively correlated with price with an *r*-squared of minus 50 percent, that the standard deviation of quantity is 10 percent, and that quantity is not autocorrelated with itself. Finally, we assume that variable cost per unit is positively correlated with quantity (*r*-squared = .7), and has a standard deviation of 10 percent.

Modeling these additional assumptions in Crystal Ball, we find that the new standard deviation of return is 31 percent, quite a bit higher than the 21 percent standard deviation that we obtained when price was the only random variable.

Increasing Confidence Bands

Although we have used constant confidence bands thus far, both common sense and the theory of econometrics suggest that confidence bands widen outside the time interval when they were estimated.

Suppose that the confidence interval widens as $\sigma\sqrt{T}$. Going back to the first set of assumptions for our 7-period project, we assume that only price is random and that its positive autocorrelation is 90 percent. Exhibit 9.10 shows the increasing standard deviation that was entered into the Monte Carlo program.

Given these standard deviations that increased through time, the overall project rate of return variance also increased from its earlier value of 21 percent to 41 percent, nearly doubling. The assumption of an increasing confidence interval had a greater impact than any of the other changes (e.g., the additional variability of quantity and variable costs).

Exhibit 9.10   Estimated standard deviations that increase through time.

Year	1	2	3	4	5	6	7
$\sigma\sqrt{T}$	10%	14.1%	17.3%	20%	22.4%	24.5%	26.5%
Price	$10	$10	$9.5	$9.0	$8.0	$7.0	$6.0
Standard deviation	$1.00	$1.41	$1.64	$1.80	$1.79	$1.72	$1.59

ESTIMATING THE COMBINED UNCERTAINTY

The first section described Monte Carlo simulations as a way of combining input in certainties (e.g., price and quantity) to estimate a single output uncertainty, the volatility of the return on the entire project. But the question remains, where can we obtain data on the variability of drivers of project uncertainty? In most cases, we use either historical data and assume that the future is like the past; or we use subjective, but forward-looking, estimates made by management.

Using Historical Data

If it seems reasonable to assume that the future will be like the past, then we may decide to use historical data to estimate the confidence bands around the variables that drive the uncertainty in our discounted cash flow model of a project or a company given no flexibility. This will be reasonable mostly when a project is a replacement investment, when we are studying a switching option to start up or shut down an existing project, or when the new project is affected by exogenous shocks in some of the same ways as the old project.

We use econometric techniques to find the best model that fits the historic data. Having done so, we use the model to forecast the expected future values of the variable, for example, price three years ahead, and then use the standard deviation of the error terms from the regression to estimate the volatility (or confidence band) called for in the Monte Carlo program.

Suppose, for example, we need estimates of confidence bands for the price, quantity, and variable costs of a new production process that will cut costs, but will still be exposed to the same market (price and quantity) risk as before. The historical volatility of the price-quantity relationship is a reasonable basis for forecasting future volatility, but the variable cost uncertainty will be different (this is discussed in the next section of the chapter).

To estimate the historic price-quantity risk, we would fit regression equations to each source of uncertainty and save information on the trends and the residuals. As discussed earlier, we can use the r-squared of the time series regression to capture the autocorrelation effect. Cross-correlation between variables (e.g., price and quantity) is captured by the r-squared between them.

The standard deviation for each of the variables is the standard deviation of the residuals that results from the time series regression, but must be adjusted for the fact that confidence bands widen for out-of-sample forecasts. This is illustrated in Exhibit 9.11.

The estimate of volatility derived from historical data becomes less certain as one forecasts further into the future, and consequently, the confidence band widens. For a simple linear regression based on time series data, the 95 percent confidence band widens according to the following formula:

$$\hat{y} \pm t(n-2, .95)\sqrt{\left(\frac{1}{n} + \frac{[x_0 - E(x)]^2}{S(x^2)}\right)s_{ey}^2}$$

This formula is the confidence band for the prediction of a random variable, y, given a level of its predictor, x. Inside the square root is the standard

Exhibit 9.11   Out-of-sample confidence band increases.

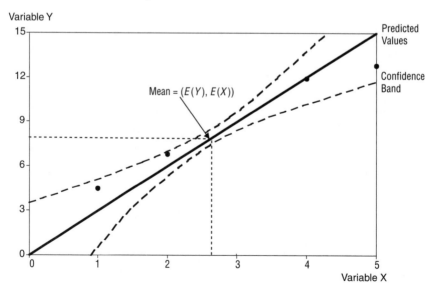

error of variable y, s_{ey}^2, multiplied by a coefficient that is smallest when x is equal to its mean, $E(x)$, and increasing as x moves away from its mean. The number of observations used in the original regression is n, and $S(x^2)$ is the sum of squared deviations of x from its mean. Finally, $t(n-2, .95)$ is the value of the t-statistic with $n-2$ degrees of freedom that provides a 95 percent confidence band (with two tails).

If the independent variable in our regression is time, then the 95 per-cent confidence band roughly follows a $\sigma\sqrt{T}$ rule, increasing with the square root of time outside of the sample period used to fit the regression equation. For example, suppose that we used 20 observations to fit the equation ($n = 20$), then the mean of x is 10 and the first out-of-sample time period is $x = 21$. The value under the square root sign is:

$$\sqrt{\left[\frac{1}{n} + \frac{X - E(x)}{S(x^2)}\right]S_{ey}^2} = \sqrt{\left[\frac{1}{20} + \frac{21-10}{S(x^2)}\right]S_{ey}^2} = S_{ey}\sqrt{\frac{S(x^2) + 20(11)}{20\,S(x^2)}} = S_{ey}\sqrt{\frac{1}{20} + \frac{11}{S(x^2)}}$$

If we go one year farther out with our forecast, the value under the square root sign becomes:

$$= S_{ey}\sqrt{\frac{1}{20} + \frac{12}{S(x^2)}}$$

Therefore, the confidence interval, out-of-sample, increase approximately as $\sigma\sqrt{T}$.*

Subjective Estimates Provided by Management

In many situations, it is impossible to estimate the uncertainties of a proj-ect by using historical data. Often the project is so new that the only cer-tainty is that the future will not be like the past. Therefore, to quantify the uncertainties, we use management estimates. This is usually a challenge,

---

* Although this seems identical to the expression of volatility for geometric Brownian motion, they can differ slightly because geometric Brownian motion is based on the rate of growth in the variable that is being modeled while the regression does not necessarily make this assumption. If it used the growth in x and the growth in y, then the two approaches would be the same.

because the traditional method of project analysis, net present value, does not require estimates of the volatility of a project—only expected free cash flows, and a discount rate that is based on systematic risk (covariance with the market). Most managers and industry experts have subjective, nonformal, nonstatistical estimates of volatility in their heads. The challenge is to develop a well-structured approach that loses none of the information used in net present value analysis, yet frames the request for additional volatility information in a way that is easy and intuitive.

We use an approach for estimating where, in addition to the expected outcome for each random variable, we ask the executives to identify a range of outcomes (specifically, either the upper or lower boundary). Suppose a project under consideration has three sources of uncertainty: price, quantity, and variable cost per unit. For each of them, we would ask the following questions. First, what is the expected value of the uncertain variable at each future point of time (each year) during the expected life of the project. This information has already been provided for the NPV calculations. Second, with 95 percent confidence, what are the highest and the lowest values that the variable could take each year?

Geometric Brownian Motion.   Initially, we will focus on subjective estimates of a single source of uncertainty in isolation. We assume that it has no autocorrelation as a starting point. One of the simplest assumptions is that the uncertainty (e.g., uncertain prices) follows geometric Brownian motion where its value next period, $V_{t+\Delta t}$, is equal to its value this period, V_t, multiplied by a continuous growth factor at rate r for an interval Δt. The growth rate, r, is a normally distributed random variable with constant expected growth ($\bar{r}$) and constant standard deviation σ:

$$V_{t+\Delta t} = V_t e^{r\Delta t}$$

At the end of one period, r lies with 95 percent confidence within the following interval:

$$r \in \left[\bar{r} - 2\sigma, \ \bar{r} + 2\sigma\right]$$

For a period of time $T = n\Delta t$, the total expected growth is normally distributed with mean of $\bar{r}T$ and standard deviation of $\sigma\sqrt{T}$. At the end of T, r, with 95 percent confidence interval, will lie within the following interval:

$$r \in \left[\bar{r}T - 2\sigma\sqrt{T}, \; \bar{r}T + 2\sigma\sqrt{T}\right]$$

The upper and lower values of the 95 percent confidence limit of r will be:

$$upper \; [r] = \bar{r}T + 2\sigma\sqrt{T}$$
$$lower \; [r] = \bar{r}T - 2\sigma\sqrt{T}$$

Because the growth rate determines the level of the random variable at time T, V_t, we have corresponding upper and lower limits for its values.

$$upper \; [V_T] = V_0 e^{\bar{r}T + 2\sigma\sqrt{T}}$$
$$lower \; [V_T] = V_0 e^{\bar{r}T - 2\sigma\sqrt{T}}$$

If the FCF model contains a specific expected path for the uncertainty, this means that there are different expected growth rates for every period–$\bar{r}_i$. For a time period $T = n\Delta t$, the total expected growth will be sum of the annual growth rates r_i with $i = [1, n]$.

$$\bar{R}_T = \sum_{i=1}^{T} \bar{r}_i$$

Correspondingly, the upper and lower 95 percent confidence interval values of the asset itself will be

$$upper \; [V_T] = V_0 e^{\sum \bar{r}_i + 2\sigma\sqrt{T}}$$
$$lower \; [V_T] = V_0 e^{\sum \bar{r}_i - 2\sigma\sqrt{T}}$$

If the uncertainty is expected to follow a steady growth, we replace the sum of the period growths Σr_i with the product of the average growth and the total number of periods $\bar{r}T$.

If the general form of the uncertainty has been determined and the expected trajectory data has been incorporated, then management can be asked a single question: "Your forecast says that at the end of period T the uncertainty (e.g., sales) will have expected value of $E(V_T)$. With 95 percent confidence, what will be the lower 95th percentile value, lower (V_T), and the higher 95th percentile value, higher (V_T)?" If the experts provide the higher or the lower values of V, we can derive the volatility of the rate of growth:

$$\sigma = \frac{\ln\left(\dfrac{V_T^{upper}}{V_0}\right) - \sum_{i=1}^{n} r_i}{2\sqrt{T}}, \quad \sigma = \frac{\sum_{i=1}^{n} r_i - \ln\left(\dfrac{V_T^{lower}}{V_0}\right)}{2\sqrt{T}} \qquad \text{(volatility estimate)}$$

Next, we go back to the Monte Carlo simulation model and for each year define the "growth of sales," r_t, as a normally distributed random variable with standard deviation σ. The value of the uncertain variable for a given year is generated for each simulation by the formula:

$$V_t = V_{t-\Delta t} e^{r_t}$$

Chapter 11 demonstrates, within the context of a case, the process for using management estimates of uncertainty to build a value-based event tree.

A More Complicated Case: Mean-Reverting Procedures. Mean-reversion represents the evolution of many uncertainties. For them, the range within which they stay is constant even as we forecast further into the future. Here the uncertainty fluctuates around a constant level. Typical categories of uncertainties that have mean reversion are commodity prices, and unit or fixed costs.

The general model for mean reversion may be written as:

$$V_t = V_{t-\Delta t} + \alpha\left(\bar{V} - V_{t-\Delta t}\right) + \sigma dz$$

$\overline{V}$ is the average level around which the uncertainty fluctuates, α is the speed with which the uncertainty returns to the average after every deviation. The value of the uncertainty in the previous period is already determined. The random variable in the model is dz, which is normally distributed with expected value of zero and standard deviation of 1. The volatility for each period, σ, is constant.

For a single period (Δt):

$$E\left(V_{t-\Delta t}\right) = \overline{V}$$
$$E\left\{\alpha\left(\overline{V} - V_{t-\Delta t}\right)\right\} = 0$$
$$E\left(\sigma dz\right) = 0$$
$$E\left(V_t\right) = E\left(V_{t-\Delta t}\right) = \overline{V}$$

For multiple periods of time, T, all of the previous parameters remain the same because of mean reversion, but the total volatility is no longer equal to the one-period volatility times the square root of the time, instead:

$$\sigma_T = \sigma_t \sqrt{\sum_{t=2}^{T}\left[(1-\alpha)^{T-t}\right]^2}$$

The formula makes intuitive sense. If the speed of return to the average α is 1, the process returns to the trend value, $\overline{V}$, at every step and volatility remains only in the last period $\sigma_T = \sigma_t$. On the other hand, if α is zero, the mean reversion disappears and the volatility becomes identical to the one from the geometric Brownian process – $\sigma\sqrt{T}$. Consequentially, at the end of period T the uncertainty V_T will lie with 95 percent confidence in the interval:

$$V_T \in \left[\overline{V} - 2\sigma_t\sqrt{\sum_{t=2}^{T}\left[(1-\alpha)^{T-t}\right]^2},\ \overline{V} + 2\sigma_t\sqrt{\sum_{t=2}^{T}\left[(1-\alpha)^{T-t}\right]^2}\right]$$

From the FCF model and other analytical work, we can obtain the average level $\overline{V}$.

What questions do we ask of management? Unlike geometric Brownian motion, here we have to determine two parameters to simulate the uncertainty: the speed of return to the average α, and the volatility per period σ. To get management estimates of α, we can ask the following question: "If the uncertainty tends to return to its average value, what percent of the one-period deviation do you expect to be eliminated on average during the next period?" To obtain the management's estimate of the volatility, we will ask a question similar to the one for the uncertainty without mean reversion: Your forecast states that for each period, the uncertainty will have expected value of $\overline{V}$. In the last period, with a 95 percent confidence what will be the lower (V_T) or the upper (V_T) actual value of the uncertainty?"

Depending on the minimum or the maximum value of V_T, the estimate of volatility can be derived through the following formulas:

$$\sigma_t = \frac{\overline{V} - V_T^{lower}}{2\sqrt{\sum_{t=2}^{T}\left[(1-\alpha)^{T-t}\right]^2}}$$

$$= \frac{V_T^{upper} - \overline{V}}{2\sqrt{\sum_{t=2}^{T}\left[(1-\alpha)^{T-t}\right]^2}}$$

Now we return to the Monte Carlo model and for each year define "standard normal variable —dz, as a normally distributed random variable with mean of zero and standard deviation of one. Then, applying the formula for mean reverting process, we get the value of the uncertainty for each period from its value at the previous period:

$$V_t = V_{t-\Delta t} + \alpha\left(\overline{V} - V_{t-\Delta t}\right) + \sigma dz$$

Having derived the volatility, we build event trees that are value based, then complete our general four-step approach by putting decisions into the tree and using real options methods to solve for the present value of the project with flexibility.

EMPIRICAL VALIDITY OF THE CONSOLIDATED APPROACH

At the project level, it is impossible to observe historical rates of return—in most cases there is no history, anyway. But it is possible, given forecasted spreadsheets, to use the consolidated approach and Monte Carlo analysis to generate an estimate of the volatility of the project. Yet it would be comforting to know that this process produces results that are realistic enough to use in practice. The problem is that project level returns are not observable. Therefore, we tried another approach.

We decided to collect 28 discounted cash flow models of companies, use a Monte Carlo analysis to generate estimates of the variance of returns on their equity, and to compare the result with actual volatility (measured historically and via the implied variance extracted from the prices of options written on the stock—forward-looking estimates).

Exhibit 9.12 lists the 28 companies used in our experiment, their equity market value, the discounted cash flow estimate of their market value, and the percentage error. All valuations were done in August 1999. We then followed these steps. We calculated the annual percentage changes in the growth of revenue, then drew randomly from these observations, which were assumed to have a uniform distribution, entered these random draws into the revenue forecast of our spread sheet, calculated the change in the entity value of the company from the base case, and subtracted the book value (a proxy for market value) of debt to estimate the market value of equity, and calculated the variance of equity returns.

Exhibit 9.13 shows the results. On the vertical axis of the chart is the historical standard deviation of the company's equity and on the horizontal axis is the standard deviation estimated from our Monte Carlo analysis.

The results show an r-squared of 63 percent. This fit is good enough to conclude that, although crude, the simple assumption that the historical variability in revenue growth (omitting other important factors such as the variability of interest rates, and the randomness of variable costs) is sufficient to explain 63 percent of the variability in the total return to shareholders. Obviously, a diligent practitioner can improve this crude approach.

Exhibit 9.12   Sample companies.

Company	Market Capitalization	DCF Value	Percentage Error
Abbott Laboratories	62,184	57,046	9.0
American Home Products	53,409	49,166	8.6
Automatic Data Processing	25,059	19,063	31.5
Bristol Myers Squibb	134,292	134,538	−0.2
Anheuser-Busch	35,705	28,670	25.0
Dow Jones	3,575	3,193	12.0
Deluxe Corporation	2,891	2,914	−0.8
EG&G Corp.	1,533	1,457	5.2
Emerson Electric	26,659	21,445	24.3
Gannett Cos.	19,528	16,830	16.0
General Electric	354,057	318,668	11.1
Heinz (H.J.) Cos.	16,890	15,397	9.7
Hewlett-Packard	106,808	81,752	30.6
IBM Corp.	223,989	181,089	23.7
Johnson & Johnson	129,056	116,612	10.7
Eli Lilly	68,642	70,397	−2.5
Masco Corp.	9,941	9,665	2.9
McGraw-Hill	9,963	8,583	16.1
3M Corp.	38,966	32,951	18.3
Merck	149,081	151,074	−1.4
Maytag	5,623	5,449	3.2
Nalco Chemicals	3,402	2,948	15.4
Pepsico	56,392	43,615	29.3
Pfizer	133,467	130,173	2.5
AT&T	157,387	160,889	−2.2
Waste Management	14,617	14,954	−2.3
Washington Post	4,570	5,172	−11.6
Worthington	1,372	1,367	0.4

CONCLUSION

The consolidated approach for estimating uncertainties is based on the philosophy that regardless of the stochastic properties of the random variables that drive future cash flows, we can rely on Samuelson's proof that properly anticipated prices fluctuate randomly to imply that we can build

Exhibit 9.13 Simulated volatility versus historical volatility.

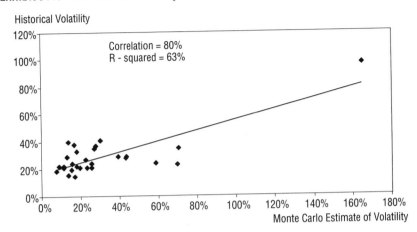

a value-based event tree. We need only to sample the causal uncertainties, estimate their joint effect on value via a Monte Carlo analysis, and estimate the volatility of percentage changes in value. This single consolidated volatility estimate and the present value of the project are then used to produce a value-based event tree that is appropriate for use as the underlying risky asset on which real options depend. This procedure works regardless of whether the causal uncertainties (e.g., price and quantity) exhibit autoregressive behavior, or whether they are cross-correlated with each other. Modern Monte Carlo programs, such as Crystal Ball or At Risk are capable of modeling these important characteristics. One should, however, be attentive to the problem that the confidence band of estimate widens when extended beyond the sample period when it was originally estimated.

We also suggested a procedure for using management estimates of volatility when historical data concerning causal uncertainties is unavailable. Management must supply a confidence band for each causal uncertainty at some future point in time (e.g., 5 years). Then we assume a sigma square root "T" rule to estimate how the confidence band changes over time. In addition, we discussed an approach to use with management when attempting to deal with mean reversion.

Finally, we attempted to test the quality of the Monte Carlo approach by using growth rates in historical sales, chosen randomly from random draws over the past 10 years to simulate future randomness, and got fairly good results. The correlation between our simulated estimates of volatility and actual volatility was 63 percent.

QUESTIONS AND PROBLEMS

For solutions go to www.corpfinonline.com.

1. Use Crystal Ball or another Monte Carlo simulation package and the model from Exhibit 9.3. Run 5,000 simulations to estimate the volatility of the project's value under each of the following conditions:

   —In addition to price, make the quantity also uncertain. For each year assume a normal distribution, calculate and insert a 10 percent standard deviation.

   —In addition to price, make the quantity also uncertain. For each year assume a log-normal distribution and insert a constant absolute standard deviation of 30.

   —To the conditions above add 25 percent autocorrelation across all periods for the quantity. Does the volatility of the project increase or decrease and why?

   —In addition to price, make the quantity also uncertain. For each year assume a normal distribution, calculate and insert a 10 percent standard deviation. Also insert a 25 percent positive correlation between quantity and price. How does the project volatility change and why?

2. What assumptions about the nature of changes in the value of the project are embedded in the use of the geometric Brownian process?

3. Price is an uncertainty for a project. It is assumed to follow a geometric Brownian motion with an expected growth of 5 percent per year and a constant volatility. Current price is $37 and with 95 percent confidence we expect that it can get as high as $70 in five years. What is its annual volatility year by year for each of the 5 years?

4. Sales quantity is an uncertainty for a project. It is assumed to follow geometric Brownian motion with first year growth of 15 percent and a constant volatility. The growth rate is expected to decrease by

one percent per year. Current sales are 100,000 and with 95 percent confidence we expect that in five years they can be at least the same. What is sales' annual volatility year by year for each of the 5 years?

5. Use Crystal Ball or another Monte Carlo simulation package and the model from Exhibit 9.3. Run 5,000 simulations to estimate the volatility of the project value under each of the following conditions:

—Price is an uncertainty that follows a geometric Brownian process with a constant volatility. With 95 percent confidence, its highest level at year seven is $14.

—Quantity is an uncertainty that follows a geometric Brownian process with a constant volatility. With 95 percent confidence, its lowest level at year seven is 70.

—Both quantity and price are uncertainties for the project with the above parameters.

REFERENCES

Bhattacharya, S. 1978. "Project Valuation with Mean-Reverting Cash Flow Streams," *Journal of Finance, 33,* 5, 1317–1331.

Bjerksund, P., and S. Ekern. 1995. "Contingent Claims Evaluation of Mean-Reverting Cash Flows in Shipping." In *Real Options in Capital Investments,* ed. L. Trigeorgis. Praeger.

Boyle, P. 1977, May. "Options: A Monte Carlo Approach," *Journal of Financial Economics, 323–338.*

Clewlow, L., and C. Strickland. 1998. *Implementing Derivatives Models.* New York: John Wiley & Sons.

Guttman, I., S. Wilkes, and J.S. Hunter, 1982. *Introductory Engineering Statistics,* 3rd edition. New York: John Wiley & Sons.

Johnston, J. 1972. *Econometric Methods,* 2nd edition. New York: McGraw Hill.

Vijverberg, W. 1997. "Monte Carlo Evaluation of Multivariate Normal Probabilities," *Journal of Econometrics, 76,* 281–307.

10 | Keeping Uncertainties Separate

In the previous chapter we learned how to model the parameters of different uncertainties and to estimate their effect on the volatility of the project's value, essentially consolidating them. Once this was done, we let the value follow a geometric Brownian process. We used it to generate a binomial event tree capable of using smaller time periods to increase the precision of the calculations. The assumption behind this methodology is that the integrated uncertainty regarding the project gets resolved continuously over time. This assumption reflects the reality for the evolution of the market value of whole companies. It is also a good assumption for single projects. However, for many projects the major uncertainties are related to technology, changes in regulation, competitor's moves, and so forth. Most of those uncertainties do not get resolved smoothly over time as in a Brownian motion process. They are resolved when the information becomes available. The actual event tree for the project may be asymmetric with changes in value occurring when a significant part of the uncertainty is resolved at certain points of time. An example is the uncertainty about an FDA approval of a new drug. When the result is announced the value of the project moves dramatically; up if the drug was approved or all the way to zero if approval was denied. As a result we can't simply estimate the volatility of the project and use it in a standard binomial model to generate the event tree. We need to build an event tree that reflects the actual resolution of the uncertainty over time so that we can get optimal execution of the available real options and correct ROA valuation. The way to do this is to keep the major uncertainties separate and to model their interaction and effect on the project's value explicitly.

In many situations the uncertainty does not get resolved by itself. Separate effort and investment are required to learn more about the conditions of the project and reduce the uncertainty. If the management has the flexibility to make this investment, it holds an option called a learning option. The decisions to invest more in geological research and find the precise amount of the ore deposits, or to invest in market testing to narrow the expected sales are both examples of learning options.

LEARNING OPTIONS—UNCORRELATED UNCERTAINTIES

This section introduces real options that are multiphased and that have two sources of uncertainty—product/market and technological. The first is based on prices that are known today and become more diffuse through time. We will assume that product/market uncertainty follows a Gauss Wiener process, thereby implying no time dependencies. Technological uncertainty is assumed to be independent of market conditions (and of time dependencies) and to be diffuse now, but reduced through time by doing research. The case example is developed in two stages. First is a compound option with only technological uncertainty. Thereafter, the solution is developed for a compound rainbow option. Product/market uncertainty is assumed to be correlated with the market and increases through time, while technological uncertainty is uncorrelated with the market and decreases through time.

Compound Option with Technological Uncertainty

The Pharma Company is considering investment in a research and development project that has a basic research phase that costs $3 million and, based on experience, has only a 20 percent chance of succeeding into the development phase. This second phase costs $60 million and has only a 15 percent chance of realizing a great product whose present value will be $600 million. It also has a 25 percent chance of developing a mediocre product with a $40 million present value. But there is a 60 percent chance of having no marketable product. To go to market, a final investment of $40 million is required to build a factory. The level perpetual cash flows start at the end of the plant construction phase (year 3) and are discounted at the weighted average cost of capital (10 percent). The risk-free rate is 5 percent. This will be the correct rate for calculating the cash flows because, given their independence of the market, their Capital Asset Pricing Model beta is zero.

The net present value model requires that we precommit either to not doing the project at all or to investing in all phases. If we make the restrictive assumption that we surrender all flexibility, the net present value of the project becomes

$$NPV = -3 + .2 \left[\frac{.15\left[\left(\frac{600}{1.05}\right)-40\right]+.25\left[\left(\frac{40}{1.05}\right)-40\right]+.60(-40)}{1.05} - 60 \right] \div (1.05)$$

$$+ .8\left[\frac{0}{1.05}-60\right] \div 1.05$$

$$= -3 + .2\left[\frac{55.23}{1.05}-60\right] \div (1.05) + .8(-60) \div (1.05)$$

$$= -3 - 1.48 - 46.86 = -51.33$$

However, if we work the tree backward, and take advantage of the fact that we have the option to invest $60 million at the end of the first time period and $40 million at the end of the second time period, we can avoid these investments if the results of the basic research or the development phase are unfavorable. This is illustrated in Exhibit 10.1.

If we have completed the research and the development phases successfully, we must decide whether to invest $40 million in a manufacturing plant. This is a good investment only if the product turns out to be great, otherwise we abandon. If we have arrived at node B with favorable results from the basic research phase, the net present value of going ahead is

$$NPV (at\ node\ B) = -60 + \left\{ \frac{.15\left[\left(\frac{600}{1.05}\right)-40\right]+.25(0)+.60(0)}{1.05} \right\}$$

$$= -60 + 75.92 = 15.92$$

Exhibit 10.1   Three-phase R&D project as a compound option.

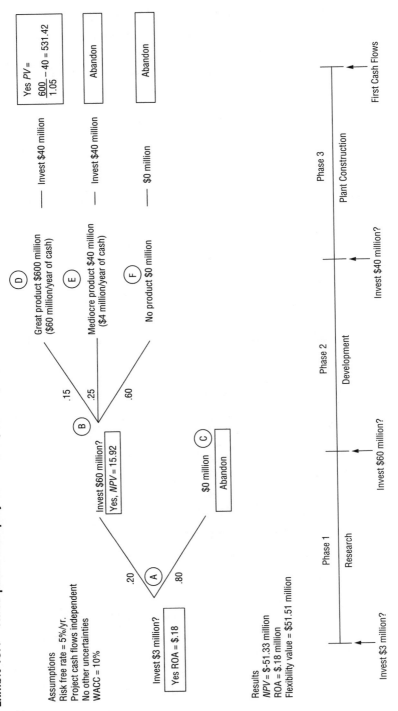

Assumptions
Risk free rate = 5%/yr.
Project cash flows independent
No other uncertainties
WACC = 10%

Invest $3 million?
Yes ROA = $.18

.20

Ⓐ

.80

$0 million Ⓒ
Abandon

Invest $60 million?
Yes, NPV = 15.92

Ⓑ

.15

.25

.60

Ⓓ Great product $600 million
($60 million/year of cash)

Ⓔ Mediocre product $40 million
($4 million/year of cash)

Ⓕ No product $0 million

— Invest $40 million

Yes PV =
$\frac{600}{1.05} - 40 = 531.42$

— Invest $40 million

Abandon

— $0 million

Abandon

Results
NPV = $-51.33 million
ROA = $.18 million
Flexibility value = $51.51 million

Phase 1
Research
Invest $3 million?

Phase 2
Development
Invest $60 million?

Phase 3
Plant Construction
Invest $40 million?

First Cash Flows

Therefore, we would proceed. However, if we arrive at the node C with unfavorable results from the first phase, we will decide not to exercise our option to invest the $60 million.

Moving back to node A, we find that the present value of the project, based on optimal decisions at node B, is

$$NPV(at\ node\ A) = -3 + \left[.2\left(\frac{15.92}{1.05}\right) + .8(0)\right] = -3 + 3.18 = .18$$

Therefore, we would proceed, given flexibility. The value of flexibility in this case is

$$
\begin{aligned}
NPV\ (with\ flexibility) &= \$.18 \\
-NPV\ (given\ precommitment) &= -(-\$51.33) \\
\hline
Value\ of\ flexibility &= \$51.51
\end{aligned}
$$

Compound Rainbow Option with Two Uncorrelated Uncertainties

Next, we complicate the problem by introducing product/market uncertainty which is correlated with the market, implying that the cash flows cannot be discounted at the risk-free rate. Although the company's marketing department believes that a great product will be worth $600 million and a mediocre one worth $40 million, they know that these estimates are affected by product/market uncertainty. In particular, they expect to spend an additional $40 million on a new factory that will produce finished products. If the product is great, perpetual cash flows will be $60 million annually (thus providing a present value of $600 million), and if it is mediocre, perpetual cash flows will be $4 million annually. These estimates, which are made today, may fluctuate up or down by 20 percent in a year.

Exhibit 10.2 shows the event trees separately for each of the two types of uncertainty. On the left-hand side is technological uncertainty. The research phase is expected to end with success 20 percent of the time and failure 80 percent. Given success in the research phase, there is a 15 percent probability that the development phase will produce a great product

Exhibit 10.2 Event tree for technological and product/market uncertainty.

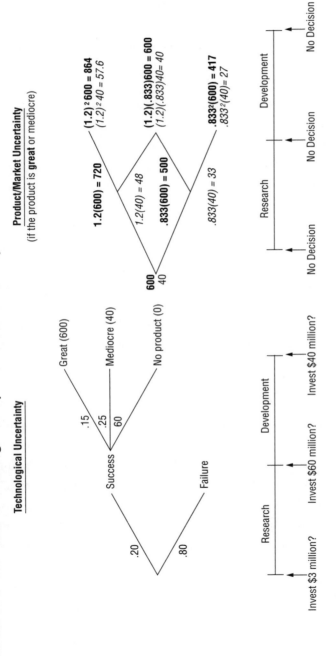

worth $600 million, a 25 percent chance that the result will be a mediocre product worth $40 million, and a 60 percent chance that no product will result. Because technological uncertainty is independent of the market, we can discount the expected values at the risk-free rate.

The second uncertainty is product/market uncertainty. The expected value can go up or down by 20 percent each year. This is illustrated in the event tree on the right-hand side of Exhibit 10.2. Note that the outcomes are contingent on whether the project turns out to be great or mediocre. We will need to value the uncertain outcomes that are resolved from product/market uncertainty by using a replicating portfolio approach because product/market uncertainty is correlated with the market (even though it is independent of technological uncertainty). If the product turns out to be great, and if the changes in the value of the product have been positive for two consecutive years, then the value of the product will be $864 million (see Exhibit 10.2). If it is mediocre, its value under the same conditions will be $57.6 million.

The project (with flexibility) is valued in Exhibit 10.3. With minimum loss of accuracy, we model the uncertainty by alternating product/market uncertainty with technological uncertainty. A more precise solution methodology called the quadranomial approach is covered later in the chapter.

The final technological uncertainty is resolved at nodes A, B, C, and D at the end of the second year. At this point in time, the decision maker must decide either to invest another $40 million to go into production, or to abandon the project. The net present value of the project at each of these nodes can take advantage of the fact that technological uncertainty is independent of the market. Therefore, the net present value is the expected value discounted at half of a year's risk-free rate, less the cost of investment (the exercise price on the real option). For example, the computation of the NPV at node D is based on the resolution of product/market uncertainty. At node D, bad news in the product/market has driven the value of the project down twice so that if the development phase proves to be a technological success (a great product), its value will be $417 million, and $27.78 million if it is mediocre. This knowledge affects the investment decision. We would invest $40 million only if the

Exhibit 10.3 R&D project as a compound rainbow option (uncorrelated uncertainties).

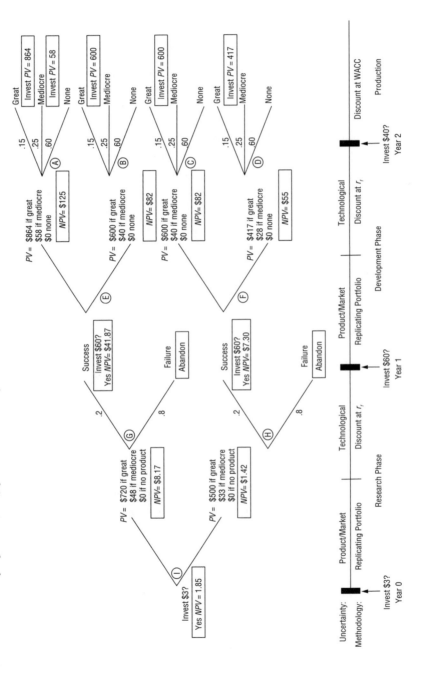

technological result is a great project. The net present value at node D is therefore calculated by discounting the expected cash flows, given the optimal investment decision, at the risk-free rate:[1]

$$NPV\,(at\ node\ D) = \frac{.15(417-40)+.25(0)+.60(0)}{1.025} = 55.17$$

Similar logic produces the NPV results at nodes A, B, and C.

Working our way back through the tree, we next focus on nodes E and F. Because product/market uncertainty is correlated with the market, we cannot simply discount expected cash flows at the risk-free rate. We must use a replicating portfolio approach. Choosing node F to illustrate, the end-of-period payoffs are $82 million in the up state, and $55 million in the down state. The beginning-of-period value of the underlying is simply the expected technological outcome from the research phase, (i.e., .15($500) + .25($33) = $83.25. The end-of-period value of the underlying in the up state, uV, is the expected outcome given an up movement in product/markets:

$$uV = .15(\$600) + .25(\$40) + .60(\$0) = \$100$$

and the end-of-period value of the underlying in the down state, dV, is

$$dV = .15(\$417) + .25(\$28) + .60(0) = \$69.55$$

Using these facts, we can form replicating portfolios for the up and down states as follows (remember that the risk-free rate is 1.025 for 6 months):

$$muV + (1+r_f)B = 82$$
$$mdV + (1+r_f)B = 55$$
$$m = .887,\ B = -6.54$$
$$Value = mV - B = .887(\$83.25) - \$6.54 = \$67.30$$

Given that the value of the project at node F is $67.30 million, we would decide to invest $60 million and proceed with the development phase.

By repeating the procedure of discounting expected values due to technological uncertainty at the risk-free rate, then alternating to use the replicating portfolio approach, we work our way back through the tree to find that the estimated net present value is $1.85 million, after spending $3 million to start the research phase.

This approach is somewhat crude, although straightforward and simple. In the next section, we introduce the quadranomial approach. It allows the uncertainties to be resolved simultaneously.

LEARNING OPTIONS—THE QUADRANOMIAL APPROACH

We provide two examples of the quadranomial approach. Th first one is similar to the previous Pharma research and development example. Product/market uncertainty is assumed to be correlated with the economy while technological uncertainty is independent of it. Later on, we give an example where both sources of uncertainty are correlated with the economy. First, however, we develop the theory of the quadranomial approach.

Introduction to the Quadranomial Approach

The quadranomial approach is a two-variable binomial tree. Consider the case of an option with payoffs based on the value of an asset driven by two sources of uncertainty. Each uncertainty is assumed to follow a Gauss-Wiener process and they may be correlated. Exhibit 10.4 illustrates the four outcomes that are possible at the end of one period, assuming that the starting value for the risky asset is V_0 and that its multiplicative up and down movements are u_1 and d_1 when driven by the first source of uncertainty and u_2 and d_2 when driven by the second source of uncertainty.

The quadranomial event tree has four branches at every node, and is a straightforward generalization of the binomial event tree that has two branches at every node. To develop the tree, we need to have estimates of the annual standard deviations of the percent changes in the value of the asset when driven by each uncertainty, σ_1 and σ_2, as well as the correlation between them, $\rho_{1,2}$. This information is equivalent to knowing the

Exhibit 10.4   Quadranomial values of the underlying and a call option after one period.

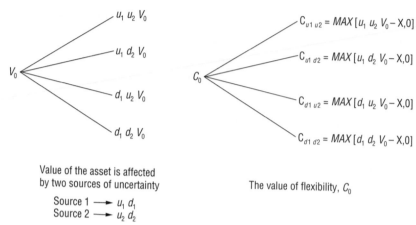

Value of the asset is affected
by two sources of uncertainty

Source 1 ⟶ $u_1\ d_1$
Source 2 ⟶ $u_2\ d_2$

The value of flexibility, C_0

joint distribution of up and down movements generated by the two uncertainties. We also need to know the exercise prices. These might be expenditures on phases of experimentation or on market development. For now, we will assume that there is only one exercise price—expenditures on experimentation.

Although we might try to use the replicating portfolio approach to solve the quadranomial, we end up with the following four equations, but only two unknowns, m and B.

$$mu_1u_2V_0 + (1 + r_f)B = C_{u1u2}$$
$$mu_1d_2V_0 + (1 + r_f)B = C_{u1d2}$$
$$md_1u_2V_0 + (1 + r_f)B = C_{d1u2}$$
$$md_1d_2V_0 + (1 + r_f)B = C_{d1d2}$$

Therefore, we proceed by solving for the risk-neutral probabilities for each branch of the quadranomial and using them in the following valuation formula:

$$C_0 = \frac{p_{u1u2}C_{u1u2} + p_{u1d2}C_{u1d2} + p_{d1u2}C_{d1u2} + p_{d1d2}C_{d1d2}}{(1 + r_f)}$$

[10.1]

If the two uncertainties are independent of each other, then the risk-neutral probability of each branch of the quadranomial is equal to the product of the risk-neutral probabilities for that branch based on each separate source of uncertainty. This fact produces four equations:

$$p_{u1u2} = p_{u1}p_{u2}$$
$$p_{u1d2} = p_{u1}p_{d2}$$
$$p_{d1u2} = p_{d1}p_{u2}$$
$$p_{d1d2} = p_{d1}p_{d2}$$

[10.2]

These risk-neutral probabilities can then be used in the above equation to value the option. Combining independent uncertainties is conceptually clear but computationally complex. By identifying all of their value combinations for a given node and the corresponding risk-neutral probabilities, we are able to properly discount the future payoffs to value the option.

The Quadranomial Approach with Correlated Uncertainties

To begin our discussion we introduce the subject of unconditional versus conditional probabilities. Assume that we have two uncertainties X and Y, and next period X can take only one of two values

$$X_t \, \varepsilon \, [X_u, X_d]$$

with probabilities p_{uX} and $(1 - p_{uX})$ respectively, and Y can take only one of two values

$$Y_t \, \varepsilon \, [Y_u, Y_d]$$

with probabilities p_{uY} and $(1 - p_{uY})$ respectively. If the two uncertainties are independent, the probability for Y going up doesn't change if we know that X has moved up. In this case the conditional probabilities for X and Y are equal to their respective unconditional probabilities.

$$p(Y_u \mid X_u) = p_{uY}$$
$$p(X_u \mid Y_u) = p_{uX}$$

As described above, given independence we can find the probability for each of the four possible combinations of $[X_u, X_d]$ and $[Y_u, Y_d]$ by simply multiplying their respective probabilities. However, when the two uncertainties are correlated, their conditional probabilities are no longer equal to their unconditional probabilities. The relationship between conditional and unconditional probabilities is provided by the Bayesian equation:

$$p\left(Y_u \mid X_u\right) = \frac{p(Y_u \cap X_u)}{p(X_u)} = \frac{p(Y_u)p\left(X_u \mid Y_u\right)}{p(X_u)} \qquad (Bayes\ Law)$$

The $p(Y_u \cap X_u)$ or p_{u1u2} represents the joint probability of X and Y moving up and corresponds to the upper most branch of the quadranomial tree. Thus, Bayes law helps to explain correlated uncertainties (see p. 294).

What follows is fairly complex. It involves a subtle point in stochastic processes: While the value of an asset follows geometric Brownian motion, the rate of return on the same asset follows arithmetic Brownian motion. For example, the price of a stock never goes negative and its movement through time can be modeled as a geometric Brownian motion process (essentially lognormal). Its rate of return, however, can have negative values and can be modeled as an arithmetic Brownian motion process. We will use this fact to model the arithmetic Brownian motion process as a quadranomial. Since the up and down movements are additive and symmetric, the quadranomial tree will be recombining.

The changes in the *value* of an asset follow a geometric Brownian motion process:

$$dV = \mu V dt + \sigma V dz \qquad [10.3]$$

One of the fundamental results in option theory is Ito's lemma, which allows us to model the changes in the value of any security (e.g., an option) contingent on another (e.g., the underlying risky asset) over a short period of time. If the contingent claim, C, is a function of only time, t, and the value of the underlying risky asset, V, it can be written as

$$dC = \left(\frac{\partial C}{\partial V} \mu V + \frac{\partial C}{\partial t} + \frac{1}{2} \frac{\partial^2 C}{\partial V^2} \sigma^2 V^2 \right) dt + \frac{\partial C}{\partial V} \sigma V dz \qquad [10.4]$$

Next, if the option is $C = \ln(S)$, then

$$\frac{\partial C}{\partial V} = \frac{1}{S}$$

$$\frac{\partial^2 C}{\partial V^2} = -\frac{1}{S^2} \qquad [10.5]$$

$$\frac{\partial C}{\partial t} = 0$$

Substituting these relationships into Ito's lemma, we obtain an expression of arithmetic Brownian motion:

$$dC = \left(\mu + \frac{\sigma^2}{2} \right) dt + \sigma dz \qquad [10.6]$$

This expression is the change in the value of the contingent claim (the option) and represents the growth rate or percent change in the value of the underlying since $\partial C = \partial V / V$. Thus the growth in the $\ln(V)$ is normally distributed with a mean of $(\mu + \sigma^2/2)$ and with a standard deviation of $\sigma\sqrt{t}$.

Now let us return to our problem, which has two underlying sources of uncertainty, each following geometric Brownian motion. We can model the problem using either of two approaches. In the first, we can represent the changes in their asset value as an expected growth rate. This expected growth rate will be affected by each of the two uncertainties. A rough analogy is the speed and direction of a yacht in Boston Harbor that is driven by the wind, which is blowing in a northeasterly direction at 30 knots plus or minus 10 knots, and by the current, which is moving in a northwesterly direction at 10 knots plus or minus 5 knots. The speed of the yacht, analogous to the value of the asset, will not be equal to the speed of the wind and current. Nor will the uncertainty about the speed be the same as the combination of the uncertainties of the wind and current. If we choose to model the value of the risky asset, we need to estimate its growth rate and uncertainty conditional on each of the two causal uncertainties (and their correlation). This is a difficult task; therefore we choose a second approach.

The more practical approach is to start with each of the causal uncertainties. We can usually observe their history or estimate them, their correlation and their growth rates. In our yacht example, they were the speed and direction of the wind and current. Without mixing metaphors, let's change back to a finance example.[2] Suppose that the two sources of uncertainty are the price per unit and the quantity of units of a new product that is being developed. Let the expected growth rate in prices be g_1 and the growth in quantity be g_2. Their respective standard deviations are σ_1 and σ_2. In a risk-neutral world, their growth rates will equal the risk-free rate, therefore we can write the equations for their growth as follows. For price, P, and quantity, Q, we have

$$d\ln(P) = \left(r_f + \frac{\sigma_1^2}{2}\right)dt + \sigma_1 dz \qquad [10.7]$$

$$g_1 = \left(r_f + \frac{\sigma_1^2}{2}\right)dt \qquad [10.8]$$

and for quantity

$$d\ln(Q) = \left(r_f + \frac{\sigma_2^2}{2}\right)dt + \sigma_2 dz \qquad [10.9]$$

$$g_2 = \left(r_f + \frac{\sigma_2^2}{2}\right)dt \qquad [10.10]$$

The growth rates will follow arithmetic Brownian motion with constant up and down changes of opposite sign (i.e., $u = -d$). The combination of their possible values is shown in Exhibit 10.5. If these two variables were independent, we would solve for the risk-neutral probabilities and for the

Exhibit 10.5 **Quadranomial combinations of price and quantity.**

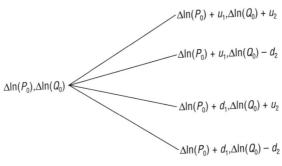

up and down movements by using a system of six equations and six unknowns. The first pair (equations 10.11 and 10.13) models expected growth, the second pair (equations 10.12 and 10.14) models the variance of growth, and a fifth (equation 10.16) is simply the requirement that the probabilities add to one. This brings our count up to a total of five equations. A sixth (equation 10.15) comes from the definition of covariance. Thus, we have six equations and six unknowns, p_{u1u2}, p_{u1d2}, p_{d1u2}, p_{d1d2}, u_1, and u_2. The six equations are

$$E(g_1)\Delta t = \left(r_f + \frac{\sigma_1^2}{2}\right)\Delta t = (p_{u1u2} + p_{u1d2})u_1 - (p_{d1u2} + p_{d1d2})u_1 \qquad [10.11]$$

$$\sigma_1^2 \Delta t = (p_{u1u2} + p_{u1d2})u_1^2 - (p_{d1u2} + p_{d1d2})u_1^2 \qquad [10.12]$$

$$E(g_2)\Delta t = \left(r_f + \frac{\sigma_2^2}{2}\right)\Delta t = (p_{u1u2} + p_{d1u2})u_2 - (p_{u1d2} + p_{d1d2})u_2 \qquad [10.13]$$

$$\sigma_2^2 \Delta t = (p_{u1u2} + p_{d1u2})u_2^2 - (p_{u1d2} + p_{d1d2})u_2^2 \qquad [10.14]$$

$$\rho_{12}\sigma_1\sigma_2 \Delta t = (p_{u1u2} - p_{d1u2} - p_{u1d2} - p_{d1d2})u_1u_2 \qquad [10.15]$$

$$p_{u1u2} + p_{d1u2} + p_{u1d2} + p_{d1d2} = 1 \qquad [10.16]$$

Solving for the system, we obtain the risk-neutral probability for each of the possible states:

$$P_{ulu2} = \frac{u_1u_2 + u_2g_1\Delta t + u_1g_2\Delta t + \rho_{12}\sigma_1\sigma_2\Delta t}{4u_1u_2} \qquad [10.17]$$

$$P_{uld2} = \frac{u_1u_2 + u_2g_1\Delta t + d_1g_2\Delta t - \rho_{12}\sigma_1\sigma_2\Delta t}{4u_1u_2} \qquad [10.18]$$

$$P_{d1u2} = \frac{u_1u_2 + d_2g_1\Delta t + u_1g_2\Delta t - \rho_{12}\sigma_1\sigma_2\Delta t}{4u_1u_2} \qquad [10.19]$$

$$P_{d1d2} = \frac{u_1u_2 + d_2g_1\Delta t + d_1g_2\Delta t + \rho_{12}\sigma_1\sigma_2\Delta t}{4u_1u_2} \qquad [10.20]$$

The other two unknowns that result from the system of equations are the up and down movements:

$$u_1 = \sigma_1\sqrt{t} \qquad [10.21]$$

$$u_2 = \sigma_2\sqrt{t} \qquad [10.22]$$

Examples Using the Quadranomial Approach

To illustrate the quadranomial approach, we use a simple example of a rainbow option. We are considering a product development project. There are two sources of uncertainty, price and quantity. The two-period project lasts 6 months and provides cash flow of $P \times Q$ in revenues less $4,000 of fixed cash cost. At the end of the second period, the cash flows become a constant perpetuity with a multiple of six. The project can be sold to a competitor (i.e., abandoned) for $50,000 at any time. Finally, the continuously compounded annual risk-free rate is 5 percent.

Exhibit 10.6 shows the two-period event tree for quantity, which is currently expected to be 1,000 units per period but its volatility is believed to be 20 percent per year. Note that the *level* of quantity is a geometric process, thus $u = 1/d = 1.105$. If the annual volatility is 20 percent, the volatility per period, given four periods per year is

$$\sigma \text{ per quarter} = \text{annual } \sigma\sqrt{.25} = .20(.5) = .10$$

Exhibit 10.6 Sales quantity.

Initial quantity $Q_0 = 1,000$

Annual volatility $= 20.0\%$

Number of periods $= 2$

Periods per year $= 4$

Volatility per period $= 10.0\% = \sigma\sqrt{T} = .2\sqrt{.25} = .10$

Up move per period $(u) = 1.1051709 = u$

Down move per period $(d) = 0.9048374 = 1/u$

Risk-free rate per period $= 1.25\%$

Risk-neutral (up) probability $= 0.5378084 = \dfrac{1 + r_f - d}{u - d} = \dfrac{1 + .0125 - .9048}{1.107 - .9048} = p$

Risk-neutral (down) probability $= 0.4621916 = 1 - p$

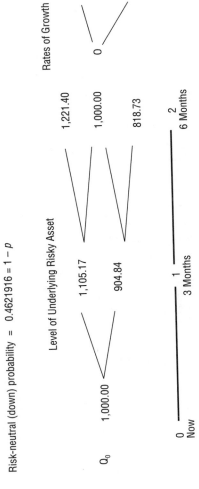

Finally, the risk-neutral probability of an upward movement, p, is

$$Q_0 = \frac{puQ_0 + (1-p)dQ_0}{1+r_f}$$

$$p = \frac{1+r_f - d}{u-d} = \frac{1+0.125 - .9048}{1.10517 - .9048} = .5378$$

Next, Exhibit 10.7 provides the two-period event tree for the price level, which is currently expected to be $10, but its annual volatility is believed to be 12 percent. The corresponding risk-neutral probabilities are also shown in Exhibit 10.7.

The next two exhibits show the price and quantity combinations (Exhibit 10.8), and the cash flows (Exhibit 10.9). The present value of the project, and the associated event tree are given in Exhibit 10.10. When

Exhibit 10.7   Price event tree.

Parameters

Initial value (P_0)	10
Annual volatility	12.0%
Periods per year	4
Volatility per period	6%
Up move per period (u)	$u = 1.0618365$
Down move per period (d)	$d = 1/u = 0.9417645$
Risk-free rate per period	$r_f = 1.25\%$
Risk-neutral (up) probability	$p = 0.5897621 = \dfrac{1+r_f - d}{u-d}$
Risk-neutral (down) probability	$1 - p = 0.4102379$

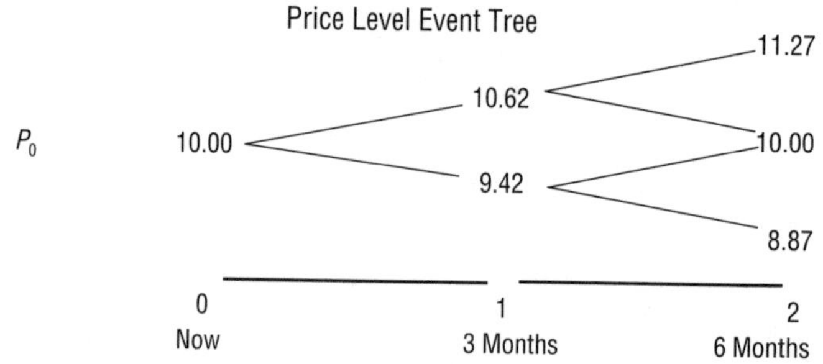

Price Level Event Tree

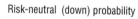

```
                                                    11.27
                                        10.62
          P_0        10.00                          10.00
                                        9.42
                                                    8.87

                      0                   1           2
                     Now             3 Months    6 Months
```

Exhibit 10.8   Event tree of quantity and price.

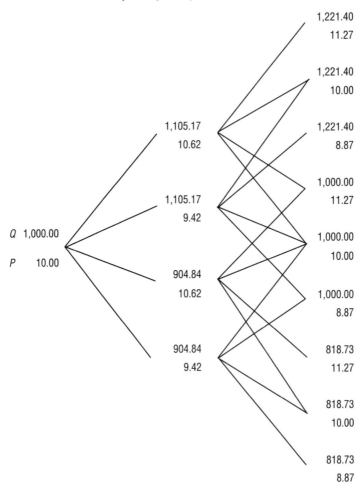

the two uncertainties, price and quantity, are not correlated, the risk-neutral probabilities are calculated using the set of four equations labeled 10.2. We obtain the present value of the project by multiplying the cash flows by the risk-neutral probabilities at each node and by dividing the result by the risk-free rate. For example, at node B we have:

$$PV_B = \frac{.32(68,398.9) + .22(57,498.2) + .27(50,924.8) + .19(42,000.0)}{1.0125} = 63,262$$

Exhibit 10.9 Event tree free cash flow and terminal value.

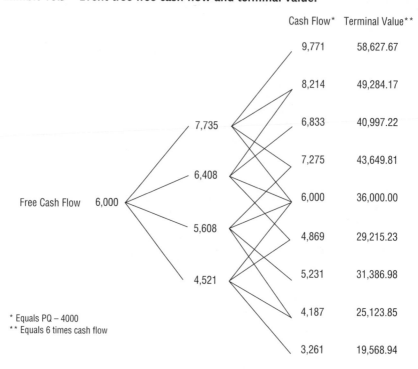

Using this event tree as the underlying risky asset on which the option is written, we turn it into a decision tree as illustrated in Exhibit 10.11. Now the payoffs reflect the abandonment put option to sell at $50,000. As before, we value the payoffs that reflect the optimal decision at each node by weighting them by their risk-neutral probabilities and discounting at the risk-free rate. Comparing the results of Exhibit 10.10, the present value of the project without flexibility, with Exhibit 10.11, the project value with flexibility, we see that the difference is $63,926 − $56,639 = $7,287. This difference is the value of flexibility in a case where the two uncertainties are uncorrelated.

Next, we assume that the two uncertainties are correlated, having a positive 30 percent correlation coefficient ($\rho_{12} = .3$). Note that the cash flows (given in Exhibit 10.9) have not changed from the case where they were assumed to be independent, however, the risk-neutral probabilities have changed. Here we have to solve the system of six equations

Exhibit 10.10   Present value when uncertainties are not correlated.

Risk-Neutral Probabilities   Present Value Tree

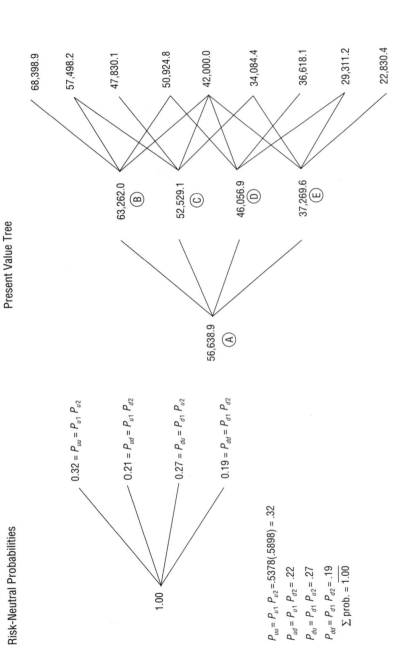

$P_{uu} = P_{u1}\ P_{u2} = .5378(.5898) = .32$
$P_{ud} = P_{u1}\ P_{d2} = .22$
$P_{du} = P_{d1}\ P_{u2} = .27$
$P_{dd} = P_{d1}\ P_{d2} = .19$
Σ prob. $= 1.00$

Exhibit 10.11   ROA valuation without correlated uncertainties.

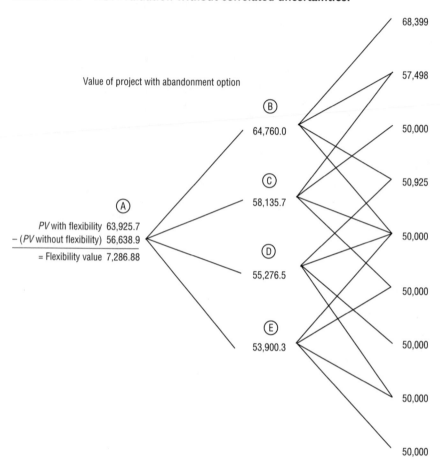

(10.11–10.16). Using equations (10.21–10.22) we calculate u_1 and u_2 which correspond to the period volatilities for the two uncertainties:

$$u_1 = \sigma_1\sqrt{t} = 0.2\sqrt{0.25} = 0.1$$
$$d_1 = -u_1 = -0.1$$
$$u_2 = \sigma_2\sqrt{t} = 0.12\sqrt{0.25} = 0.06$$
$$d_2 = -u_2 = -0.06$$

Now, using equations 10.8 and 10.10, we calculate the expected growth of the natural logs of price and quantity in the risk neutral world:

$$g_1 = \left(r_f + \frac{\sigma_1^2}{2}\right)dt = \left(0.05 + \frac{0.2^2}{2}\right) \times 0.25 = 0.0075$$

$$g_2 = \left(r_f + \frac{\sigma_2^2}{2}\right)dt = \left(0.05 + \frac{0.12^2}{2}\right) \times 0.25 = 0.0107$$

Finally, we find the values of the four probabilities from equations (10.17–10.20):

$$p_{u1u2} = \frac{0.1 \times 0.06 + 0.06 \times 0.0075 + 0.1 \times 0.0107 + 0.3 \times 0.2 \times 0.12 \times 0.25}{4 \times 0.1 \times 0.06} = 0.39$$

$$p_{u1d2} = \frac{0.1 \times 0.06 + 0.06 \times 0.0075 - 0.1 \times 0.0107 - 0.3 \times 0.2 \times 0.12 \times 0.25}{4 \times 0.1 \times 0.06} = 0.15$$

$$p_{d1u2} = \frac{0.1 \times 0.06 - 0.06 \times 0.0075 + 0.1 \times 0.0107 - 0.3 \times 0.2 \times 0.12 \times 0.25}{4 \times 0.1 \times 0.06} = 0.20$$

$$p_{d1d2} = \frac{0.1 \times 0.06 - 0.06 \times 0.0075 - 0.1 \times 0.0107 + 0.3 \times 0.2 \times 0.12 \times 0.25}{4 \times 0.1 \times 0.06} = 0.26$$

Note that if the correlation is zero, the formulas above produce probability identical with the ones where the price and the quantity are independent.

$$p_{u1u2} = \frac{0.1 \times 0.06 + 0.06 \times 0.0075 + 0.1 \times 0.0107}{4 \times 0.1 \times 0.06} = 0.32$$

$$p_{u1d2} = \frac{0.1 \times 0.06 + 0.06 \times 0.0075 - 0.1 \times 0.0107}{4 \times 0.1 \times 0.06} = 0.22$$

$$p_{d1u2} = \frac{0.1 \times 0.06 - 0.06 \times 0.0075 + 0.1 \times 0.0107}{4 \times 0.1 \times 0.06} = 0.27$$

$$p_{d1d2} = \frac{0.1 \times 0.06 - 0.06 \times 0.0075 - 0.1 \times 0.0107}{4 \times 0.1 \times 0.06} = 0.19$$

Using the quadranomial probabilities with correlation and Bayes' Law, we can derive the conditional binomial probabilities for the two uncertainties. For example, the conditional probabilities for the quantity going up given that the price is up or down are:

$$p\left(Q_u \mid P_u\right) = \frac{p(Q_u \cap P_u)}{p(P_u)} = \frac{0.39}{0.59} = 0.66$$

$$p\left(Q_u \mid P_d\right) = \frac{p(Q_u \cap P_d)}{p(Q_d)} = \frac{0.15}{0.41} = 0.36$$

We can see that with 30 percent correlation, the quantity is almost twice as likely to move up when the price moves up. With no correlation the probability of the quantity increasing is constant.

$$p\left(Q_u \mid P_u\right) = \frac{p(Q_u \cap P_u)}{p(P_u)} = \frac{0.32}{0.59} = 0.54$$

$$p\left(Q_u \mid P_d\right) = \frac{p(Q_u \cap P_d)}{p(Q_d)} = \frac{0.22}{0.41} = 0.54$$

Positive correlation has resulted in greater probability on the extreme values and as a result an increased volatility of the project, as shown in Exhibit 10.12. The change in the probabilities does not affect the present values at the end of the tree, but changes them in the previous nodes.

For example, the present value of the project at node B is

$$PV(B) = [.39(6839) + .15(57498.2) + .20(50924) + .26(42000)] \div (-0.0125)$$
$$= 63,390.8$$

When we assumed that price and quantity were uncorrelated, the value at node B was $63,262—a less extreme value. Similarly, the value at node E, where both price and quantity have moved down, is $37,269.6 if they are uncorrelated and $37,363.2 if they are correlated.

As a result, the present value of the project has increased from 56,638.9 to 56,877.7. The economic reason for the higher present value is that we have increased the probability of taking full advantage of higher prices being correlated with higher sales—a good result—and a corresponding higher probability of lower prices accompanied by smaller sales—a bad result, but not as bad as the alternative of lower prices with high sales (implying larger losses). Now we will use this event tree as the underlying risky asset and apply the option to abandon to transform it into a decision tree as illustrated in Exhibit 10.13.

Exhibit 10.12 Present value event tree with correlation of 30 percent.

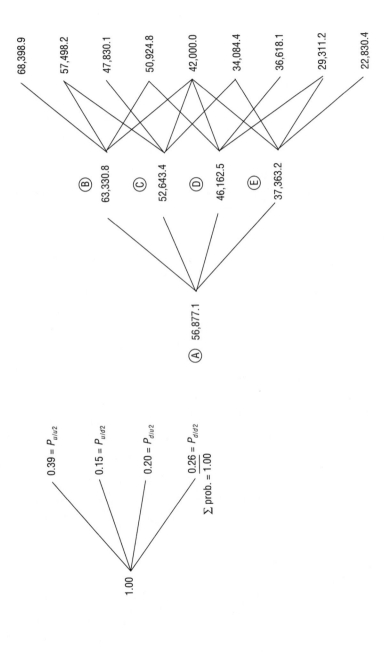

Risk-Neutral Probabilities

PV Event Tree

$0.39 = P_{u/u2}$

$0.15 = P_{u/d2}$

$0.20 = P_{d/u2}$

$0.26 = P_{d/d2}$

Σ prob. = 1.00

1.00

(A) 56,877.1

(B) 63,330.8

(C) 52,643.4

(D) 46,162.5

(E) 37,363.2

68,398.9

57,498.2

47,830.1

50,924.8

42,000.0

34,084.4

36,618.1

29,311.2

22,830.4

Exhibit 10.13   Quadranomial example ROA valuation with correlated uncertainties at 30 percent.

We calculate ROA with correlation in the same manner as it was calculated without correlation.

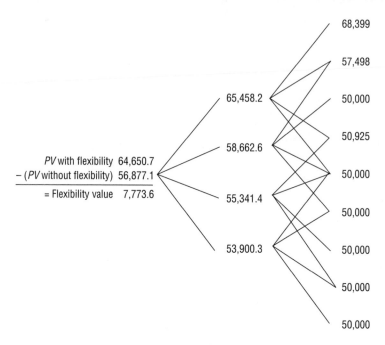

Again, we set the value of the project at each node for an optimal execution of the option. We then calculate expected value for each set of four nodes, using the risk-neutral probabilities and discounting backward at the risk-free rate. The present value of the project with flexibility and correlated factors is 64,650.7, compared with a value of 56,877.1 without flexibility—a difference of 7,773.6. Note that introduction of positive correlation between price and quality has resulted in an increase in the value of the flexibility. The value of the option has declined when the volatility of the project has increased.

CONCLUSION

This chapter has looked into real options situations where it is desirable to keep one source of uncertainty separate from the others. Decision makers may choose to do so because technological uncertainty is resolved discontinuously in time (e.g., when the results of an experiment become available).

We worked solutions of increasing complexity. When the problem is a compound option with a single source of uncertainty, technological uncertainty that is independent of the economy, the solution is easy because we can discount at the risk-free rate. Next, we introduced a second source of uncertainty, product-market uncertainty, that while correlated with the market, is independent of technological uncertainty. Initially, we used an ad hoc solution by splitting each subinterval into two—then alternated the uncertainties. We discounted cash flows during technological uncertainty regimes at the risk-free rate, and used replicating portfolios during product-market regimes. An alternate, more precise but more complicated approach—the quadranomial—was also used.

Finally, we showed how to use the quadranomial approach for two correlated uncertainties, and with compound options (i.e., true compound rainbow options).

Questions and Problems

For solutions go to www.corpfinonline.com.

1. Suppose that we want to value a lemonade franchise on a Caribbean island. Its value depends on the number of tourists and the present value of a supply of lemons, which is the market price of a lemon tree. We have the right to buy the lemonade stand for an agreed price of X dollars for the next two months. How do we design our approach for solving the problem? Should we use a consolidated or a separated approach for dealing with uncertainties?

2. Change the problem statement of question 1 slightly. Now we already own the lemonade stand, but can spend money to do market research about the number of tourists and to buy more lemon juice. Does this change our approach for solving the problem? If so, how?

3. Use the data for the problem described on pages 286–288. Assume that the two uncertainties are not correlated. Will the value of the put option as a percent of the total ROA value go up or down and why

under one of the following changes? (Prove your answer with detailed calculations.)

—The initial price increases from $10 to $15.

—The volatility of the quantity decreases from 20 percent to 15 percent.

—The fixed cost increases from $4,000 to $6,000.

4. Use the data for the problem described on page 286. Assume that the two uncertainties are positively (30%) correlated. Will the value of the put option as a percent of the total ROA value go up or down and why under one of the following changes? (Prove your answer with detailed calculations.)

—The correlation increases from 30 percent to 50 percent.

—The correlation increases from 30 percent to 40 percent, and the price increases from $10 to $15.

—The correlation becomes negative 20 percent.

5. For all the cases in problem 4: Find the conditional probabilities for the price to move up or down when the quantity has increased and when it has decreased. In the same fashion, find the conditional probabilities for the quantity to move up or down when the price has increased and when it has decreased.

REFERENCES

Boyle, P. 1988. "A Lattice Framework for Option Pricing with Two State Variables," *Journal of Financial and Quantitative Analysis, 23,* 1–26.

Boyle, P., P. Eunine, and S. Gibb. 1989. "Numerical Evaluation of Multivariate Contingent Claims," *Review of Financial Studies, 2,* 241–250.

Chang, C., and J. Chang. 1996. "Option Pricing with Stochastic Volatility: Information-Time versus Calendar-Time," *Management Science, 42,* 7, 974–991.

Clewlow, L., and C. Strickland. 1998. *Implementing Derivatives Models.* New York: John Wiley & Sons.

Hull, J., and A. White. 1987. "The Pricing of Options on Assets with Stochastic Volatilities," *Journal of Finance, 42,* 2, 281–300.

Kamrad, B., and P. Ritchken. 1991. "Multinomial Approximating Models for Options with k State Variables," *Management Science, 37,* 1640–1652.

PART III

11 | Case Examples

Now that you have wrestled with the details of real options methodology, let's look at a few examples that illustrate solutions to fairly realistic cases. In the first we value an Internet portal and in the second a research and development project. The first case illustrates the solution methodology that combines uncertainties (Chapter 9). The second keeps uncertainties separate, using the quadranomial approach (Chapter 10).

Valuing an Internet Project—The Portes Case

The high prices paid for Internet companies, especially those that are small with emerging growth, have led many experts to comment that stock valuation is either a mystery or a sign of the market's "irrational exuberance."[1] This case attempts to demystify the valuation of Internet companies using real options—an approach that seems to be viable for small high-growth companies that are undiversified in the sense that the whole company is made up of one or two projects. The company and the data in the case are fictional, however, we have worked with similar companies in our consulting practice.

Case Statement

Boston-based Portes, Inc. is a software company that has been in operation for 10 years in the United States. Its flagship product is systems recovery software (called Recover™) that enables firms to recover data from damaged hard drives. The product has to be customized to client needs and the value of each product unit is high. The firm was founded by its current CEO, Diane Mullins, who is a software expert with an entrepreneurial bent. She studied computer science as an undergraduate, worked for four years in a reputable U.S. software firm, then went on to do an MBA at INSEAD in France. Immediately upon completing her MBA, Diane moved back to the United States and started her own company, Portes, Inc. The company now employs 60 people, most of whom are trained programmers.

A few years ago, Diane started to suspect that Portes, Inc. had reached a plateau with its systems recovery product. The rapid growth of the early years had waned, although the product was still quite profitable. Diane felt that one problem with Recover was that since it had to be customized to client needs it could not be mass marketed or sold in great volume. Therefore, even though some of Portes' distributors advertise their product on the Web, almost none of the sales take place on the Internet. Even though it meant loss of customization service revenues, Diane thought that Portes needed to step up its R&D activity to come up with mass-appeal software that did not need any customization. As a result of directing energy and resources in this direction, Portes, Inc. now has a portfolio of standardized high-end data recovery software. One advantage with these products is that they can be sold over the Internet. Although Portes was using its existing distribution channels to sell these products on the Web, the commission charged by the distributors was considered to be too high compared to the value of the product. Not having their own Internet presence before, Diane feels that it may be too late for Portes, Inc. to enter the U.S. business-to-business Internet space, since it is already quite crowded. She is also afraid of annoying the company's current distributors by selling directly to customers.

Diane discussed these issues with Olivier, a friend from her INSEAD days, and he made a suggestion which could lead to the perfect solution. Olivier is a Frenchman who worked in Paris for several years before moving to the United States to work at an Internet startup firm. He is very knowledgeable about the French software market. He expects that due to the high demand for data protection and recovery products there, and the fact that Portes has no commitments to local distributors, the ideal place to sell the newly developed software of Portes, Inc. is over the Internet in

France. According to him, the business-to-business (B2B) e-commerce market in France is, as yet, not as crowded as that in the United States. There is a huge potential for starting Internet-based selling firms in France because although the U.S. Web-based sellers are accessed from France they cannot seem to satisfy the French market, mainly due to a lack of knowledge about the local conditions and the language barrier. Moreover, when French buyers access U.S.-based sites for purchases, they face high mailing costs, as well as import duties. Olivier thinks that if the new software can be adapted for use in France, Portes, Inc. should invest in setting up an Internet-based selling facility in France. It can be used, not only to sell existing software, but subject to the popularity of the site, it can also be used to sell other products from other vendors. In addition, establishing a presence there now would also provide Portes, Inc. with valuable information about the specific software needs of the French market. Software developed by Portes to meet these needs could then be marketed using its then-existing site as a platform.

Diane is thoroughly convinced by Olivier's arguments. She calls Bill, her CFO, and explains that she would like him to evaluate the investment opportunity very seriously. Diane makes it clear that she is in favor of the idea for strategic reasons.

Bill and his staff do some research to find out more about the costs and revenues of the potential business in France. There is an initial investment in hardware. There are high continuing costs of advertising both in the printed media and on the net. There are costs of running the site. It is a challenging job to estimate the cost of capital of this business. There seems to be a lot of uncertainty. Bill performs NPV calculations and finds that the project has a negative $319 thousand NPV (see Exhibit 11.1).

Portes was expecting to sell 200 of its programs in the first year of operations and to double its annual sales to 400 within the next five years. During the same period, the price erosion should reduce the expected initial unit price of $30,000 to $20,000. Bill's team forecasted that the COGS/unit would be significantly higher than in the United States due to smaller quantities and more complex logistics. The first year of operation, every program will have COGS of $9,000 with the expectation of dropping to $7,000 by the sixth year.

Exhibit 11.1   NPV analysis of the investment proposal.

Item	Year 0	Year 1	Year 2	Year 3	Year 4	Year 5	Year 6	Year 7
Quantity (units)		200	230	264	303	348	400	
Continuous annual growth rate		13.9%						
Price per unit ('000s)		30.00	27.66	25.51	23.52	21.69	20.00	
Continuous annual growth rate		-8.1%						
Cost per unit		9.0	8.6	8.1	7.7	7.4	7.0	
Revenues		6,000	6,355	6,732	7,130	7,553	8,000	
Cost of goods sold		1,800	1,966	2,148	2,346	2,563	2,800	
Gross income		4,200	4,389	4,584	4,784	4,990	5,200	
Gross margin %		70%	69%	68%	67%	66%	65%	
Rent		200	200	200	200	200	200	
S&A expenses		600	636	673	713	755	800	
EBITDA		3,400	3,554	3,711	3,871	4,034	4,200	
Depreciation		3,500	3,500	3,500	3,500	3,500	3,500	
EBIT		(100)	54	211	371	534	700	
EBIT *growth*			-154%	294%	76%	44%	31%	
Taxes		0	21	84	148	214	280	
Net income		(100)	32	126	223	321	420	
Depreciation		3,500	3,500	3,500	3,500	3,500	3,500	
Initial investment	35,000							
Free cash flow	(35,000)	3,400	3,532	3,626	3,723	3,821	3,920	
Change in FCF			4%	3%	3%	3%	3%	
Continuing value								50,960
Discount rate	13%							
PV	34,681	36,096	37,575	39,165	40,880	42,735	44,748	
NPV	(319)	39,496	41,107	42,792	44,603	46,555	48,668	
FCF as a % of PV		8.6%	8.6%	8.5%	8.3%	8.2%	8.05%	

Portes would have to rent some office and storage space with an expected fixed annual cost of $200,000. Based on the company's experience, The selling and administrative (S&A) expenses were projected to be 10 percent of the revenue.

The project would require an initial investment of $35 million, expected to be depreciated over a 10-year period. Portes was very profitable in the past five years and currently carried no debt. The company was planning to finance the project in France.

The expected tax rate in France is 40 percent with no loss carry-forward allowance. In the recent years, for similar projects in the United States, the company was using a 10 percent to 11 percent expected rate of return. To capture the higher market risk and the foreign currency risk of the project, Bill decided to apply a 13 percent expected rate of return.

Bill and his team feels that they cannot reliably forecast the revenues and the costs with the same level of detail after the sixth year. To capture the continuing value of the project, they used a simple growing annuity formula with free cash flow expected to grow at 4 percent and expected rate of return at 12 percent forever.

Bill shares his analysis of the project with Diane. She finds it hard to believe that the NPV is negative and questions in detail every assumption Bill has made. At the end of a long discussion about the numbers, Diane repeats all the arguments she and Olivier have gone through and insists that this is a great opportunity for the company to grow internationally and to establish its own Internet presence. She asks Bill to go back to the drawing board and consider all the value the project could generate for the company one more time and report back in two weeks.

As a first step in expanding the analysis, Bill asked Eric, a recent MBA, to identify, model, and forecast the key risk factors that would affect the profitability of the project. He wanted to perform a Monte Carlo simulation and see what range the NPV would lie within.

Eric identified the annual unit sales and price per unit as the two major risk factors for the project. For the first run of the Monte Carlo simulation he assumed the quantity and the price to be uncorrelated. Working with people from marketing, Eric developed 95 percent confidence ranges for each of the factors. The consensus was that in the sixth year, the lower 95 percent confidence level for the unit sales was 190, with an expected level of 400. Analogously, the consensus lower limit for the price in year six was $15 with an expected level of $20.

Bill spent a significant amount of time researching and thinking about how to clarify and quantify the strategic sources of value for the project. He is of the opinion that in addition to the cash flows from software sales of the current product, the main strategic value of the project would derive from being able to use the Web site as a platform to sell another related product once the Web site became popular with companies in France. The other product Bill has in mind is PreventLoss. This product, which was in the final stages of development, is an intelligent real-time back-up software, that, if installed, increases the chance and quality of data recovery (using Recover) in case of hard-drive damage. There is perfect complementarity between the two products—Recover and PreventLoss. Bill discusses this idea with Diane, who completely agrees.

In the course of their conversation, they note an important point about the expansion opportunity. Since the additional investment will be made at the time of the expansion, they are not committed to the expansion right now. Given that the amount of investment required for the introduction of the new product will almost certainly be sizeable, their decision to expand (and thus the timing of expansion as well) will depend on how well their existing sales are doing at that time. If the sales of Recover are sufficiently large, by assuming that a percentage of those buyers will also buy PreventLoss, they can introduce the latter product profitably. Their conviction is that this will happen sometime within the next five years. Therefore, there is an important added dimension—that of flexibility of deciding whether and when to introduce PreventLoss to the French market.

Diane thinks there may be other possibilities along the way as well. For instance, if for some reason Portes, Inc. does not perform well in France, they should be able to sell out their investment in hardware in that country. A phone call to Olivier confirms this. After reviewing the project's technical specifications, Olivier thinks that Portes, Inc. should be able to get about $15 million for its hardware investment at any time during the next six years. With these ideas, Diane asks Bill to get an estimate of the amount of investment that will be required to introduce PreventLoss to the French market, and the likely increase in value that this will generate.

According to Bill's estimate, based on collaboration with the engineering and the marketing teams, the introduction of PreventLoss will require an additional investment of about $10.5 million. When implemented, it can be expected to increase the remaining future free cash flows by 30 percent.

Case Solution

Exhibit 11.2 shows the process that was used to solve the case.

Step 1 The DCF Value. The first step is to calculate the DCF value of the project without flexibility. The free cash flow of the project has the usual profile (see Exhibit 11.3) with a significant initial investment followed by a small positive cash inflow over the forecasted period and a considerable continuing value.

By discounting the free cash flow at 13 percent cost of capital, we obtain the present value of the project for each year and its NPV today. Exhibit 11.4 illustrates this (a negative NPV of $319 thousand) and shows how the project's present value evolves through time. Each period, as the project generates a positive cash flow that is taken away as a profit, the remaining value decreases by the same amount.

Exhibit 11.2 Portes, Inc. solution process.

Steps	Compute base case present value without flexibility using DCF valuation model	Model the uncertainty using event trees	Identify and incorporate managerial flexibilities creating a decision tree	Calculate real option value (ROA)

Actions	• Use the expected values of price, quantity, cost investments, terminal value, and WACC to compute Free Cash Flow.
	
	 • Compute NPV of FCFs.
	
	 • Obtain expected PV evolution over time, (i.e., compute the PV of all future FCF for each point in time).
		• Specify price and quantity uncertainties.
		  • Provide the lowest values for price and quantity in year six with 95% confidence.
		  • Obtain volatilities of price and quantity.
		
		 • Run Monte Carlo simulation on price and quantity assuming they are independent.
		
		 • Translate uncertainty in price and quantity to PV growth uncertainty.
		  • Obtain standard deviation of PV growth.
		
		 • From standard deviation compute "up" and "down" factors for PV growth.
		
		 • Obtain PV event trees (use ratio of FCF to PV for "ex-dividend").
			• Identify all the real options available to Portes.
			
			 • Starting at the last period, compute the value of each option at each node.
			  • Compute the value manually for node X. The rest will be done by the program.
			
			 • At each node compare the value of the real option with the investment required.
			  • Mark the alternative that has the maximum value at each node.
				• Value the total project using replication methodology.
				
				 • Identify the optimal exercise paths for the real options.
				
				 • Subtract NPV from ROA to find the combined value of all options.

Exhibit 11.3   Project expected free cash flows.

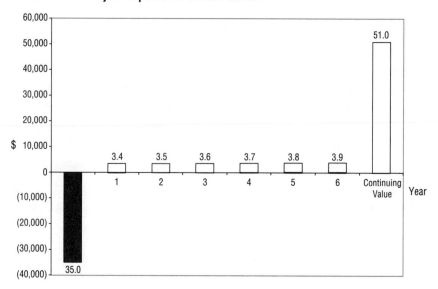

Exhibit 11.4   Evolution of the present value of the project (without flexibility) through time.

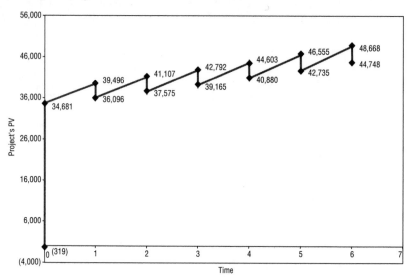

Step 2 The Event Tree. The second step models the causal uncertainties and feeds them into a Monte Carlo simulation model based on the original NPV analysis. From the simulation we get an estimate of the expected volatility of the project's value. Then we use the volatility to build a value-based event tree. The quantity of unit sales per year and the unit price were identified as the two major uncertainties for the project.

Using the material developed in Chapter 9 we can use the information supplied by management to develop the 95 percent confidence intervals shown in Exhibits 11.5 and 11.6.

From the NPV analysis, we know that the current price level is 30 and is expected to decline on average at a constant −8.11 percent rate for the next six years to reach 20:

$$P_6 = P_1 e^{Tr} = 30 e^{5(-8.11\%)} = 20$$

Exhibit 11.5 Inputs for the Monte Carlo simulation: Units sold (95% confidence interval).

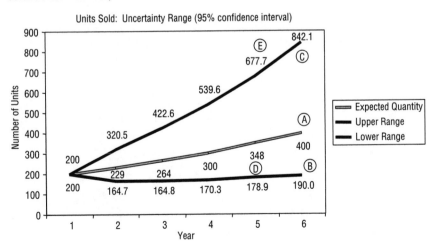

Exhibit 11.6 Inputs for the Monte Carlo simulation: Price per unit (95% confidence interval).

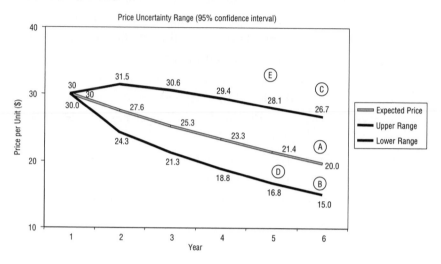

For the sales, we know that the current year sales are currently 200 and are expected to grow on average at a constant 13.86 percent for the next six years to reach 400:

$$Q_6 = Q_1 e^{Tr} = 200 e^{5 \times 0.1386} = 400$$

For each uncertainty, the only parameter we are missing for the Monte Carlo simulation of the project is its volatility. Depending on the volatility the actual price level in year six will lie within the following 95 percent confidence interval:

$$P_6 = \left[30 e^{5(-8.1\%) - 2\sigma\sqrt{5}}, 30 e^{5(-8.1\%) + 2\sigma\sqrt{5}} \right]$$

The management estimate of the 95 percent confidence interval of price is obtained indirectly by asking: "In the NPV analysis we expect the price at year six to be 20. We all understand that this is an average estimate. We need to ascertain, with 95 percent confidence, your estimate of how low (or how high) the actual price can fall at year six."

The management then provides a value for the lower limit of the interval just shown. If this value is 15 then we can derive the annual volatility by using the volatility estimate equation in Chapter 9.

$$\sigma = \frac{\sum_{i=1}^{n} r_i - \ln\left(\frac{P_T^{lower}}{P_0}\right)}{2\sqrt{T}}$$

$$\sigma = \frac{5 \times (-8.1\%) - \ln\left(\frac{15}{30}\right)}{2\sqrt{5}} = 6.43\%$$

Next, we build the confidence interval around the expected level of the price for each year in the model. For year six, points B and C, Exhibit 11.6, the two limits are:

$$Lim_u[P_6] = P_1 e^{\Sigma r_i + 2\sigma\sqrt{T}} = 30 e^{5 \times (-0.081) + 2 \times 0.0643\sqrt{5}} = 26.7$$

$$Lim_l[P_6] = P_1 e^{\Sigma r_i - 2\sigma\sqrt{T}} = 30 e^{5 \times (-0.081) - 2 \times 0.0643\sqrt{5}} = 15$$

Similarly, the 95 percent confidence interval for year five, points D and E, Exhibit 11.6, is:

$$Lim_u[P_5] = P_1 e^{\Sigma r_i + 2\sigma\sqrt{T}} = 30 e^{4 \times (-0.081) + 2 \times 0.0643\sqrt{4}} = 28.1$$

$$Lim_l[P_5] = P_1 e^{\Sigma r_i - 2\sigma\sqrt{T}} = 30 e^{4 \times (-0.081) - 2 \times 0.0643\sqrt{4}} = 16.8$$

The confidence interval is widening as we predict further in the future. Similar to the price forecast, the actual sales quantity in year six will lie with 95 percent confidence within the interval:

$$P_6 = \left[200 e^{5(139) - 2\sigma\sqrt{5}}, \ 200 e^{5(139) + 2\sigma\sqrt{5}}\right]$$

To obtain management's estimate of the annual volatility of the units sold, we ask a similar question: "Given that the expected average sales for year six is 400, what is the level where we can expect with 95 percent confidence that the actual sales will be higher or equal?" As before, we are asking management to provide the lower limit of the interval.

Assuming that the estimate is 190, we can derive the value of the sales volatility, using the volatility estimate equation in Chapter 9:

$$\sigma = \frac{5 \times 13.86\% - \ln\left(\dfrac{190}{200}\right)}{2\sqrt{5}} = 16.65$$

Having estimated the volatility, we can obtain the lower and the upper limits of the 95 percent confidence interval for year six (points B and C, Exhibit 11.5):

$$Lim_u[Q_6] = Q_1 e^{\Sigma r_i + 2\sigma\sqrt{T}} = 200 e^{5 \times .1386 + 2 \times .1665\sqrt{5}} = 842.1$$
$$Lim_l[Q_6] = Q_1 e^{\Sigma r_i - 2\sigma\sqrt{T}} = 200 e^{5 \times .1386 + 2 \times .1665\sqrt{5}} = 190$$

Analogously, the limits of the confidence interval for year five are:

$$Lim_u[Q_5] = Q_1 e^{\Sigma r_i + 2\sigma\sqrt{T}} = 200 e^{4 \times .1386 + 2 \times .1665\sqrt{4}} = 677.7$$
$$Lim_l[Q_5] = Q_1 e^{\Sigma r_i - 2\sigma\sqrt{T}} = 200 e^{4 \times .1386 - 2 \times .1665\sqrt{4}} = 178.9$$

Now we can model both uncertainties in the Monte Carlo simulation of the original DCF model. For each year we define two normally distributed random variables: "Price annual growth," r_{Pt}, with mean (−0.0811) and standard deviation 0.0643, and "Annual growth of units of sales," r_{Qt}, with mean 13.86 percent and standard deviation of 0.1665. For each simulation, we generate price and sales quantity for each year with the formulas:

$$P_t = P_{t-1} e^{r_{Pt}}$$
$$Q_t = Q_{t-1} e^{r_{Qt}}$$

Using this process we obtain many simulated sets of prices and sales quantities for the forecasted years. They have very important characteristics.

First, for each year the averages of all drawings for the price and the sales approach their expected values in the NPV model. Second, for each year 95 percent of the drawings reside within the confidence intervals outlined above. In this way, even though the price and the sales behave as random variables, their average characteristics reflect the information embedded in the NPV analysis and generated by the management.

For example, the mean of sales for year six after 1,000 simulations is 416, and the mean for the price is 20.10. Both numbers are very close to the respective expected values of 400 and 20, and by increasing the number of simulations, the differences decrease. The distributions of the price and the sales approximate lognormal shape as their evolution is defined as a Geometric Brownian Motion (Exhibit 11.7).

Now we can complete the Monte Carlo simulation, and run the uncertainties through the NPV model to get an estimate for the volatility of the project's value. For 1,000 trials, the distribution of the rate of return is approximately normal with a mean value of 12 percent (Exhibit 11.8).

$$E\left[\ln\left(\frac{PV_1 + CF_1}{PV_0}\right)\right] = 0.12$$

Exhibit 11.7   Distribution of sales units (Monte Carlo analysis).

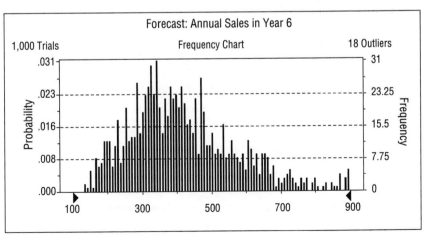

Exhibit 11.8   Distribution of rates of return (based on value).

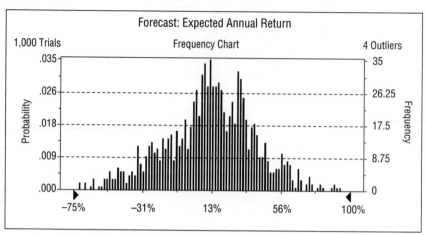

The volatility (standard deviation) of the rate of return is 30 percent. Having combined management estimates of uncertainty about price and quantity into a single uncertainty of the value of the project, we build a value-based event tree as shown in Exhibit 11.9. Recall that the net present value of the project is −$319,000. Adding back the initial $35 million investment yields the present value of the project at node A, namely $34.681 million.

Step 3 The Decision Tree.   The third step is to identify the real options that management can exercise, their effect on the remaining present value, their exercise prices, and their timing. We can identify two options in this case. The first is an abandonment put. Olivier's estimate is that the company can be sold for $15 million any time, just for the value of its hardware investment. Second is an expansion option, namely the introduction of PreventLoss, which would cost $10.5 million and when implemented, is expected to increase the company's cash flow from that point on by 30 percent.

Step 4 Real Options Analysis.   As in all other examples, we start at the end of the tree and analyze the optimal execution of the two options at

Exhibit 11.9 The present value event tree for the project without a follow-up investment.

PV Uncertainty Tree

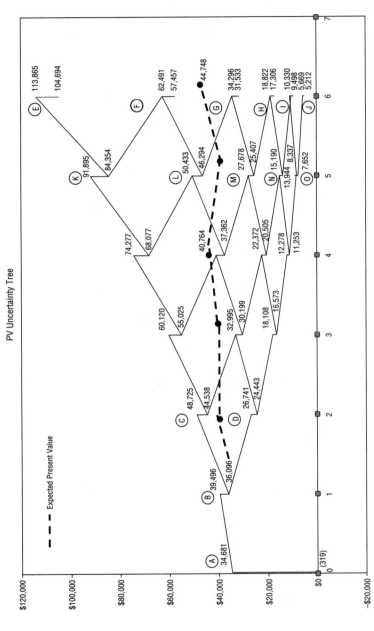

Note: We have assumed that uncertainty evolves from year 1. Alternately, one could assume that it starts immediately and that there are two branches rather than one.

each final node (Exhibit 11.10). The maximum value of the project after paying out free cash flow is the maximum of its intrinsic value and the values of the expansion or abandonment options. For example, at the node on Exhibit 11.10, highlighted by the magnifying glass, the maximum value is:

$$MAX\ Value = MAX(present\ value,\ value\ given\ expansion,\ value\ given\ abandonment)$$
$$= MAX[104,694,\ 104,694 \times 1.3 - 10,500,\ 15,000]$$
$$125,602 = MAX[104,694,\ 125,602,\ 15,000]$$

The total *PV* of a project at this point is the maximum present value plus the free cash flow:

$$134,774 = 125,602 + 9,172$$

Exhibit 11.10   Real options calculations for a final node of the event tree.

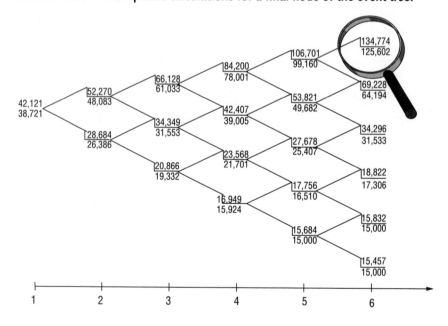

Using the replicating portfolio technique to discount, we move backward along the branches of the decision tree, identifying all the nodes where the execution of expansion or the abandonment option is optimal. At the beginning of the tree we get the ROA value of the project with flexibility.

Exhibit 11.11 shows the optimal exercise of the expansion and the abandonment options. Both the option to expand and the option to abandon add to the flexibility of the project as they will be executed in many possible scenarios. As can be expected, the option to expand will be optimally executed if the project does well and the option to abandon will be executed if it does badly.

Because of the project's high level of uncertainty, the flexibility has added a significant value. By enhancing the project's upside in case of success, and bounding the down side in case of failure, the options have moved its net present value from negative $319,000 to positive ROA value with flexibility of $1,986,000 (Exhibit 11.12).

Conclusion. The ROA value is over $2 million higher than the NPV value that fails to value flexibility. The ROA analysis confirms Diane

Exhibit 11.11 Optimal decisions resulting from the real options analysis.

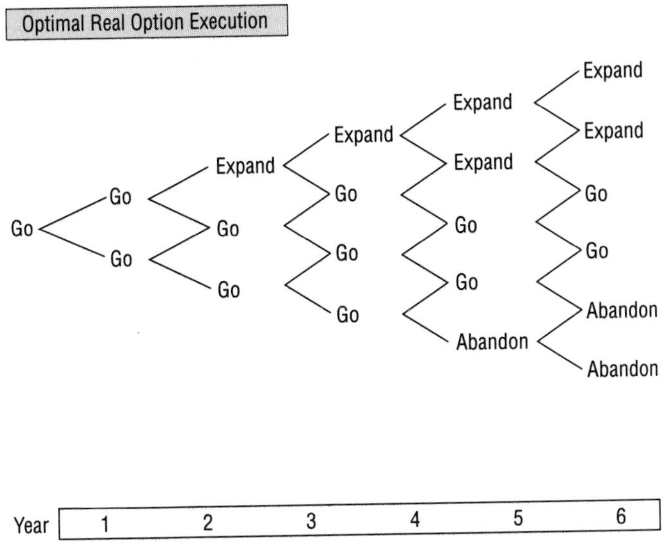

Exhibit 11.12   Project's value with flexibility.

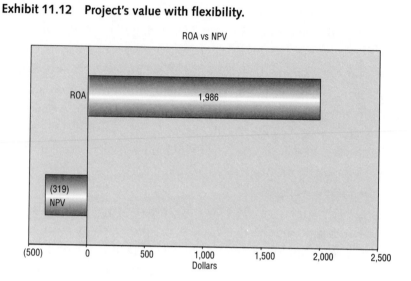

Mullins' intuition and the extra value of flexibility makes the project worthwhile.

REVISITING PRECOMMITMENT IN A MULTIPERIOD SETTING

Before we move on to discuss the next case, which is a compound rainbow option—a pharmaceuticals research and development investment—we need to point out the distinction between what we shall call naïve net present value analysis, sophisticated scenario-based NPV, decision tree analysis (DTA), and real options analysis (ROA). Turn to Exhibit 11.13, a compound option with a single source of uncertainty. Managers have to decide whether to invest $50 today to start the first stage of a project and $70 at the beginning of the second period. The state contingent free cash flows are shown in Exhibit 11.13. Assume a 25 percent discount rate, and that the risk-free rate is 5 percent.

Naïve net present value assumes that it is necessary to precommit at time zero to either making both investments or none at all. Given this strong assumption, the net present value of the project is calculated by

Exhibit 11.13 Naïve NPV event tree (precommitment—no flexibility).

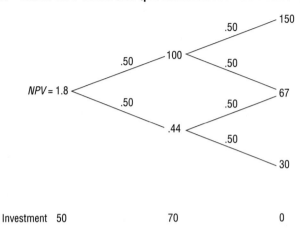

discounting the expected cash flows at the weighted average cost of capital:

$$Naive\ (NPV) = -50 + \frac{.5(100) + .5(44) - 70}{1.25} + \frac{.5(.5)150 + 2(.5)(.5)67 + .5(.5)30}{(1.25)^2}$$
$$= -50 + 1.6 + 50.2 = 1.8$$

This analysis is naïve because, given the information that we have today, we know that if the down state of nature turns up at the end of the first time period, we would choose not to invest $70 because the present value of future cash flows given that state of nature is the present value of the cash flows at the end of the second year, namely [.5($67) + .5($30)]/(1.25) = $38.4. Therefore, we know at the start of the project that we would not invest at node E, and precommitment simply does not make sense.

It turns out that the next two decision criteria, sophisticated NPV (scenario analysis) and decision tree analysis (DTA) are two names for the same thing. Both use information available today to eliminate states of nature where precommitment to investment is foolish. Exhibit 11.14 shows that scenario planning or DTA would construct the payoffs by rationally assuming that no investment will take place in states of nature

Exhibit 11.14   DTA and sophisticated NPV event tree (with flexibility).

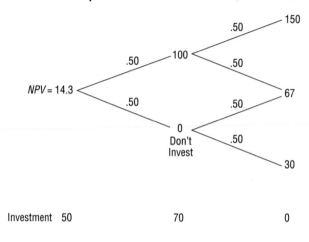

where it makes no sense to do so. Therefore, the sophisticated NPV of the project is:

$$Sophisticated(NPV) = DTA = -50 + \frac{.5(100-70) + .5(44)}{1.25}$$

$$+ \frac{.5(.5)150 + .5(.5)67 + 2(.5)(.5)0}{(1.25)^2} = -50 + 29.6 + 34.72 = 14.3$$

This value is obviously higher because any scenario-based approach can use the information that is available today to eliminate investing in states of nature (scenarios) where it would not make sense to do so. We believe that while some companies use the assumptions of naïve NPV (i.e., total inflexibility), there are many others who use the assumptions of the sophisticated NPV or decision tree approach.

Real options analysis is an improvement over sophisticated NPV and DTA because it obeys the law of one price and therefore prices the project in a way that eliminates arbitrage possibilities—which is another way of saying that relative prices are properly established. Exhibit 11.15 shows the value-based event tree for the no flexibility case (the earlier version was cash-flow based). The NPV is the same as before but we need to base our ROA analysis on the value of the underlying without flexibility. The ROA solution for the example problem that we are working on is given in

Exhibit 11.15   Value-based event tree (precommitment).

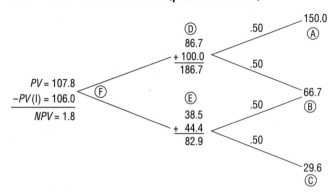

Exhibit 11.16. There are no decisions to be made at the end nodes, A and B, therefore the present value at node D remains the same as before. Therefore at node D in Exhibit 11.16, the choice is between investing $70 to get a present value of $86.70 in return, or choosing not to invest and getting $0. The total value at node D is therefore $16.70 plus the $100 cash flow that period—a total payoff of $116.70. At the other node at the end of the first year, node E, we choose not to invest because the present value of cash flows is only $38.5 which is much less than the required $70 investment. Therefore, the total payoff at node E is $0 plus the cash flow of $44. Due to the exercise of flexibility at node E, the risk of the payoffs has changed from the base case NPV without flexibility and

Exhibit 11.16   ROA valuation.

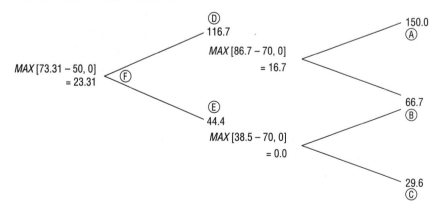

we must use the replicating portfolio approach to calculate the ROA value. The algebra is shown as follows:

$$At\ node\ D:\ muV_0 + (1 + r_f)B = C_u$$

$$At\ node\ E:\ mdV_0 + (1 + r_f)B = C_d$$

Therefore:
$$m = \frac{C_u - C_d}{V_0(u - d)} = \frac{116.7 - 44.4}{107.8(1.5 - .67)} = .805$$

And
$$B = \frac{C_u - muV_0}{1 + r_f} = \frac{116.7 - .805(1.5)107.8}{1.05} = -13.47$$

Consequently, the present value of the option is

$$C = mV_0 + B = .805(107.8) - 13.47 = 73.31$$

Since the value of the option is greater than the $50 exercise price, we would invest in the project, with flexibility. The net present value estimated via the ROA approach is $73.31 – $50 = $23.31. In this example, the DTA approach undervalues the project by $9.

The purpose of this section of the chapter is to point out the difference between the naïve NPV approach, which assumes no flexibility at all, and a more sophisticated NPV approach that uses information that is available today to make correct state-contingent decisions. It turns out that this more sophisticated scenario-based approach is equivalent to decision tree analysis. Neither are correct because they use the weighted average cost of capital that is appropriate for the project without flexibility to discount the real options values. Finally, we used replicating portfolios to correct the risky cash flows of the project with flexibility.

In the pharmaceutical company research and development case that is described next, we compare the sophisticated NPV approach to the ROA approach.

VALUING A PHARMACEUTICAL RESEARCH AND DEVELOPMENT PROJECT

The second case is a compound rainbow option with uncorrelated uncertainties. We keep one of them, namely technological uncertainty, separate from the others and use the quadranomial approach. A team of scientists provides objectively determined estimates of experimental success at each stage and historical data is used to provide estimates of product-market uncertainty.

Case Statement

PharmX Inc. is about to launch research into a new treatment for Parkinson's disease—a drug that is expected, if successful, to eliminate all symptoms of cogging (neurotransmitter tremors) without side effects (such as drowsiness) and to actually cure the disease. Dr. Timothy Parks, head of research, wants the economic analysis of the project to be done two ways—the usual net present value approach, and the new real options approach that he has been reading about recently.

The project will have three compulsory testing phases, each necessary for approval by the Federal Drug Administration (FDA), followed by either going straight to market, or by taking an additional year to perform an indications test phase that is a comparative test of the new drug (nicknamed PDX) versus other emerging drugs, that, if successful, will increase sales by allowing additional therapeutic claims.

This seemed to be a complex decision tree, so Dr. Parks drew a schematic (Exhibit 11.17) that seemed to capture the relevant decisions up to the product launch. The objective probabilities of success or failure of each phase are given in the exhibit. Note that the cumulative probability of success in all three stages of clinical testing is 47.8 percent. Dr. Parks noted that the NPV approach seemed to require evaluation of two mutually exclusive alternatives at the end of phase 3 of research. Either they would go straight to market or they would conduct comparative testing—but not both. It seemed, however, that the real options approach would provide a single present value estimate because it worked backward through time, making optimal decisions at each node, conditional on the outcomes of technological and product-market uncertainty. He was anxious to discuss this difference between the two approaches with his colleagues.

As indicated by Exhibit 11.18, the cumulative investment for the three research phases, comparative testing, and product launch is expected to be $92 million, if PharmX decides to do comparative testing.

Exhibit 11.17 Pharma R&D decision.

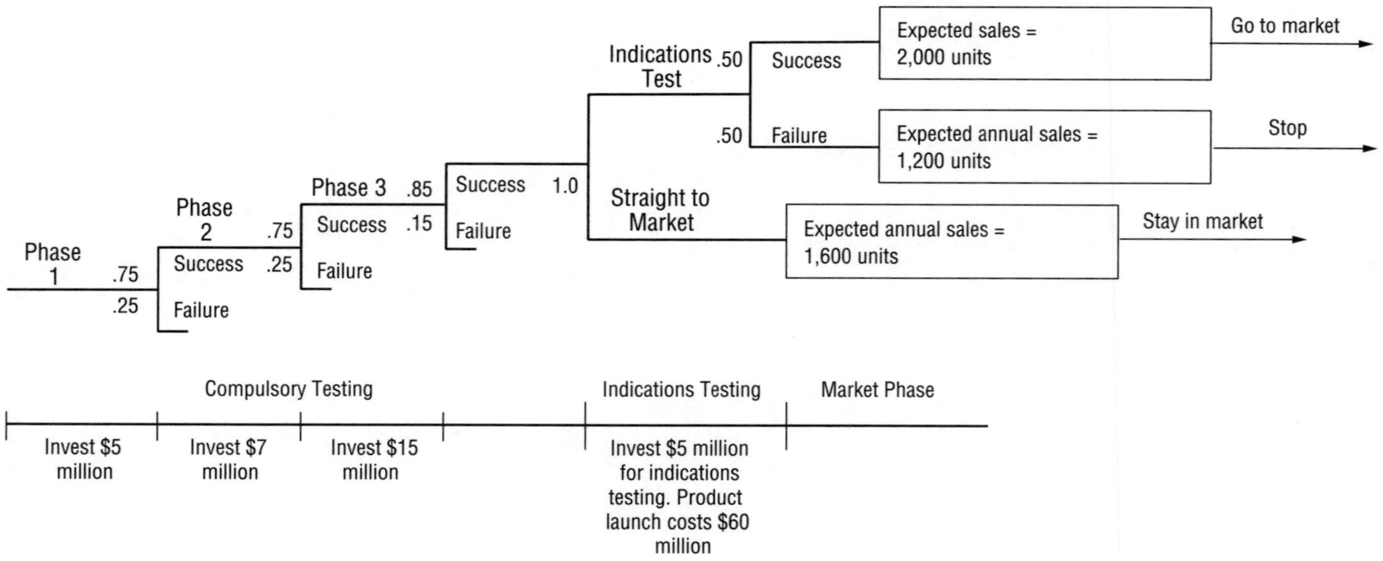

Exhibit 11.18 **Cumulative investment (with indications testing).**

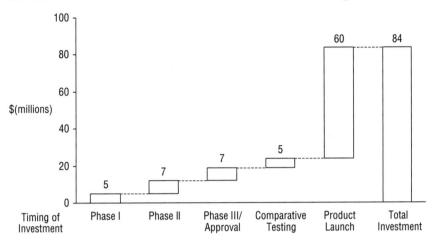

In addition to technological uncertainty, PharmX faces product/market uncertainty. The company estimates that the drug could sell for $10 per unit were it available now, however, this estimate can shift 10 percent per year. The quantity of sales is also uncertain. As shown in Exhibit 11.17, the estimated annual growth of sales is contingent on whether the decision is to go straight to market (expected sales of 1.6 million units per year), or to conduct further indications testing (either 2.0 or 1.2 million units per year depending on the results). Once the drug goes to market its value is estimated to be seven times its cash flow.

To simplify the estimation of free cash flows, Dr. Parks defines them as total revenues (price times quantity) minus total costs (variable cost per unit of $2 times the total units minus fixed costs of $1 million). The weighted average cost of capital is 7 percent and the risk free rate is 5 percent.

Case Solution

Because we want to keep technological uncertainty separate from market uncertainty (i.e., price and quantity uncertainty), we use the four-step process shown in Exhibit 11.19. It starts with modeling the uncertainties

Exhibit 11.19   PharmX case project analysis overall approach.

	Step 1	Step 2	Step 3	Step 4
	Model the Uncertainty Using Event Trees	Compute Base Case Present Value without Flexibility	Identify and Incorporate Managerial Flexibilities Creating a Decision Tree	Calculate Real Option Value (ROA)
Objectives	• Identify major uncertainties in each stage • Understand how those uncertainties affect the PV	• Compute base case present value without flexibility at t = 0	• Analyze the event tree to identify and incorporate managerial flexibility	• Value the total project using a simple algebraic methodology
Comments	• Explicitly estimate uncertainty		• Incorporating flexibility transforms event trees into decision trees • The flexibility continuously alters the risk characteristics of the project, and hence the cost of capital	• ROA includes the base case present value without flexibility plus the option (flexibility) value • Given high uncertainty and managerial flexibility option value will be substantial
Output	• Detailed event tree capturing the possible values of the major uncertainties	• Project's PV without flexibility	• A detailed decision tree combining possible events and management responses	• ROA of the project and optimal contingent plan for the available real options

using event trees, then computes the base case net present value by using risk-neutral probabilities and the risk-free rate to discount end of branch free cash flows backward in time. The third step adds decisions to the tree and the fourth recalculates present values with flexibility.

Step 1 Modeling Uncertainties.   Remember that technological and product/market uncertainty evolve simultaneously through time. Technological uncertainty is assumed to be independent of the economy and is illustrated in Exhibit 11.20.

Exhibit 11.21 shows the evolution of price uncertainty through time, starting with a price of $10 per unit were the drug available immediately and having an annual standard deviation estimate of 10 percent. For a multiplicative binomial lattice, this translates into annual up and down movements of

$$u = e^{-1} = 1.1052$$

$$d = \frac{1}{u} = .9048$$

Exhibit 11.20 Technological uncertainty.

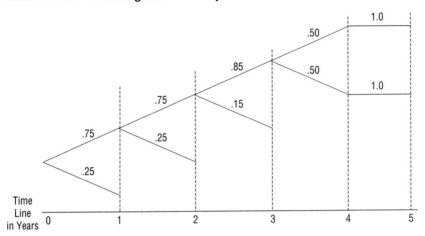

Exhibit 11.21 Price uncertainty.

Assumptions

- The drug today would sell for $10 per unit today
- The price is expected to grow on average at 8% annually
- The forecast assumes the price can fluctuate by 10% annually

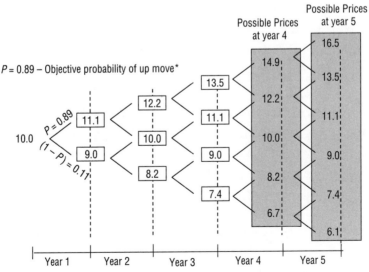

*Based on the theory of lattice representation of options: $u = e^{0.1}$, $d = \dfrac{1}{u}$, $p = \dfrac{(1 + 0.08) - d}{u - d} = 0.89$

Furthermore, if the price per unit is expected to grow at 8 percent annually, the objective probability of an upward movement is determined by the fact that today's price multiplied by one plus the growth rate must equal the expected price. The corresponding equation is

$$P_0(1+g) = puP_0 + (1-p)\,dP_0$$
$$(1+g) = pu + d - pd$$
$$p = \frac{1+g-d}{u-d} = \frac{1.08 - .9048}{1.1052 - .9048} = .89$$

The third source of uncertainty is the number of doses of the drug that might be sold each year. We are told that the unconditional expectation is 1.6 million units if we go straight to market after phase 3 clinical testing. Alternatively, we may choose to spend an additional $5 million for indications testing and forego any sales for an additional year, to learn whether the market for the product is 2.0 million units, or whether it is 1.2 million units.

The final task needed to complete step 1 of our process is to build a quadranomial event tree that combines price and quantity uncertainty into a single source called product/market uncertainty. This is illustrated in Exhibit 11.22. Cash flows, contingent upon the state of nature, appear at each node. We assume that technological and product/market uncertainty are independent of each other.

Step 2 Calculating the Base Case NPV. We know that the net present value approach must view the choice of going straight to market as mutually exclusive to the alternative of indications testing for a year before going to market. This section of the chapter shows how to estimate the NPV of each alternative starting with the alternative of indications testing. The calculations will show its NPV to be −$36.4 million while the alternative of going straight to market has an NPV of −$35.1 million. Thus, the standard NPV analysis would favor going straight to market, but since the NPV of both approaches is negative we would not precommit to going ahead.

Exhibit 11.22   Quadranomial event tree for the uncertainties.

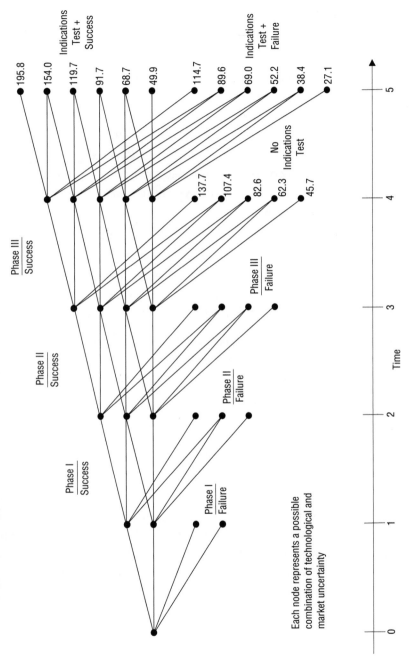

Each node represents a possible
combination of technological and
market uncertainty

329

To analyze the indications testing alternative, we start by calculating the present value of expected investment outlays

$$PV(I) = 5 + \frac{7}{1.05} + \frac{15}{(1.05)^2} + \frac{5}{(1.05)^3} + \frac{60}{(1.05)^4}$$
$$= 5 + 6.67 + 13.61 + 4.32 + 44.36 = 78.96$$

Note that we have discounted these investment outlays at the risk-free rate because they are exercise prices of call options whose value depends on technological uncertainty that is independent of the market economy. Note also, that we assume that the expenditure of $60 million to go to market is a Precommitment.

Exhibit 11.23 shows the event tree of values (assuming that we do the indications testing) conditional on the market price per dose and on the quantity of doses in each state of nature. For example, the present value at node A is calculated by estimating the cash flows and capitalizing them by using a multiple of seven. At node A, if the indications testing is successful

$$CF = [(P - VC)Q - F] = (\$16.5 - \$2)\ 2\ million - \$1 = \$28\ million$$
$$Value = CF \times 7 = \$196\ million$$

If it is unsuccessful (node G)

$$CF = (16.5 - 2)\ 1.2\ million - 1\ million = \$16.4\ million$$
$$Value = CF \times 7 = \$114.8\ million$$

Similar calculations provide the end-of-tree values at nodes B to L.

Next, we use risk-neutral probabilities to estimate the certainty equivalent cash flows that we will discount at the risk-free rate. Only price uncertainty is market related. From Exhibit 11.21 and the accompanying assumptions we know that the beginning price is $10, and that its annual volatility is $\sigma = 10$ percent, therefore, its binomial up and down movements are

$$u = e^{\sigma} = e^{.1} = 1.1052$$
$$d = \frac{1}{u} = 0.9048$$

Exhibit 11.23 NPV calculations with indications testing.

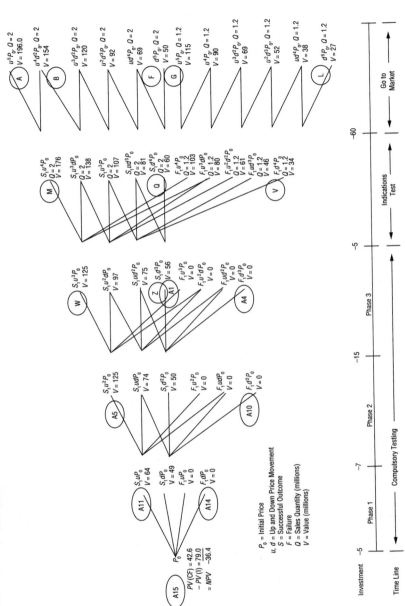

We are also told that the price grows at 8 percent per year and that the risk-free rate is 5 percent. We know that the expected end-of-period price, given its growth, will equal the objective probabilities times the payoffs,

$$P_0 e^g = pu V_0 + (1-p) dP_0$$

$$\frac{e^g - d}{u - d} = \frac{e^{.08} - .9048}{1.1052 - .9048} = p = .83$$

To calculate risk-neutral probabilities, the price will grow at the risk-free rate, so that we have

$$\frac{e^{r_f} - d}{u - d} = \frac{e^{.05} - .9048}{1.1052 - .9048} = p' = .73$$

Now we use the risk-neutral probabilities to calculate the value at each node, working backward in the tree shown in Exhibit 11.23. For example, at node M

$$V_M = \frac{p' 196.0 + (1 - p') 154}{1 + r_f} = \frac{.73(196.0) + (.27)154}{1.05} = 175.6$$

Note that years five and beyond have only price uncertainty because all technological uncertainty was resolved by the end of indications testing in year four. Therefore, there were only two branches from each period 4 node.

If we move back in time to calculate the value at node W, there are two sources of uncertainty, that are independent of each other, and four branches—a quadranomial tree. To determine the value at node W, we need to estimate four risk-neutral probabilities—one for each branch. Because price and quantity uncertainty are independent, we can multiply their risk-neutral probabilities as shown in Table 11.1. The value at node W is calculated by multiplying the payoffs by the risk-neutral probabilities and discounting the result at the risk-free rate:

$$V_W = \frac{.365(176) + .135(138) + .365(103) + .135(80)}{1.05} = \frac{131.265}{1.05} = 125$$

Table 11.1 Quadranomial risk-neutral probabilities (indications phase).

		Price	
		Prob. Up = .73	*Prob. Down = .27*
Quantity	Prob. Up = .5	.365	.135
	Prob. Down = .5	.365	.135

Similar arithmetic is used to calculate values at nodes W through A4, and back through the tree to the root node, A15 where the present value of the project is $42.6 million. Don't forget, however, that the risk-neutral technological risk probabilities (also equal to the objective probabilities) are different at each phase of testing.

The mutually exclusive alternative is an event tree (Exhibit 11.24) without indications testing where we precommit to going straight to market. The process for calculating the project NPV is exactly the same as before, however, the loss in wealth is slightly less, −$35.1 million, therefore we would choose going straight to market as the better of the two mutually exclusive alternatives—even though we would reject both.

Next, we turn to real options analysis to estimate the value of the project with flexibility—in this case, the option to abandon, and compound options to invest. Exhibit 11.25 shows the ROA calculations and the optimal decisions. At the end of each of the first two compulsory test phases, the decision is either to exercise the option to go ahead by making the required investment, or to abandon. At the end of the third phase, however, we have three options to consider. Either we spend $5 million to do indications testing, spend $60 million to go straight to market, or abandon. To illustrate, let's go through the calculations at point W. If we decide to do indications testing, the results could be successful or a failure with either a high or low price. Exhibit 11.26 shows the quadranomial risk-neutral probabilities, the payoffs for each state of nature and the value at node W,

$$Test\ V_W = \frac{.365(116) + .135(78) + .365(43) + .135(20)}{1.05} = \frac{71.265}{1.05} = 67.87$$

Exhibit 11.24 NPV calculations without indications testing.

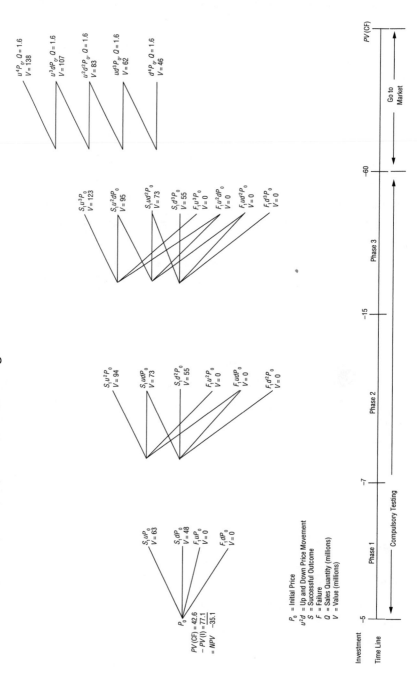

P_0 = Initial Price
u^2d = Up and Down Price Movement
S = Successful Outcome
F = Failure
Q = Sales Quantity (millions)
V = Value (millions)

$$PV(\text{CF}) = 42.6$$
$$-PV(\text{I}) = 77.1$$
$$= NPV \quad -35.1$$

P_0

S_1uP_0 $V = 63$
S_1dP_0 $V = 48$
F_1uP_0 $V = 0$
F_1dP_0 $V = 0$

$S_1u^2P_0$ $V = 94$
S_1udP_0 $V = 73$
$S_1d^2P_0$ $V = 55$
$F_1u^2P_0$ $V = 0$
F_1udP_0 $V = 0$
$F_1d^2P_0$ $V = 0$

$S_1u^3P_0$ $V = 123$
$S_1u^2dP_0$ $V = 95$
$S_1ud^2P_0$ $V = 73$
$S_1d^3P_0$ $V = 55$
$F_1u^3P_0$ $V = 0$
$F_1u^2dP_0$ $V = 0$
$F_1ud^2P_0$ $V = 0$
$F_1d^3P_0$ $V = 0$

u^4P_0, $Q = 1.6$ $V = 138$
u^3dP_0, $Q = 1.6$ $V = 107$
$u^2d^2P_0$, $Q = 1.6$ $V = 83$
ud^3P_0, $Q = 1.6$ $V = 62$
d^4P_0, $Q = 1.6$ $V = 46$

Investment
Time Line

-5
Phase 1

-7
Phase 2

-15
Phase 3

-60
Go to Market

PV (CF)

Compulsory Testing

Exhibit 11.25 ROA calculations and optimal decisions.

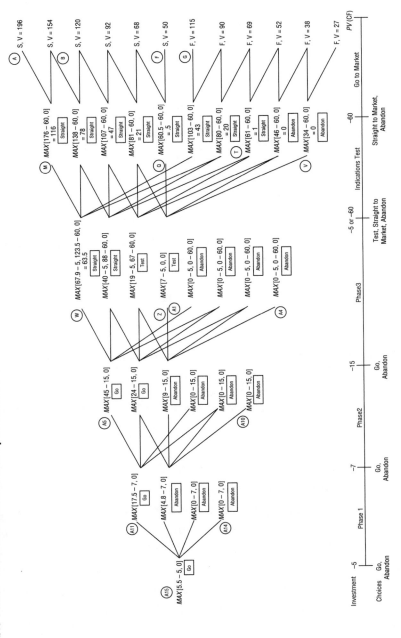

Exhibit 11.26 Indications testing the results could be successful or a failure.

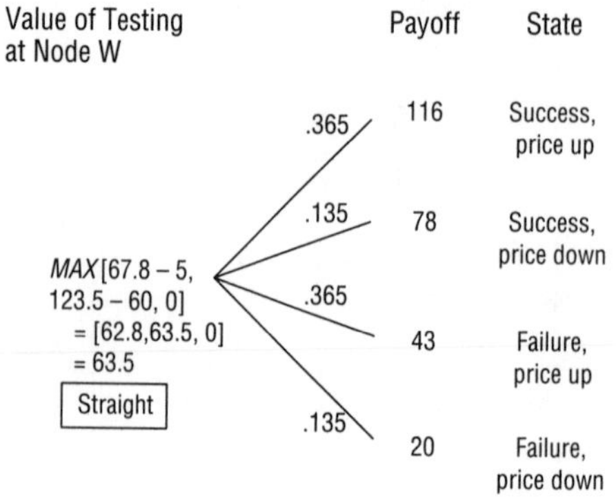

		Price Up	Price Down
Quantity	Success .5	.365	.135
	Failure .5	.365	.135

The other investment opportunity at node W is to go straight to market, which costs $60 million, and has the following present value:

$$\textit{Straight to market } V_W = \frac{.73(138) + .27(107)}{1.05} = 123.46$$

Since the net present value of going straight to market is greater than the NPV of indications testing,

$$MAX[123.4 - 60.0] > MAX[67.87 - 5.0]$$
$$63.46 > 62.87$$

we decide to go straight to market at node W. Similar calculations are made at the other nodes.

Working all the way back to the root node we find that the ROA valuation of the project is positive, $5.3 million, therefore we would go ahead and invest the initial $5 million to begin phase 1 of compulsory testing. At the end of the third phase of compulsory testing, we go straight to market in those states of nature where prices are high, but decide to do indications testing when prices are lower. The decision at node T is also interesting. Along one of the two paths that reach it, we conducted an indications test that was unsuccessful in the sense that it indicated low demand (only 1.2 million doses per year). Nevertheless, we decide to go straight to market because the market price is high.

CONCLUSION

This chapter has presented two cases, each fairly realistic, and each illustrating a different approach for handling multiple input uncertainties. The Portes case used ROA to value an Internet portal project that could expand operations (an American call) or abandon (an American put). The sources of uncertainty included the price per unit and the number of units sold. Using Monte Carlo analysis, these uncertainties were combined into the standard deviation of return on the company's value. From this single volatility estimate and from the NPV of the project, we built the value-based event tree that was used to value the project.

The PharmaX case was a compound option with three phases of mandatory testing followed by the possibility of voluntary comparative testing of indications—a complication that traditional NPV handles via mutually exclusive alternatives. There were two sources of uncertainty— technological uncertainty independent of the market, and product/market (i.e., price and quantity) uncertainty that was correlated with the market. We chose to keep the uncertainties separate in this case, and therefore used the quadranomial approach. Not only did the ROA approach capture the value of flexibility, but it also eliminated the fiction of mutually exclusive alternatives.

QUESTIONS AND PROBLEMS

For solutions go to www.corpfinonline.com.

1. Use the data in the Portes case. Will the ROA value go up or down and why under one of the following changes? What will happen with the project's volatility? (Prove your answer with detailed calculations).

    —The expected floor for the quantity sold in year six goes down to 120.

    —The expected floor for the price in year six goes up to $18.

—There is a 35 percent positive correlation between in the random component of the growth rate for quantity and price.

—There is a 45 percent negative correlation between the random component of the growth rate for quantity and price.

—The terminal value discount rate drops from 12 percent to 8 percent.

2. Use the data in the Portes case. Will the ROA value go up or down and why under one of the following changes? How will the optimal execution of the expand and abandon options change? (Prove your answer with detailed calculations.)

—Only the expansion option is available.

—Only the abandonment option is available.

—The abandonment value increases from $15 million to $25 million.

—The incremental value increases when the expansion option drops from 30 percent to 20 percent.

—There is an additional contraction option. It allows management to reduce operations by 20 percent and save $7 million.

3. Use the data in the Portes case. How much is the option to abandon worth? How much is the option to expand worth? How much are the two options worth together and why?

4. Use the data in the PharmaX case. Will the ROA value increase or decrease under each of the following conditions and why? How will the optimal execution of the abandon option and the option to perform the additional test change?

—The volatility of the price increases from 10 percent to 20 percent.

—The initial expected price increases from $10 to $13, and the chance of a successful marketing test drops from 50 percent to 30 percent.

—The initial price expectation drops to $5, and the expected terminal value multiple increases from 6 to 8.

—The probability of failure for Phase 2 decreases from 0.25 to 0.1.

5. Use the data in the PharmaX case. Will the ROA value increase or decrease under each of the following conditions and why? How will the optimal execution of the abandon option and the option to perform the additional test change?

—There is no option to perform the additional test.

—At any time during the development stage we have the option to sell the project for $3 million.

6. Use the data in the PharmaX case. How much is the option to abandon worth? How much is the option to perform the additional test worth? How much are the two options worth together and why?

7. Why is the option to perform the additional test a learning option? What change in conditions would have made the option more valuable?

REFERENCES

Greenspan, Alan. 1996. Excerpt from a speech given by the Federal Reserve Chairman.

Mitchell, G., and W. Hamilton. 1988, May–June. "Managing R&D as a Strategic Option," *Research Management, 31,* 15–22.

12 | Final Thoughts and Unfinished Business

Real options analysis is a significant step forward for thinking about flexibility and especially how to value it. Some of the methodology that is in this book may be thought of as a simple extension of the work that has preceded it, but one can also argue that it pushes the frontiers of applicability quite far. Much remains to be done and we encourage those who find the valuation of flexibility as fascinating as we, to help push applications even further.

The first part of this short chapter discusses simple extensions of the basic approaches that are described in the first 11 chapters, then more complex extensions—some with solutions and others without. We then register our complaint that the empirical evidence of the validity of real options analysis is scarce. And finally, we discuss the relationship between game theory, which endogonizes uncertainty, and real options analysis which keeps it exogenous.

SIMPLE EXTENSIONS

Plain vanilla call options, such as the right to expand a project, are easy to describe. One has the right, but not the obligation, for a fixed period of time to expand operations (and therefore the present value) by a predetermined percentage by investing a fixed amount of dollars. To solve the problem we need to estimate the volatility of the project, its net present value, and we need to determine the risk-free rate. What happens if we relax some of the implicit assumptions?

Suppose the exercise price increases over time in a non random way? This is usually the rule rather than the exception. The cost of constructing extra capacity, for example, usually increases through time. In a lattice, this problem is easy to solve. We change the exercise price each period, then solve in the usual way. If you go back to Chapter 5 and solve problem 3 or Chapter 7, problem 7, you will have mastered the problem.

What if the project can be exercised at some points in time but not others? Again, this is a common problem. For example, the results of research and development usually come in periodically at inconstant intervals of time—after three months of animal testing, five months of human testing, and so forth. The lattice framework provides an easy solution to this problem simply by dividing the life of a project into more subintervals than decision points and by modeling decisions only when they are physically possible. Problem 8 of Chapter 7 illustrates a problem of this type.

Switching options—their extensions and ramifications—merit a lengthier discussion than we can present here. The simplest switching option has no switching costs and no inventory. It is simply the option to exchange one risky asset for another—a problem that is analogous to pricing an option with a stochastic exercise price (the price of the asset for which it can be switched). The methodology described in Chapter 6 can be used to solve this problem, as well as the more difficult problem that assumes positive switching costs from mode A to mode B and vice versa. Note that we did not discuss how to use lattices for solving switching option problems when the underlying assets are not perfectly correlated. Although we believe that a quadranomial approach is feasible, its use in switching option problems is beyond the scope of this book.

There are three extensions to the switching problem that are potentially useful. First, what happens if the problem is modeling the extraction of an exhaustible natural resource and the two modes of operation are fast versus slow extraction? If prices are high, one would think that faster extraction might be sensible, however, it also implies that the resource is exhausted faster, and consequently that opportunities to exploit even higher prices are eliminated. See end-of-chapter problem number 2, Chapter 6 for an example to work on. A second extension is more than two modes of operation. What do you do if the rate of extraction is high, medium, or low? And a third is a sequence of several switching options. An example would be a switching technology of one type that might be upgraded at a fixed cost into another type of switching technology. We know of no literature and no published solutions for these problems.

Throughout the book we assumed that the volatility of the underlying was constant through time. Often this is a strong assumption that needs to be relaxed. If the volatility changes in a deterministic way (so that the change in volatility is not a random variable), it can be modeled by changing the up and down movements in the lattice each period. However, when we make this modification the event tree becomes non-recombining (see Exhibit 12.1). Problem 1 at the end of this chapter is a simple example of how to handle this problem.

Finally, there are combinations of options that are interesting. One example is the combination of deferral with learning options. An example would be the decision to open a mine. Suppose there are two sources of uncertainty—the price of gold and the quantity of gold in the ground. The only way to reduce uncertainty about the quantity of gold is to open the mine and start digging. The deferral option is more valuable if exercised later in time, but the learning option is more valuable when exercised earlier. Consequently, depending on the parameters of the problem,

Exhibit 12.1 Decision trees with constant and changing volatility.

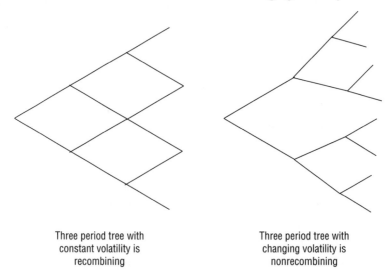

Three period tree with
constant volatility is
recombining

Three period tree with
changing volatility is
nonrecombining

there may be an interior optimum, it may be best to open the mine immediately, or it may be best to defer as long as possible.

REAL OPTIONS AND STRATEGY

It is worth reiterating that real options thinking radically changes traditional approaches to thinking about strategy. Traditionally we develop a set of mutually exclusive strategies, use some strategy metric (often the value impact) to compare them, then select one of them. In effect, we are using net present values of mutually exclusive alternatives. In Chapter 6, we suggested that real options, switching options in particular, provides a better framework for evaluating strategies. Why? Because executives know that once they select a strategy and begin to implement it, very often new information arrives that indicates it would be better to switch to another strategy.

If switching costs are low and uncertainty is high, then it is fairly obvious that highly flexible strategies dominate those that are inflexible. Therefore, strategists should not think of the strategic choice as a set of mutually exclusive alternatives, but rather as a switching option exercise where the amount of uncertainty and the cost of switching are as important as the expected cash flows of the strategic paths that may be undertaken.

REAL OPTIONS AND GAME THEORY

One of the implied assumptions of real options analysis is that uncertainty is exogenous. It is treated as a parameter that affects the value of a real option, not as part of the solution. It is an input, not an output. This is a particularly vexing assumption when we are dealing with deferral options. These are American options, and if the underlying pays no dividend, they are optimally exercised only at expiration. This can lead to silly results. For example, suppose that you are in a competitive race to develop a new drug. If you treat the volatility of the value of the hoped for end product as exogenous, and therefore unaffected by your decisions and the competitive response of other companies, then you will defer the start of your research until the last possible moment—a foolhardy decision.

Clearly, you are in a competitive game where your decisions affect the other company and vice versa.

Academic research on the relationship between option pricing and game theory is in its infancy with articles by Grenadier (2000), Smit and Ankum (1993), and Trigeorgis (1996). The work by the latter authors embeds a two-person prisoner's dilemma game into each node of a decision tree. However, the more complicated problem of an N-person game remains to be solved.

Let's review the work of Smit and Ankum (1993). They analyze deferral options in the context of competitive equilibrium. One example is the competition between Schiphol airport in Holland and the nearby Brussels airport in Belgium to become the major hub of operations in Northwestern Europe. Both airports are considering major investments to expand. Consequently, they find themselves in a two-person game called the "prisoner's dilemma" as illustrated in Exhibit 12.2. If they both choose to expand, their payouts will be low. If one expands and the other does not, the payoff to the aggressive airport is high while the payoff to its competitor is low. Finally, if both choose to forego expansion, both receive a moderate payoff.

There are many assumptions that we can make about competitive behavior and a duopoly is only one of them—one that we shall return to shortly. Smit and Ankum (1993) discuss several possibilities: a monopoly

Exhibit 12.2   Prisoner's dilemma payoff table.

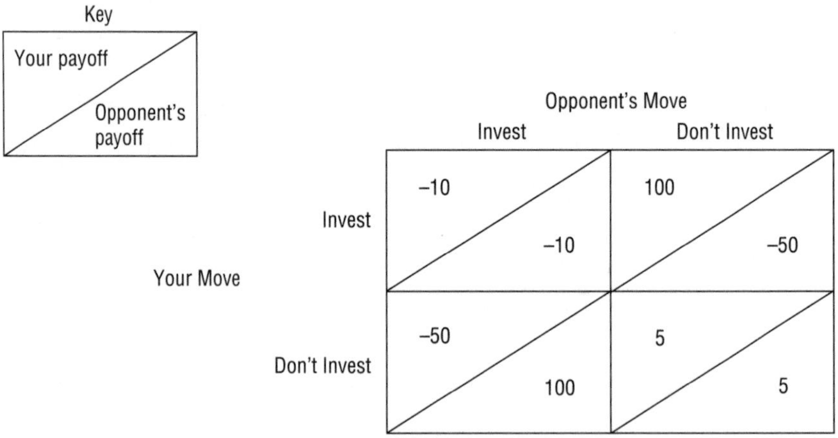

case where the economic rents on a project are assumed to remain undiminished throughout time (due to a barrier to entry), a competitive reaction function where economic rents are assumed to come down over time (in a nonstochastic fashion) until the project earns a competitive return, and finally, the aforementioned duopoly. They go on to discuss the effect of the market power of duopolists (symmetric or asymmetric) on the problem solution.

Reaction Functions

We will review the competitive solution first because one can think of it as a type of reaction function that solves the problem by assuming that the initial competitive advantage produced by a new product will erode over time in a predictable way due to competition. The monopoly case is simply a competitive reaction curve where there is no erosion of economic rents.

To use a specific example to illustrate how reaction curves can be embedded into an option pricing framework, start with the following assumptions:

1. It costs $1,000 to invest in a project that will go on forever ($I =$ $1,000).
2. Each year the project produces two types of cash flow or dividend. First, $k = 20\%$ is a normal or competitive return on the $1,000 investment. Second, is an expected economic rent (or excess return) that starts at $100 the first year but shrinks by 20 percent per year due to anticipated competition.
3. The risk free rate of return, r_f, is 5 percent and the cost of capital, k, is 20 percent.
4. The value of the project can go up by a factor of $u = 1.7$ each year or down by $d = 1/u = .588$.
5. There is a three year deferral option.
6. Dividends are assumed to be proportional to the present value of the project cum dividend.

To solve the problem, we first figure out the evolution of the present value of the project through time. The present value at time zero is:

$$PV_0 = \frac{D_1}{1+k} + \frac{D_2}{(1+k)^2} + \frac{D_3}{(1+k)^3} + \ldots + \frac{D_N}{(1+k)^N}$$

$$= \frac{kI+100(1-.2)}{1+k} + \frac{kI+100(1-.2)^2}{(1+k)^2} + \ldots + \frac{kI+100(1-.2)^N}{(1+k)^N}$$

$$= \sum_{t=1}^{N} \frac{kI}{(1+k)^t} + \sum_{t=1}^{N} \frac{100(1-.2)^t}{(1+k)^t}$$

The first term is an infinite constant annuity and the second is an infinite growing (shrinking) annuity, therefore we can rewrite the expression for PV_0 as follows:

$$PV_0 = \frac{kI}{k} + \frac{100}{k-(-.2)}$$

$$= 1000 + \frac{100}{.2+.2} = 1250$$

If we were using the net present value rule, we would invest because the NPV of the project is positive

$$NPV = PV - I = 1250 - 1000 = 250$$

To finish our calculation of the evolution of the present value through time, let's figure out PV_1 from the definitions of PV_0 and PV_1 which are written as:

$$PV_0 = \frac{D_1}{1+k} + \frac{D_2}{(1+k)^2} + \frac{D_3}{(1+k)^3} + \ldots + \frac{D_N}{(1+k)^N}$$

$$PV_1 = \frac{D_2}{(1+k)} + \frac{D_3}{(1+k)^2} + \ldots + \frac{D_N}{(1+k)^{N-1}}$$

Therefore,

$$PV_1 = \left[PV_0 - \frac{D_1}{(1+k)} \right](1+k)$$

$$= PV_0(1+k) - D_1 = 1250(1.2) - (kI+100)$$

$$= 1500 - (200+100) = 1200$$

By repeating this process we obtain the expected value of the project through time as illustrated in Exhibit 12.3

Next, we introduce uncertainty about the underlying risky asset by multiplying the values ex-dividend by the assumed up and down movements. This is illustrated in Exhibit 12.4. Remember that we have assumed that dividends are proportional to the value of the project cum dividend.

Finally, we insert decisions into the event tree for the value of the underlying and then use risk-neutral probabilities to evaluate them. The results are shown below in Exhibit 12.5. The risk-neutral probability is

$$p = \frac{1 + r_f - d}{u - d} = \frac{1.05 - .588}{1.7 - .588} = .415$$

Therefore, the value of the live option at node H is

$$C = \frac{pCu + (1-p)}{1 + r_f}C_d$$
$$= \frac{.415(1376) + (1 - .415)146}{1.05}$$
$$= \frac{656}{1.05} = 625$$

Exhibit 12.3 Expected value of the project.

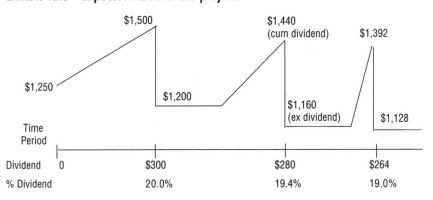

| | | $1,500 | | $1,440 (cum dividend) | $1,392 |
| $1,250 | | $1,200 | | $1,160 (ex dividend) | $1,128 |

Time Period

| Dividend | 0 | $300 | $280 | $264 |
| % Dividend | | 20.0% | 19.4% | 19.0% |

Exhibit 12.4   Event tree for value of underlying (assumes a competitive reaction curve).

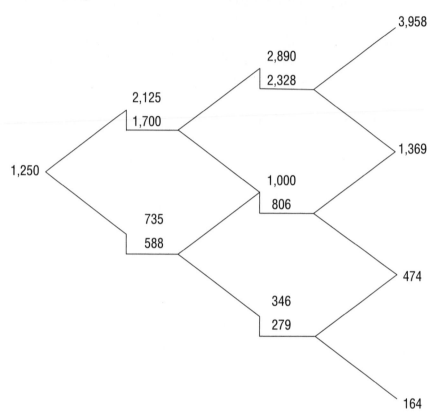

As before, we solve the tree recursively to determine that the value of the project with the right to defer is $309 versus a net present value of $250. Note also, that the assumed decline in economic rents causes us to invest as early as period 2.

OPTIONS WITH ENDOGENOUS UNCERTAINTY

Smit and Ankum solve the option problem with two non-cooperating competitors by embedding a two person game at each node of the decision tree as shown in Exhibit 12.6. The example we just analyzed demonstrates how the Real Options framework can be used to model and

Exhibit 12.5   Real option analysis (competitive reaction curve).

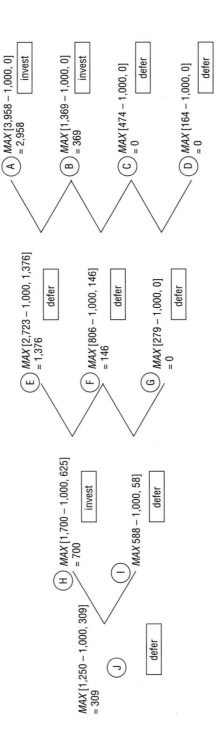

A   MAX [3,958 – 1,000, 0]
    = 2,958   invest

B   MAX [1,369 – 1,000, 0]
    = 369   invest

C   MAX [474 – 1,000, 0]
    = 0   defer

D   MAX [164 – 1,000, 0]
    = 0   defer

E   MAX [2,723 – 1,000, 1,376]
    = 1,376   defer

F   MAX [806 – 1,000, 146]
    = 146   defer

G   MAX [279 – 1,000, 0]
    = 0   defer

H   MAX [1,700 – 1,000, 625]
    = 700   invest

I   MAX 588 – 1,000, 58]
                               defer

J   MAX [1,250 – 1,000, 309]
    = 309   defer

Exhibit 12.6   Decision tree with prisoner's dilemma embedded.

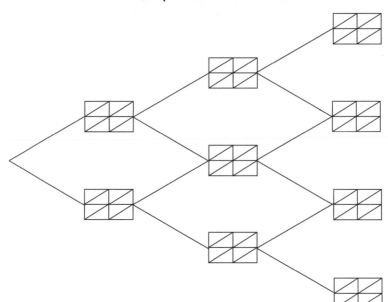

analyze strategic interaction between competitors without significant complications. The common feature in this type of real options model is the exogenous character of the competitor's actions. In the example above we just assumed that the competitors enter the market and reduce the abnormal rent over time no matter what the company does. In this context the company only optimizes its competitive response to a pre-determined competitor's action.

A more realistic situation is when both competing firms recognize each other's optimizing behavior and adjust their actions accordingly. This is the type of situation where Game Theory works as a powerful analytical tool. We can model different market structures from monopoly through duopoly, oligopoly, and perfect competition. We can also select from a broad set of competitive actions for each firm like setting price or output levels. The most insightful are the so-called dynamic games. Here we identify not only an optimal strategic action for each participant at a given moment of time, but a sequence of actions across time. This approach is much closer to management's understanding of strategy as a way to compete over time.

All dynamic games assume that the discounting of future values is taken into account when optimizing current decisions. At the same time by capturing the future change in business conditions and the flexibility for each competitor, the dynamic games reflect the change in the project's risk profile. As with regular options (real and financial) we know that the discount rate changes across time and across scenarios to reflect the change in the risk of the investment. Here is where Game Theory and Real Option complement each other. While the first models the value created by each firm in a combative situation, the second helps to discount this value properly and to formulate and evaluate correctly a dynamic competitive strategy.

SUMMARY AND CONCLUSION

This chapter has discussed some of the extensions and limitations of real option analysis. Lattice frameworks enable the practitioner to model situations that are more cumbersome and sometimes impossible for closed form stochastic calculus approaches. It is even possible to embed game theory into a binomial lattice. Of course, much remains to be done.

QUESTIONS AND PROBLEMS

For solutions go to www.corpfinonline.com.

1. An asset's current value is $100, its annual volatility is 30 percent, and its expected annual growth rate is zero. What is the value of a three year option to abandon for a price of $60?

   How does your approach and your answer change if the annual volatility changes over time from 30 percent the first year to 20 percent the second to 10 percent the third year?

2. Using the example developed in the chapter, determine the optimal timing of the invest and the value of the firms flexibility under each of the following conditions:

   —The abnormal rent doesn't decline over time. (What type market structure would this situation represent?)

   —The investment does not provide free cash flow the first three years.

—The up-ward movement declines from 1.7 to 1.5.

—The abnormal rent declines by 50 percent annually.

REFERENCES

Grenadier, S. (ed.). 2000. *Game Choices: The Intersection of Real Options and Game Theory.* Risk Books.

Grenadier, S. 2000. "Option Exercise Games: The Intersection of Real Options and Game Theory," *Journal of Applied Corporate Finance, 13,* 2, 99–108.

Smit, H. and L. Ankum. 1993. "A Real Options and Game-Theoretic Approach to Corporate Investment Strategy Under Competition," *Financial Management, 22,* 241–250.

Smit, H. and L. Trigeorgis. 1993. "Flexibility and Commitments in Strategic Investment," working paper, Tinbergen Institute, Erasmus University.

Trigeorgis, L. 1991. "Anticipated competitive entry and early preemptive investment in deferrable projects," *Journal of Economics and Business, 43,* 2, 143–156.

Trigeorgis, L. 1996. *Real Options: Managerial Flexibility and Strategy in Resource Allocation.* Cambridge, MA: MIT Press, chapter 9.

APPENDIX A

Areas under the Normal Curve

					Areas under the Standard Normal Distribution Function $\int_0^z f(z)\,dz$				

z	.00	.01	.02	.03	.04	.05	.06	.07	.08	.09
0.0	.0000	.0040	.0080	.0120	.0160	.0199	.0239	.0279	.0319	.0359
0.1	.0398	.0438	.0478	.0517	.0557	.0596	.0636	.0675	.0714	.0753
0.2	.0793	.0832	.0871	.0910	.0948	.0987	.1026	.1064	.1103	.1141
0.3	.1179	.1217	.1255	.1293	.1331	.1368	.1406	.1443	.1480	.1517
0.4	.1554	.1591	.1628	.1664	.1700	.1736	.1772	.1808	.1844	.1879
0.5	.1915	.1950	.1985	.2019	.2054	.2088	.2123	.2157	.2190	.2224
0.6	.2257	.2291	.2324	.2357	.2389	.2422	.2454	.2486	.2517	.2549
0.7	.2580	.2611	.2642	.2673	.2704	.2734	.2764	.2794	.2823	.2852
0.8	.2881	.2910	.2939	.2967	.2995	.3023	.3051	.3078	.3106	.3133
0.9	.3159	.3186	.3212	.3238	.3264	.3289	.3315	.3340	.3365	.3389
1.0	.3413	.3438	.3461	.3485	.3508	.3531	.3554	.3577	.3599	.3621
1.1	.3643	.3665	.3686	.3708	.3729	.3749	.3770	.3790	.3810	.3830
1.2	.3849	.3869	.3888	.3907	.3925	.3944	.3962	.3980	.3997	.4015
1.3	.4032	.4049	.4066	.4082	.4099	.4115	.4131	.4147	.4162	.4177
1.4	.4192	.4207	.4222	.4236	.4251	.4265	.4279	.4292	.4306	.4319
1.5	.4332	.4345	.4357	.4370	.4382	.4394	.4406	.4418	.4429	.4441
1.6	.4452	.4463	.4474	.4484	.4495	.4505	.4515	.4525	.4535	.4545
1.7	.4554	.4564	.4573	.4582	.4591	.4599	.4608	.4616	.4625	.4633
1.8	.4641	.4649	.4656	.4664	.4671	.4678	.4686	.4693	.4699	.4706
1.9	.4713	.4719	.4726	.4732	.4738	.4744	.4750	.4756	.4761	.4767
2.0	.4772	.4778	.4783	.4788	.4793	.4798	.4803	.4808	.4812	.4817
2.1	.4821	.4826	.4830	.4834	.4838	.4842	.4846	.4850	.4854	.4857
2.2	.4861	.4864	.4868	.4871	.4875	.4878	.4881	.4884	.4887	.4890
2.3	.4893	.4896	.4898	.4901	.4904	.4906	.4909	.4911	.4913	.4916
2.4	.4918	.4920	.4922	.4925	.4927	.4929	.4931	.4932	.4934	.4936
2.5	.4938	.4940	.4941	.4943	.4945	.4946	.4948	.4949	.4951	.4952
2.6	.4953	.4955	.4956	.4957	.4959	.4960	.4961	.4962	.4963	.4964
2.7	.4965	.4966	.4967	.4968	.4969	.4970	.4971	.4972	.4973	.4974
2.8	.4974	.4975	.4976	.4977	.4977	.4978	.4979	.4979	.4980	.4981
2.9	.4981	.4982	.4982	.4982	.4984	.4984	.4985	.4985	.4986	.4986
3.0	.4987	.4987	.4987	.4988	.4988	.4989	.4989	.4989	.4990	.4990

NOTES

CHAPTER 1: GETTING STARTED

1. For example, see T. Copeland, T. Koller, and J. Murrin, *Valuation: Measuring and Managing the Value of Companies,* 3rd edition, New York: John Wiley & Sons, 2000.
2. Some of the work was done while employed at McKinsey between 1987 and 1998 and some while at Monitor, 1998 to present.

CHAPTER 2: THE CHANGE PROCESS

1. Everett M. Rogers, *Diffusion of Innovations,* 4th edition, Free Press, 1995.

CHAPTER 3: NET PRESENT VALUE

1. The CAPM theory posits that the expected rate of return on any security in equilibrium is equal to the risk-free rate, r_f, plus the expected market risk premium, $E(R_m) - R_f$, times the systematic risk of the security, β_j. Note that $E(R_m)$ is the expected return on the market portfolio of all risky assets.
2. The covariance is defined as

$$COV(x, y) = \frac{\sum_i p_i[x_i - E(x)][y - E(y)]}{\sum_i p_i[x_i - E(x)]^2}$$

It is the same as the slope of a linear regression of the dependent variable, *y*, on an independent variable, *x*.
3. Beta in the Capital Asset Pricing Model is defined as

$$\beta = \frac{COV(R_i, R_m)}{VAR(R_m)}$$

CHAPTER 4: COMPARING NET PRESENT VALUE, DECISION TREES, AND REAL OPTIONS

1. We are also assuming that the increase in volatility is uncorrelated with the market so that the discount rate does not change.

CHAPTER 5: NUMERICAL METHODS FOR SIMPLE OPTIONS

1. For example, the geometric average payoff in the first time period of Exhibit 5.1 is $[(uV_0)(dV_0)]^{1/2} = V_0$ since $ud = 1$.
2. If either $p \neq q$ or $u \neq |\,d\,|$ the distribution becomes asymmetric (skewed).
3. If the continuous rate is 5 percent per year, the equivalent annual discrete rate is

$$e^j = (1 + r_f)$$
$$e^{.05} = (1 + r_f)$$
$$1.0513 = 1 + r_f$$
$$r_f = 5.13\%$$

The quarterly risk-free rate is therefore

$$(1 + \frac{j}{m})^m = 1 + r_f$$
$$\frac{j}{4} = (1.0513)^{.25} - 1$$
$$\frac{j}{4} = 1.258\%$$

4. In general, with multiperiod problems, early exercise of an American call option will be possible when the option is written on the post dividend value.

CHAPTER 6: COMPOUND AND SWITCHING OPTIONS

1. It is obvious that the payouts are both less than the exercise price of $400 and that the first option would not be exercised in this state.

CHAPTER 8: A FOUR-STEP PROCESS FOR VALUING REAL OPTIONS

1. The derivation of this formula starts by writing the infinite geometric series for payments of $b every odd-numbered period forever, discounted at rate r:

$$PV(odd) = \frac{b}{1+r} + \frac{b}{(1+r)^3} + \frac{b}{(1+r)^5} + \dots + \frac{b}{(1+r)^{2N-1}}$$

If we let $u = 1/(1 + r)$, this formula can be simplified, then multiplied by u squared to obtain a second equation that, when subtracted from the first, eliminates all of the middle terms, as follows:

$$PV(odd) = bu + bu^3 + bu^5 + \dots + bu^{2N-1}$$
$$-u^2[PV(odd) = bu^3 + bu^5 + \dots + bu^{2N-1} + bu^{2N+1}]$$
$$= PV(odd) - u^2 PV(odd) = bu - bu^{2N+1} = bu(1 - u^{2N})$$

$$= \frac{bu(1 - u^{2N})}{1 - u^2}$$

In the limit, as N goes to infinity, the second term within parentheses in the numerator goes to zero, and the final expression is $PV(odd) = bu/(1 - u^2)$. The derivation for payments in even-numbered years is similar.

CHAPTER 9: ESTIMATING VOLATILITY: CONSOLIDATED APPROACH

1. Covariance, COV, is defined as $\Sigma p_i[x_i - E(X)][(Y_i - E(Y)]$ where X_i and Y_i are the two random variables with means $E(X)$ and $E(Y)$, and p_i is the joint probability of observing $(X_i$ and $Y_i)$. The intuitive explanation is that covariance is a measure of the simultaneous departure of X from its mean and Y from its mean. If both random variables tend to be simultaneously above or simultaneously below their means, then the covariance will be positive (and vice versa).

CHAPTER 10: KEEPING UNCERTAINTIES SEPARATE

1. Note that we discount at the risk-free rate for only half a year.
2. The discussion of the quadranomial approach with correlated uncertainties can be found in Clewlow and Strickland (1998), pp. 44–51. These methods were introduced by Boyle (1988), and Boyle, Eunine, and Gibbs (1989).

CHAPTER 11: CASE EXAMPLES

1. Alan Greenspan, 1966. Excerpt from a speech given by the Federal Reserve chairman, December 5, 2000.

ABOUT THE AUTHORS

Tom Copeland is Managing Director of Corporate Finance at Monitor Group, where he is leader of the Finance Practice. Tom has been a consultant to over 200 companies in 34 countries around the world and is a leading authority on valuation.

Tom has also written about real options in his co-authored book on *Valuation,* in three *McKinsey Quarterly* articles entitled "Managing Uncertainty," "Making Real Options Real," and "What is Flexibility Worth?," and in a new book entitled *e-Commerce.* Tom is also acknowledged as a leading practitioner having been involved in over a dozen option pricing studies. He has given presentations on real options at MIT, Wharton, Northwestern, The University of Virginia, the American Finance Association, and the Financial Management Association. *Real Options: A Practitioner's Guide* is his fifth book.

Before joining Monitor, Tom was Director of Corporate Financial Services at McKinsey & Company (1987–1998) and was a tenured full Professor of Finance at UCLA (1973–1987), where he served as Chairman of the Finance Department and Vice Chairman of the Graduate School of Management. In addition, he was an adjunct professor at MIT and NYU. He received his B.A. in Economics from Johns Hopkins University in 1968, his M.B.A. in Finance from the Wharton School, where he graduated second in his class, in 1969, and his Ph.D. in from the University of Pennsylvania in 1973.

He is co-author, with J. Fred Weston, of *Financial Theory and Corporate Policy,* a widely used advanced-level finance text, and of Managerial Finance, the well-known intermediate-level corporate finance text. With Tim Koller and Jack Murrin, he co-authored *Valuation: Measuring and*

Managing the Value of Companies, a book that shows how top management can take an action-oriented approach to enhancing shareholder value, and instructs staff on the methodology of doing valuations. It has sold over 200,000 copies and is used as a textbook at over 100 universities. His books have been translated into eleven languages. His publications include articles about stock splits, market trading activity, receivables policy, leasing, exchange offers, bid-ask spreads, spin-offs, pension fund management, portfolio performance measurement, corporate recapitalizations, foreign exchange hedging, capital productivity, asset options, growth through acquisition, LBOs, and experimental economics. He is a member of the Editorial Board and Board of Directors of *Financial Management* and has served as chairman of the Practitioner's Board of Directors of the Financial Management Association.

Vladimir Antikarov joined Monitor Group in 1992. His work spans a wide area of domestic and international corporate strategy, traffic flows and network economics analysis, modeling and optimization, screening and valuation of M&A targets, acquisition and bidding strategic support. He has extensive experience in the telecommunications services and equipment industries. Recently, Vladimir has been concentrating on building Monitor's capabilities and serving clients with real options. With Tom Copeland, he has developed methodologies and led the building of software tools to apply real options in the management of R&D, product development, foreign investment analysis, investment in switching capacity and other applications.

Vladimir has an M.B.A. from Boston University and is currently a doctoral student in Finance at Boston University. His undergraduate degree is from the University for National and Global Economy, Sofia, Bulgaria. He is a recipient of a Fulbright Scholarship, a member of Beta Gamma Sigma, the Honor Society for Collegiate Schools of Business, and of Phi Beta Delta, the Honor Society for International Scholars.

INDEX